Cleansing FIRE Healing STREAMS

Experiencing

God's Love

Through Prayer

Kent A. Hansen

Pacific Press® Publishing Association
Nampa, Idaho
Oshawa, Ontario, Canada
www.pacificpress.com

Cover design by Gerald Lee Monks
Cover photo dreamstime.com; iStockphoto.com
Inside design by Steve Lanto

Additional copies of this book are available by calling toll free 1-800-765-6955
or by visiting http://www.adventistbookcenter.com.

ISBN 13: 978-0-8163-2179-7
ISBN 10: 0-8163-2179-5

07 08 09 10 11 • 5 4 3 2 1

Dedication

For Patricia,
who speaks the truth with love.

Acknowledgments

Gratitude is the fruit of prayer because it is the realization that we are not alone and that we owe our very life to God and the loved ones and friends whom He brings along side us to share it. I am a grateful man for some dear people without whom this book would not be possible.

Terry Acosta is my legal assistant and friend who has worked with me for fourteen years at this writing. She took the raw muddle of my manuscript; looked it over, and said, "Stay out of my way till I get this done!" She organized and formatted and retyped my chapters until they could be shared with others as a coherent whole. She herself is a praying woman of faith, and her intelligence, competence, taste, and laughter bless my days.

My son, Andrew, honored me using his computer skills and talent for words to help Terry with the word processing of the manuscript. This book contains many stories about him, and he grew up with me writing across the hall from his bedroom. His commitment to Christ, insights, wry humor, and understanding heart are a source of joy and inspiration to me.

Patricia is my best friend and spouse of thirty years. She is my muse and proofreader. Her tender heart for Christ and for me has healed and deepened my soul. Her rigorous objectivity and refusal to "settle" for anything less than the true and the good have taught me the power of consecration.

We learn the scope and power of prayer by praying with others. Many friends have shared prayer and thoughts with me over the years that encouraged my walk with Christ and my desire to pray. I am grateful for all I have experienced with Heidi, Ed, Cyndi, Paul, Joyce, Jill, David H., Debbie, Richard, Shirley J., Linda, Dave C., Dolores, Dave S., Lori, Preston, Helen, Kelly, Rosie, Tom, Sue, Cliff, Dee, Terry C., Art, Al, Steve, Fran, Ginny, David W., Alvin, and my brother Gus.

My hardest working days are made into sanctuaries of grace and delight by the fellowship, prayer and support of my "homies": Shon, Barbara, Steve O., Pev, Mignon, Sandy, Michael, Melanie, Pat, Beth, Linda M., Mark, Deanna, Patti, Dulce, Gwen, Ignatious, Lizette, Neva, Ginny, Myrna, Donna, Roland, Kerry, Nate, and Susan. They have each in their own way encouraged me along the way of writing this book.

Dr. Lyn Behrens, the president of the Loma Linda University Adventist Health Sciences Center, has been my client, mentor, colleague, friend, and sister-in-Christ for many years. She and I have walked through the "fire" together with much prayer. God has blessed our collaboration with success, trust, and understanding. Her single-minded devotion to Christ is a beacon in my prayer life.

Derrill Yaeger brought me to my law firm in 1982 and opened many doors for me as a young lawyer. We have been through many victories and a few tough defeats together. Much of my understanding of my work as prayer comes from watching Derrill's passionate service to his God, his church, and his community.

Don Pursley is another mentor and friend who taught me that "the only thing worth losing sleep over is talking with God."

My brother Terry introduced me to reading great books on prayer and to the discipline of silence as a catalyst of prayer. No one else hugs "as good" as Terry. His life was saved through divine grace in response to fervent prayer just as I finished the manuscript. I told him, "Some of us live the story, and some of us write about it."

My profound thanks goes to Bonnie Tyson-Flyn of Pacific Press, who edited this book. I am grateful for the patient professionalism that she brought to clearing the "thickets of my prose."

I pray that these pages will bless you with the grace and truth of Christ that these good people have shown me.

Kent A. Hansen
Corona, California
January 9, 2007

Contents

Introduction

I never liked mathematics until I discovered how statistics empowered baseball strategy, business planning, and politics. Diagramming sentences held no appeal for me until I learned that writing a compelling lead paragraph for a news story or a legal brief determined whether or not it would be read. Dating was a nuisance until I met a woman whose conversation was more interesting and attractive than that of anyone else I'd ever met.

Reality, please—no game playing for me. That's why I pray. God is too important to pretend, hypothesize, posture, or speculate about. We can speak to Him and listen to Him. No guesswork or pretense is required.

The most real and significant thing that ever happened to me is learning that God loved me, not because He had to do so as a theological principle, but because He delighted in me and wanted to love me. I acquired this knowledge by praying and listening.

Of course I had read and memorized Scripture at home, school, and church during my childhood and youth. But God breathed life into the Word in my soul when I began to pray to Him because nothing else answered the longing in my heart.

I couldn't have been any busier than I was back then. My standing in my profession and community was high, but my soul was fraying around the edges, and my spirit was low. The thrill of becoming a new dad barely brought a lull to my workaholic frenzy.

What hadn't registered with me was that my drive for achievement and success was a search for love. Somehow, I never seemed to do what my teachers wanted or to satisfy the expectations of my mother or to care enough about what other people thought I should. I was tough enough to go my own way, but the words of disappointment and disapproval left me bruised and aching inside.

I enjoyed college and achieved success in academics and leadership. This recognition medicated my longing, self-doubting heart like a drug.

My means of obtaining more of the drug was to work harder and do more than anyone else. I even disparaged Jesus' parables of grace because He just didn't seem to appreciate hard work and merit enough for me.

Any recovering addict will tell you that one problem is that you need more and more of whatever makes you high until you pass the point of what your body and mind can tolerate, and you break down or die. I began to fill every moment with work until I poured everything I had in the way of energy, ability, and spirit into effort—and that wasn't enough.

By that time, I was way beyond the support of family, friends, and colleagues. They couldn't keep up with me, and I despised them in my mind for not caring enough about what I cared about. Of course, love and friendship are mutual support activities, and I never stayed still long enough to give reliable support or to let them support me. I was on my own and needed nothing, or so I thought.

A great sadness began to well up in me when I was alone, driving or working late at night. Every external indicator said that I was a rising young attorney and civic leader. Every internal indicator said that I was nothing but a high-maintenance shell of a man.

My most authentic spiritual moments came when I sat down at the piano and played hymns late at night or on weekends. I would remember the words about Jesus who came a long way and gave up His life for me so that I could go home with Him and rest. I'd been told that He was my Friend and I could tell Him anything. I knew people who lived and died in faith that His love was true for everyone and anyone. But why would He love me? When would I ever do enough to earn His love?

It occurred to me that I should pray, but what would I pray about if I weren't trying to pass a test, make a deal, or win a case? What difference would words uttered into space make if the real work and performance I was delivering every day left me feeling sad and empty?

I tried to pray, to no avail. I had nothing to say. There I was—brought up in a Christian family, a lifetime of church attendance and seventeen years of Christian school, a livelihood that depended on my eloquence—and I had nothing to say to God.

Then, two mornings in a row, I stood up in a hotel room and muttered, "God, I'd like to talk to You, but I don't know how." These were feeble, but honest words. God's answer was genuine and blunt. It convinced me that I had to give up my frenzied effort and learn to trust Him.

Mine was no miracle conversion. It has taken years of examination, struggle, and joys and failures to come to a belief in my heart as well as my head that God loves me.

Introduction

The road on that journey to accept the embrace of God has been and continues to be my prayer. I have learned that there are times when I have to set my books aside—even the Bible and devotional reading—stop planning and working; and kneel, sit, stand, lie down, or walk before Him and just tell Him how much I love Him and want to hear from Him. Then, I need to listen for His voice leading me to the understanding or acceptance of His will for me that always begins and ends with His love for me.

Coming to understand that God sent His Son Jesus Christ to rescue me and bring me home because He loves me was the most important event of my life. Christ is the Light that extinguishes all other lights by His brightness.

There comes a point in a relationship with Christ, if one is intent on intimacy, that He becomes the compelling influence in one's schedule, priorities, relationships, and performance.

The apostle Paul urged the Ephesian believers to "pray in the Spirit at all times."[1] He told the Thessalonians to "pray without ceasing."[2] The literal mind in its limitations asks, "How could this possibly happen?" Paul was speaking the truth that every lover, parent, and good friend knows. A real relationship requires frequent and honest communication.

Love is not realized until it is expressed in words or action. That is what prayer does. It places our longing souls in proximity to our Lover so we can hear why He made us and loves us still in spite of everything, and He can hear from us how much we need and adore Him. As understanding and intimacy grow, it often is enough for lovers to sit together in silence watching the light of dawn or sunset on the water.

The first rule of prayer is to show up. The second rule is to leave your heart and mind wide open to the possibilities of God at all times. Devotion requires a flexibility and openness of soul and spirit rather than a rigidity of routine.

A prayerful heart is ready and waiting for what God may say or do at any time and in every situation. It is willing to yield its own desires, conveniences, and expectations to respond with obedience to the impulse of God's love.

I am an opinionated, verbally combative attorney. I have been described as "passionate," but learning to fight harder and smarter did not transform me. Surrender did.

The original meaning of *passion* was "to give oneself over to a deep, overwhelming power." There is no way that one can be taught to do this. It is a choice to give way to God's superior strength. Prayer is the time when my mind is changed and my hard heart softens because I surrender to God's power.

9

Surrender is the essence of prayer. True prayer is an admission that God—the Father, Son, and Holy Spirit—is God and that we are not God. No matter how good we are, we can never be good enough. No matter how hard we work, we can never earn God's love. No matter how strong our will, we can never will His love into our lives. It takes some of us longer than others to learn this, but sooner or later every knee in heaven, earth, and hell will bend, and every tongue . . . confess that Jesus Christ is Lord, to the glory of God the Father.[3]

Prayer gets us before His throne in heaven now rather than later and opens all the delights of His kingdom to us. To pray is to recognize that our lives and beings are gifts of a God who loves us.

Each person brings his or her personality, experience, convictions, dreams, and needs to prayer. Solomon observed that "that heart knows its own bitterness, / and no stranger knows its joy."[4] Jesus said that He has a special voiceprint as the Good Shepherd, and His sheep will hear it and respond to it as uniquely speaking to their need for life.[5]

That is why I have not written an instruction book and offer no secrets to you for successful prayer except to come before the Lord your God with an honest, open, and surrendered heart. What I have written for you are field reports and observations of God's love experienced through prayer.

If you are going to get something out of this book, you are not going to rush through it. There are fifty-two chapters, each written for you to pray, read, reflect, and pray some more about what God is speaking to your life through my words. What word or words particularly speak to you in the ideas and stories shared in the chapter? What joy or concern rises in you from what you have read? What action is the Holy Spirit calling you to take because of what you have read?

If I've accomplished what God has called me to do with this book, at the end of reading it you will have a deeper acceptance of God's love for you, your love for Him will have grown, and you will be looking and listening to Him everywhere you go.

I invite you to experience the words of Psalm 34:8: "O taste and see that the LORD is good; / happy are those who take refuge in him."

Under the mercy of Christ,

Kent Hansen
Corona, California
August 2006

Myths and Truths
About Prayer

1

The Myths That Separate Us From Our Father

Prayer is an open door through which the child of God can reach the heart of the Father.

I don't know whether it takes courage or *chutzpah* to write about something as personal as prayer. Everyone has an opinion about prayer, it seems. It is even a political lightning rod between the "red" states and the "blue" states. Yet Jesus says it is one thing that we ought to do in the closet.

There is a longing for something more in the hearts of men and women who look thoughtfully at the world, who consider their own human condition and limitations. These longings are exposed in the music we listen to about love and peace, in the efforts we make to end our loneliness, and in the delight that we take in the mysteries and grandeur of nature. Sometimes while carpooling to work, sharing a meal, or talking with a stranger on a plane, we will share our hopes and doubts and longings.

These deep thoughts and feelings are too precious and real to expose for long. Fearing rejection and humiliation, we stuff them back into our hearts, where they grow even stronger. Meanwhile, we wait and wonder, *Am I all alone in this? Does anyone else think and feel the way I do?*

Where information is withheld and truth is obscured, human souls are tyrannized by ignorance and fear. Nowhere is this more evident than in the falsehoods told about talking with God. Over the centuries, these falsehoods have been repeated until they have gained the stature of tradition and the authority of religiosity. The children of God have been separated from their Father, who longs to speak with them and to share His love for them and discuss His plans with them. This separation is so strong and wrong that the myth can be countered only by speaking truth so that men and women may find their rightful place with the Father who loves us. Prayer is the way to find that place, so I have decided to challenge the myths and write about the truth of prayer to my brothers and sisters.

Several specific, pernicious myths about prayer hinder our intimate relationship with God:

• God knows everything and really doesn't need our prayers.
• Prayer connects only when we ask God for the "right" thing.
• God communicates only with "good" persons.
• We have to know the "right" words in order to pray.
• We must be careful what we ask God, because He may give it to us and we won't be able to handle it.

Prayer is essential to our salvation. A great commentator on prayer wrote, "Everyone is capable of praying, but many have the mistaken idea that they are not called to prayer. Just as we are called to salvation, we are called to prayer. Scripture commands us to 'pray without ceasing.' (1 Thess. 5:17). Prayer is nothing more than turning our heart toward God and receiving in turn His love."[1] Prayer is *that* important.

I am frequently asked in small-group meetings or after talks, "How can I know God is talking to me?" or "How can I know the will of God for my life?"

The answer is, "You'll never know if all you do is speculate about it." Author and raconteur Garrison Keillor says that "you can no more become a Christian just by going to church than you can become a Cadillac by sleeping in a garage." An effective relationship requires communication. A dynamic relationship with God requires prayer. Prayer is "hands-on" faith.

In spiritual terms, there are only two kinds of people: those to whom God is an intense reality and those to whom He is not. That difference is expressed in prayer.

We read many slogans about prayer: "Prayer changes things," "Prayer doesn't change things; it changes us," "Handle with prayer," "When the going gets tough, the tough get praying." Many prayer "products" are available: prayer bumper stickers, "praying hands" salt and pepper shakers, prayer cloths, prayer incense, and 1-800 prayer lines. Our society seeks to fulfill its nutritional needs through "junk food" and its spiritual needs through "junk prayer."

What does such a prayer have to do with Jesus Christ, who said, " 'I am the way, the truth and the life. No one comes to the Father except by me' "?[2] Absolutely nothing! Jesus said this about prayer: "When you pray, do not be like the hypocrites, for they love to pray standing in the synagogues and on the street corners to be seen by men. I tell you the truth, they have received their reward in full. But when you pray, go into your room, close the door and pray to your Father, who is unseen. Then your Father, who sees what is done in secret, will reward you. And when you pray, do not keep on babbling like pagans, for they think they will be heard because of their many words. Do not be like them, for your Father knows what you need before you ask Him."[3]

Everything we need to know about prayer is contained in these words of Jesus:

- **Jesus says, "When you pray . . ."** Jesus doesn't say, "If you pray . . ." Prayer is essential, not elective, in the Christian life.
- **Jesus says, "Close the door . . ."** Prayer is private. It's between you and God and no one else. Hypocrites pray for show. Honest people seek out God in private.
- **Jesus says, "Don't babble . . ."** Prayer is direct. "Ask" is Jesus' simple instruction.
- **Jesus says, "Pray to your Father . . ."** Prayer is intimate. Prayer isn't talking to the wall or some mysterious "other." Jesus came to show us that His Father is our Father. He called Him Abba. In the colloquial Aramaic language that Jesus used, *Abba* is a personal, intimate name for Father like our *Dad* or *Daddy*. This expression of intimacy with God shocked the religious elite around Jesus, but Jesus knew and taught that a real relationship exists on a first-name basis.

Some persons have such damaged relationships with their own parents that they can't identify with calling God "Father." This is tragic. God, however, is the Parent none of us ever will have on earth. Even if you can't speak to your own parents, prayer opens up a real relationship with God. Andrew Murray, a wonderful writer on prayer, says, Jesus "wants us to know the secret of effective prayer: a heart filled with the Father-love of God. It is not enough for us to know that God is a Father. He wants us to understand fully all that the name implies. Take the best earthly father we know. Think of the tenderness and love he gives to the request of his child, and the joy with which he grants every reasonable desire. Then think in adoring worship of the infinite love and fatherliness

15

of God and consider with how much more tenderness and joy He sees us come and gives us what we ask."[4]

Theologian Roberta Bondi wrestled with relationship with God in the light of her emotionally abusive relationship with her own father. She wrote of that struggle:

> A long time passed after that in which through my everyday prayer I actually began to learn something firsthand about the trustworthiness of the God I couldn't yet address as Father. Then, several things happened that allowed me to become desperate enough as well as brave and trusting enough to do the work of prayer I needed to do around the issue of calling God "Father." I pored over scripture for help, and in God's presence I began to be able to understand in my own heart . . . about the radical implications I heard in Jesus' words when he said to Philip, "The one who has seen me has seen the Father."
>
> As I continued to bring my own past and present experience into painful, direct conversation with God through the help of this and other passages of scripture, I found myself increasingly freed from my secret belief that the way my father had been with me as a child was somehow a normative description not just of God but of the power men have a right to exercise over women in the world.
>
> But remember, I said that I pray the Lord's Prayer for formation in love of God and neighbor together, so you will not be surprised to know that learning to understand God's fatherhood in new ways also helped me significantly with my pain over my human father. Once having stopped confusing my father with God, I was able to forgive my father for his failures toward me and let my father be who he was—not God, but simply a human being with ordinary weaknesses. It was allowing my father to be no more than human, as much as anything else, that made it possible for me to experience myself as his fully adult child. Then, at last, I could be reconciled with him and learn to love him, enjoy him for the actual man he was, and care for him in a way appropriate to him.[5]

I once awoke after a serious surgery to see my own father standing beside my bed. He smiled at me. He kissed my forehead. He didn't say a word. He didn't have to say anything. His presence was enough. I have found this to be true of my heavenly Abba when we visit in prayer. In my favorite book on prayer, Ole Hallesby, a Norwegian theologian, wrote the following:

> My little boy came in one day and stuck his little head into the doorway of my study. Now he knew that he was not supposed to disturb me during working hours. And his conscience troubled him a little on account of this. But he looked at me nevertheless with his kind, round baby eyes and said, "Papa, dear, I will sit still all the time if you will only let me be here with you!"
>
> That he received permission when he approached my father-heart in that way, every father knows. . . .
>
> Is not that just the way we often feel with regard to our heavenly Father? We do so love to be with Him, just to be in His presence! Moreover, we never disturb Him, no matter when we come nor how often we come! . . .
>
> As evening drew nigh, and our little fellow had played until he was tired, I noticed that he drew closer and closer to his mother. At last he found the place he was longing for, mother's lap. He did not have a great deal to say then either. He simply lay there, and let his mother caress him into sleep.
>
> We, too, become tired, deathly tired, of ourselves, of others, of the world, of life, of everything! Then it is blessed to know of a place where we can lay our tired head and heart, our heavenly Father's arms, and say to Him, "I can do no more. And I have nothing to tell you. May I lie here a while and rest? Everything will soon be well again if I can only rest in your arms a while."[6]

Is it our perverse pride that makes our approach to God seem harder than it is? We so easily succumb to the myths and falsehoods that keep us apart. Yet, we are dying without Him. If we can't break the hold that these myths have on us, we need to ask Him directly to set us free.

Questions for Reflection

1. What is your fondest longing about prayer?
2. How have human relationships influenced your prayer life?
3. How have you experienced the presence of God through prayer?

2

Myth: Prayer Makes No Difference

Prayer is a real and active connection between the living God and the children He loves.

"To pray is nothing more involved than to open the door, giving Jesus access to our needs and permitting Him to exercise His own power in dealing with them."[1] The question is, Does Jesus need that access and permission? This is a fundamental question about prayer.

One myth is that prayer is naive and unnecessary because God already knows what we need—so it's pointless to talk about it. A pastor was recruiting me to lead prayer and small-group ministries in his congregation. I made my decision not to take the position when I attended a meeting in which he stated that prayer makes no difference at all—except to people who were in the same room where the prayer was being prayed. "The effect of prayer is only psychological," he said. "God is going to do what God is going to do, and it makes no difference what we tell Him about it."

Let's consider several biblical passages relevant to the myth that prayer is wasted words to a God who ignores our feelings and needs.

1. Prayer at heart is our expressed belief in God. "Without faith it is impossible to please God, for whoever would approach him must believe that he exists and that he rewards those who seek him."[2] Implicit in the text is the requirement of belief in God's existence and His positive engagement with those who believe. The apostle James says that one who doubts, "being double-minded and unstable in every way, must not expect to receive anything from the Lord."[3] Even our struggles with doubt and unbelief are a legitimate subject of prayer. "Help my unbelief!" is a prayer that God will hear and that He will answer. [4]

2. Jesus instructs us to pray. "Don't babble, ask . . ." He says.[5] "Ask your Father," Jesus says. "Ask and it will be given to you; seek and you will find; knock and the door will be opened to you. For everyone who asks receives; he who seeks finds; and to him who knocks, the door will be opened." [6] This is prayer—a direct, simple, honest conversation with the One who can do something about our concern.

Jesus modeled prayer. "In the morning, while it was still very dark, he got up and went to a deserted place, and there he prayed."[7] The Gospels record Jesus' prayers for Himself, for His friends, for the entire world, and for the glory of His Father.

Prayer was the most apparent connection between the man Jesus and God. Jesus taught that prayer was the key to spiritual freedom[8] and changed circumstances.[9] The biblical narrative is replete with interactions between God and humans such as Moses, Elijah, Deborah, David, Solomon, Jeremiah, Nehemiah, Daniel, Mary, Peter, John, a Roman centurion, servants, kings, fishermen, and shepherds. These all realized the grace of God in release, relief, justice, healing, or provision. Sin is what separates fallen humanity from God, and the prophet Samuel observed that not to pray was a sin.[10]

3. God likes us to ask. This is abundantly clear in Scripture. Richard Foster says, "We like our children to ask us for things that we already know they need because the very asking enhances and deepens the relationship. P. T. Forsyth notes, 'Love loves to be told what it knows already. . . . It wants to be asked for what it longs to give.' "[11]

4. A true and deep relationship is a shared relationship. Abraham was God's confidant over His distress at the sin of Sodom.[12] "The LORD used to speak to Moses face to face, as a one speaks to a friend."[13] Jesus loved us enough to become one of us. Jesus loves us so much that He would rather have died than live without us. Jesus called His disciples His friends and prayed to His Father that all of us—Father, Son, and believing children—become one in shared, faithful relationship.[14] Brennan Manning repeats this story of how relationship becomes true in the sharing of hearts: "An old Hasidic rabbi, Levi Yitzhak of Berdichev in the Ukraine, used to say that he discovered the meaning of love from a drunken peasant. Entering a tavern in the Polish countryside, he saw two peasants at a table, both deep in their cups. Each was protesting how much he loved the other, when Ivan said to Peter: 'Peter, tell me what hurts me?' Bleary-eyed, Peter looked at Ivan: 'How do I know what hurts you?' Ivan's answer was swift: 'If you don't know what hurts me, how can you say you love me?' "[15]

No one enjoys being taken for granted. Familiarity breeds contempt. (Have you ever heard the Lord's Prayer recited like so many lines of the telephone book?) However, intimacy, the ability to safely share the thoughts and secrets of the heart, is the fruit of assured love. This assured love is to be found in the intimacy of prayer.

Somehow, this intimacy of prayer usually eludes us, much as intimacy is all too rare in our human relationships. This lack stems from our own denial and self-delusion. Do you ever notice how we tend to talk to everyone except the person who can fix our problem? We want everyone to feel sad or outraged with us because we want to justify ourselves. But we frequently feel alone and empty because others don't share our sadness or outrage. Prayer makes a difference when we open our heart to the One who can do something for us.

Carolyn worked as a secretary in my law office. She was a great employee: intelligent, conscientious, skilled, and cheerful—a delight in every way.

Each Valentine's Day, the women in the office received flowers from their spouses or boyfriends, but Carolyn never did.

Her husband, a well-educated executive, could afford flowers, but he never sent them. "You know how I feel about sending flowers," he told Carolyn. "It's a waste of money. I work hard for you and the kids—and that's enough."

The next Valentine's Day came, and lots of flowers were sent to the office. Again, Carolyn received none. When this happened, she would always go out and buy something expensive and charge it to her husband. This time she bought expensive clothing. She came back and told the other women, "It cost Sam a lot this time."

Some of the women, as a practical joke, took flowers from their arrangements and made a bouquet for Carolyn. They put a ribbon on it and made a card as if Sam had sent it.

Carolyn was thrilled when she received the flowers. She joyfully showed off the bouquet all over the office. Finally, when Carolyn was dialing Sam to tell him "thanks," Joyce, the office manager, interceded to tell Carolyn that it was a joke. The two laughed together at first, but then Carolyn broke into sobs.

Joyce comforted her. Then she asked, "Does Sam know how much you're hurting?"

"I don't hurt; I'm just mad," said Carolyn.

"You're mad 'cause you hurt so much, aren't you?" said Joyce.

"Yes."

"You should tell Sam how you feel."

So that evening, when Sam came to pick up Carolyn, she told him.

"You know I never send you flowers—you know how I feel about that," he said.

Carolyn responded, "And now you know how I feel about it."

Why do we never say how we feel or what we really want until it is too late? Pride? Stubbornness? Fear of rejection? And if we are that way with the persons closest to us, it figures that we will be even more distant with our Father in heaven whom we do not see. "Out of sight, out of mind," the saying goes.

It's a lack of trust. It's a matter of risk—putting aside our fear to state our feelings. What kills this trust in us? Probably a lot of things. One childhood day, we ask for love and it's denied us. Parents may abuse us. Teachers may be too strict and unfeeling. The pain that confronts us may be too intense, and we retreat into an emotional fortress. The standards may be too high for us to reach, and nobody gives us help or hope. Someone we love may betray us or be lost to us.

How do we regain this trust? How do we build the hope that invites us to ask? There is no formula. There is only a choice to accept Jesus' invitation: "Come unto me you who are entangled and thrashing and looking for love in the wrong places or who have given up the hope of love, and I will hold you and wipe your tears and tell you I love you and I will never let you go."

Knowing this, assured of this we can move out in freedom into real and lasting change. Prayer is a relationship, and we cannot grow in that relationship unless we are reborn and accept our life and inheritance as children of God. David sang out about this acceptance of our life as a gift of a loving God: "The Lord be exalted, who delights in the welfare of his servant."[16]

Frederick Buechner writes, "We are children, perhaps, at the very moment when we know that it is as children that God loves us—not because we have deserved his love and not in spite of our undeserving; not because we try and not because we recognize the futility of our trying; but because he is our Father; and all our efforts, fruitful and fruitless, to do good, to speak truth, to understand, are the efforts of children who, for all their precocity, are children still in that before we loved him, he loved us, as children, through Jesus Christ our Lord."[17]

Without this realization that we are the beloved children of a good and gracious God, our prayers are nothing more than spitting into the wind.

Our son Andrew is adopted. He came into Patricia's and my arms within hours of his birth. Often during his childhood, when we prayed just before he went to sleep, I told him, "Andrew, you know if every kid in the world was lined up and I could pick any one of them, I would pick you."

"A-w-w, Dad," he would say because he'd heard this from me for as long as he could remember. "You always say that."

He was right. I always have said that—and I always will. But even of more assurance: Our heavenly Father says it to us.

How long is eternity anyway? That is how long God will love you.

"Though the mountains be shaken
 and the hills be removed,
yet my unfailing love for you will not be shaken
 nor my covenant of peace be removed,"
 says the LORD, who has compassion on you.[18]

God longs to hear from you with whatever is on your heart. God wants to help you. Just say, "Jesus sent me," and tell Him what you need.

Questions for Reflection

1. If God knows the future, why does prayer matter?
2. How can you experience prayer as a relationship?
3. How do you feel about sharing the deepest longings of your heart with God?

3

Myth: Prayer Connects Only When We Ask for the Right Thing

God initiates prayer in our hearts and minds to return us
to the fullness of life with Him.

Don't believe anyone who tells you that prayer is heard by God only when we ask Him for the "right thing."

The truth is that God initiates prayer; we don't. This is evident in Scripture. God spoke directly to Abraham, who was a sheik of an idol-worshiping, nomadic people, led him to a new land, and established a relationship with him through faith.[1] The Bible records that God spoke to Moses as man speaks with his friend.[2] Jesus told His disciples, "No longer do I call you servants, for the servant does not know what his master is doing; but I have called you friends, for all that I have heard from my Father I have made known to you. You did not choose me, but I chose you."[3] The book of Hebrews begins, "In many and various ways God spoke of old to our fathers by the prophets; but in these last days he has spoken to us by a Son."[4]

Jesus says, "Here I am! I stand at the door and knock. If you hear my voice and open the door, I will come in and eat with you, and you will eat with me."[5] Our prayers are not the first step initiating contact with Jesus. It is Jesus who stirs us to pray. He comes to the doors of our hearts. He knocks. He lets us know that He wants to enter in. Our prayers give Him permission to access our needs and permit Him to share the bread of life with us.

Psychiatrist and author John White describes the importance of God-initiated prayer: "Two facts necessarily follow. 'If you are his friend, He will share His thoughts and plans with you. If you are His partner, He will be concerned about your views on His plans and projects. Whatever else prayer may be, it is intended to be a sharing and a taking counsel with God on matters of importance to Him. God has called you to a celestial board meeting to deliberate with Him on matters of destiny.' "[6]

We, who do not see the end from the beginning, may indeed ask God for the "wrong things." I typed this message on a computer. Each computer has default settings. The computer will reset itself automatically to a format after we vary from that format. Our lives also have a default setting. It is revealed in that much-abused verse, "Take delight in the LORD, / and he will grant you the desires of your heart."[7] This verse does not mean that if we desire a new Mercedes-Benz, God will give us a new Mercedes-Benz. We may have no need for a car, or we may own a perfectly serviceable Chevrolet. The promise does mean that if we yield our will to God, since the Lord is both our source and our supply, He will literally re-create our very desires into a desire for God.

God is the default setting of our heart. Many Bible passages express this truth: "He has made everything beautiful in its time. He has also set eternity in the hearts of men."[8] "And now, O Lord, what do I wait for? / My hope is in you."[9]

> O God, you are my God, I seek you,
>   my soul thirsts for you;
> my flesh faints for you,
>   as in a dry and weary land where there is no water.[10]

"My flesh and my heart may fail, / but God is the strength of my heart and my portion forever."[11] "And this is eternal life, that they may know you, the only true God, and Jesus Christ whom you have sent."[12] Our truest desire is to live with God who made, redeems, and sustains us.[13]

Jesus said, " 'Do not worry, saying, "What shall we eat?" or "What shall we drink?" or "What shall we wear?" For the pagans run after all these things, and your heavenly Father knows that you need them. But seek first his kingdom and his righteousness, and all these things will be given to you as well.' "[14] Our honest prayer returns us to God, the default setting of our heart.

Eugene Peterson paraphrases Psalm 42:8 this way:

God promises to love me all day,
    sing songs all through the night!
    My life is God's prayer.[15]

To live our lives as a prayer breathed into the world by our Creator and Redeemer is grace personified. At the Source, it is never an issue of things, right or wrong. "[God] is the source of your life in Christ Jesus, who became for us wisdom from God, and righteousness and sanctification and redemption."[16] In Christ, we receive life and breath and all things, "for 'in him we live and move and have our being.' "[17] The apostle John took this to the next step. "Let what you heard from the beginning abide in you. If what you heard from the beginning abides in you, then you will abide in the Son and in the Father. And this is what he promised us, eternal life. . . . As for you, the anointing that you received from him abides in you, and so you do not need anyone to teach you. But as his anointing teaches you about all things, and is true and is not a lie, and just as it has taught you, abide in him."[18]

The first thing to know about prayer is that God wants to talk to you so much that He starts the conversation. The second thing to know is that praying is the best way to stay close to Him.

Questions for Reflection

1. What moves you to pray?
2. Do you worry about what words to use with God? Why?
3. What can you do to make it easier for God to start a conversation with you?

4

Myth: God Hears and Answers Only the Prayers of "Good" People

*God loves sinners and gives them access to His grace
in their time of greatest need.*

I have a friend who is an infectious disease specialist and a retired professor of medicine. He is a devoted follower of Christ who leads the Medical Evangelism Training Seminar ("METS") affiliated with Campus Crusade for Christ at the Loma Linda University Medical Center. Medical and nursing students from all over the United States come to this inspiring summer program to learn how to integrate their faith into their patient care as health-care professionals.

One evening I attended a small reception for the administration of Loma Linda University and Medical Center in which some medical students who had trained in the program gave their testimonies. At the end of the evening, my friend told a story that inscribed the gospel of Jesus Christ into my heart as few stories ever have.

My friend contracts with a public health department and serves as a physician for its sexually transmitted disease clinic. Men and women who believe they may have an STD come to the clinic for evaluation, testing, and treatment. The clinic visit may not be pleasant, but it is a necessary aspect of programs to control STDs that are pandemic throughout the world, including our southern California community.

One day a young woman came into the clinic. She kept her head down and avoided eye contact as she mumbled the answers to my friend's questions. He performed a physical examination and took an appropriate laboratory specimen. After the woman dressed again, my friend returned to talk with her. Not once during the exam had she raised her head. My friend noticed this and responded, "You seem to be troubled."

"I shouldn't have done it," she said, obviously referring to the conduct by which she had caught the disease.

"Is that what you really think?" asked my friend.

"I know I shouldn't have done it. I'm a Christian," she said, her eyes still focused on the floor.

"Have you told God how you feel?" he asked.

She nodded, "Yes."

"Has God forgiven you?" he asked her.

She shrugged.

My friend took out his pocket New Testament and read from 1 John 1:9, " 'If we confess our sins, he is faithful and just and will forgive us our sins. . . .' Do you believe that God would lie to you?"

"No," she said softly.

"What did God promise to do when you confessed your sins?"

"Forgive me."

"You confessed your sins, am I right?"

"Yes."

"Then what has God done?"

"He has forgiven me," and as she said this, her head moved up ever so slightly and she looked at my friend.

"What does that make you?"

After a pause, she said, "Forgiven."

"OK," he went on. "There's more to the verse. It says, 'If we confess our sins, he is faithful and just and will forgive us our sins and purify us from all unrighteousness.' When God purifies us, how pure do we become?"

"Pure."

"Well, how pure? Fifty percent pure? Ninety percent pure?"

She was getting a little annoyed at him with this one and replied, "One hundred percent pure."

"You believe that God wouldn't lie, and His Word says that He will forgive you if you confess your sins—and you have done that. He also says that He will purify you from all unrighteousness. What does that make you?"

She thought about it for a moment in the florescent hum of the examining room.

For the first time, she sat straight up, smiled, and said, "I am one hundred percent pure."

I think of this story in the context of a question asked me by a "church lady," whose life and experience was a world apart from that STD clinic. As she listened to me talk to a small group about God's desire to hear and answer our prayers, she began to fidget. Then she asked me bluntly, "Kent, how can you say that God hears the prayers of a sinful person? Doesn't the Bible say, 'If I had cherished iniquity in my heart, the Lord would not have listened' to my prayer?[1] Are you really telling us that a holy and righteous God can be approached by a sinful person?"

Her question raises another myth about prayer—that God communicates only with "good" people. If God talks only to well-scrubbed, clear-thinking individuals who keep the Ten Commandments without exception, we all are in real trouble. In that case, 1 John 1:9 would be a lie to that young woman in the STD clinic. A lot of us have the idea that God will hear and respond only to high spiritual achievers. This misconception began when we were given gold stars as children when we said our Bible memory verses correctly or when our parents or teachers told us, "God loves only good little boys and girls."

Consider this radical statement of Jesus to religious bootlickers: " 'You are the ones who justify yourselves in the eyes of men, but God knows your hearts. What is highly valued among men is detestable in God's sight.' "[2] When the religious establishment criticized Jesus for eating with marginal, messed-up persons, He replied, " 'It is not the healthy who need a doctor, but the sick. But go and learn what this means: "I desire mercy, not sacrifice." For I have not come to call the righteous, but sinners.' "[3]

How does Jesus' statement relate to prayer? It says that God loves desperate souls, and that people in trouble have ready access to Him. It means that Jesus Christ identifies with our screw-ups and mistakes. The Bible tells us that Jesus sympathizes with our weaknesses and was "tempted in every way, just as we are—yet was without sin."[4] That text concludes, "Let us then approach the throne of grace with confidence, so that we may receive mercy and find grace to help us in our time of need."[5]

Contrary to what you may have been told most of your religious life, the Bible says that God loves sinners and that you have access to Him in prayer in your time of greatest need, not when you're all "spiffed up" and in your right mind. When is your time of greatest need—when you're lonely, angry, tired, guilty, ashamed, despairing, drunk, damaged? The Word of God says you can be confident in those moments to approach God through Jesus and receive His mercy and His grace to help you.

What about the Bible text the church lady quoted? What did King David mean when he wrote, "If I had cherished iniquity in my heart, the Lord would not have listened to my prayer"? It means that dishonest prayer—prayer in which we pay lip service to God while holding on to our own secret agenda—gets us nowhere. Effective prayer requires our utter honesty. Even if specific sins don't come to mind, we can pray with David, "Who can detect their errors? Clear me from hidden faults."[6]

The only time that Jesus expressly called a person "justified," made right with God, was following an honest prayer by an acknowledged, distressed sinner: " ' "God, be merciful to me, a sinner!" ' "[7] God seeks our undivided hearts, and it's our honesty that is essential.

I was truly startled and resistant a few years ago, when I first read these thoughts from Watchman Nee:

> I have a friend who was preaching in a certain city. A woman sought him out and he talked to her and preached Christ to her. He spoke of her sin, and of the punishment for sin, and of the Lord who came to save. But the woman said to him, "I don't think you know how nice sin is; you have never tasted its delights. I like to sin. Life would be empty otherwise." After a while my friend suggested that they pray. The woman said, "What could one so sinful as I say to your God? I cannot find repentance in my heart. I have nothing I could say that would be acceptable to him." But my friend replied: "My God understands. He is *near* to you and he can hear *any* prayer; so you say to him just what you have said to me." She was amazed, for till now she had only heard the kind of formal prayer where you have to say what you do not believe, for politeness sake! Then he showed her the verse in Acts 11 where it says of the Gentiles on whom the Holy Ghost fell that God "granted" them repentance unto life. So she prayed, and told it all to the God who understands sinners. "Though I do not want to repent," she pleaded. "O God, help me and grant me repentance." And he did! She had opened to his Spirit's illumination the windows of her heart, and she arose from her knees a saved woman.
>
> Here then is a principle, that because Jesus is the Friend of sinners, and because the Holy Spirit undertakes to do what men themselves cannot do, therefore sinners can come to God just as they are. . . .

There is not one other condition necessary to being saved except that of being a sinner and being honest enough to say so to the Lord. That condition is enough to allow the Holy Spirit to begin its convicting and transforming work. . . . Oh, it is wonderful what our God can do! When you go out preaching the gospel, never lose sight of the fact that he is a living God, ready to act in mercy. Even if men and women could be a little better than they are it would not help matters, and if they were much worse it would not hinder. All he looks for is "an honest and good heart." And never forget that the Holy Spirit is present in power to move men's and women's hearts to God.[8]

King David carried on an adulterous affair, murdered his lover's husband, and married her. He tried to assuage his guilt with religious ritual and diligent sacrifice. After God sent the prophet Nathan to confront him with his sins, David prayed probably the most heart-rending, honest prayer in Scripture. It includes these lines:

O Lord, open my lips,
    and my mouth will declare your praise.
For you have no delight in sacrifice;
    if I were to give a burnt offering, you would not be pleased.
The sacrifice acceptable to God is a broken spirit;
    a broken and contrite heart, O God, you will not despise.[9]

What makes a broken heart a good heart? God's presence. "Only God is good," said Jesus.[10] What makes a heart contrite and humble? Casting all our cares upon the Lord. Peter betrayed Christ and committed many impetuous sins and mistakes out of his pride and bluster. Near the end of his life he wrote,

"God opposes the proud,
    but gives grace to the humble."
Humble yourselves therefore under the mighty hand of God, so that he may exalt you in due time. Cast all your anxiety upon him, because he cares for you.[11]

If we think we cannot go to God in prayer unless and until we have cleaned up our mess, we are not practicing humility because we are reserving a role for ourselves. "Cast *all* your care upon me," Jesus says. If we say, "God, my sin is too great for you to forgive," we are not being humble because we think our sin is too great for Jesus' sacrifice to cover us. We are deluded when we think that we can out-sin God's mercy. Paul wrote, "Where sin increased, grace abounded all the more."[12] If we think our concerns are too insignificant for God to care about, we are not humble and hold ourselves outside of God's care for us.

I don't know where you are when you read this or what you've done or what the person on your heart today has done, but I will tell you this: Neither you nor your loved ones are outside the earshot of God or outside of His power to heal and forgive in the person of Jesus Christ.

Even when we are battered and broken, damaged and shamed, if we give our hearts to God with honesty, He will not despise our condition but will tenderly heal us and cleanse us from our shameful stains. Jesus, who did not hesitate or flinch before touching a leper, will not hesitate to touch us in love, regardless of our loathsome condition. His love, after all, is unconditional! We are distasteful to God only if we deny our broken, wretched, naked, blind, pitiful condition in the pretense that we are OK and need nothing.[13]

Since childhood, I have always been moved to tears by the words of the hymn "The Love of God," by F. M. Lehman.

> The love of God is greater far
> Than tongue or pen can ever tell;
> It goes beyond the highest star,
> And reaches to the lowest hell:
> The guilty pair, bowed down with care,
> God gave His Son to win;
> His erring child He reconciled,
> And pardoned from his sin.
>
> Oh, love of God, how rich and pure!
> How measureless and strong!
> It shall for evermore endure—
> The saints, and angels' song.

In 1989, I was a successful attorney representing my church, honored in my community, and . . . I was miserable. A lifelong "Christian," I discovered in great emptiness in a hotel room that I couldn't even pray. Distressed and shamed, I blurted out to God a kind of incoherent cry,

"God, I want to talk to You, but I don't know how." It was a pathetic prayer, but it was honest.

Oh, how Abba answered me in love and mercy, taking me by the hand and teaching me to talk to Him as Patricia and I talked to our baby Andrew until he could mouth his first words in reply. He is the same loving Father who reached out to his shamed daughter with forgiveness and cleansing in the examining room of the STD clinic.

He is the same loving God who is available to you, twenty-four hours a day, seven days a week. All He asks is that you level with Him. There is nothing that you have said, thought, or done that He can't handle. His grace is sufficient for you. He will not despise your broken spirit and wounded, but contrite heart. He longs to take it from you and give you a new, tender, clean heart. He waits patiently for your prayer asking Him to do that very thing.

Only God manifest in Jesus Christ can make us 100 percent pure, and He promises to do this for you and me.

"If we confess our sins, he is faithful and just and will forgive us our sins and purify us from all unrighteousness."[14]

> O taste and see that the LORD is good;
>   happy are those who take refuge in him.[15]

Questions for Reflection

1. What makes a broken heart a good heart?
2. How is giving all your cares to God an act of humility?
3. What have you said or done that God can't handle?

5

Answering the One Who Taunts Me

*Prayer is the path to the knowledge that God loves us now and forever,
and that love is our salvation.*

Here is a basic truth to remember: You can never love anyone more than you believe you are loved yourself. I write about how I came to know this truth.

There is a story of a man who came to see the famous psycho-analyst Carl Jung for help with depression. Jung told him to cut back his fourteen-hour work day to eight, go directly home, and spend the evenings in his study, quiet and all alone. So the man tried. He went to his study, shut the door, read a little Hesse or Mann, played a few Chopin etudes or some Mozart. After some weeks of this he returned to Jung complaining that he could see no improvement. On learning how the man had spent his time, Jung said, "But you didn't understand. I didn't want you to be with Hesse or Mozart or Mann or Chopin. I wanted you to be all alone with yourself." The man looked terrified and exclaimed, "I can't think of any worse company." Jung replied, "Yet this is the self you inflict on other people fourteen hours a day" (and, Jung might have added, "the self you inflict on yourself").[1]

This story explains why I was on an 8,700-foot peak in Arizona's White Mountains at 6:30 A.M., on July 30, 1994, reading Psalm 119. I could no longer live with the self that I was inflicting on others or me. I had learned in childhood to distrust whether I was really loved or not. So to prevent the pain of finding out that I wasn't loved, I learned to keep those closest to me at bay by routinely using an emotional flame thrower to clear the space around me and readjust my boundaries.

I have known many others who, fearing that they were not loved, turned promiscuous, throwing themselves at anyone whom they thought might love them. My problem was the flip side of promiscuity: If you don't let people get close, they can't hurt you. An irate mechanic might pick up a wrench to drive the object of his anger out of his shop. Anger was my tool/weapon of choice to drive those I didn't trust away from me. I learned to think the worst of everyone and ascribe bad motivations to them. That way, I would be able to cut them off when they let me down. However, when you acquire persons in your life who are committed to you no matter what—such as a spouse, a child, and law partners—the habit becomes counterproductive.

Relationships that I valued were broken in my rages. People I loved and who loved me came to fear me and distrust my responses. But the behavior pattern was strong, and I perpetuated the cycle.

Christ had seized my life five years before, and He simply refused to coexist with the flaming heart of anger within me. The fact that my habitual response was a reaction to childhood wounds was no excuse. Paul, in writing of the preeminence of love in the life of the Christ-follower, said, "When I was a child, I spoke like a child, I thought like a child, I reasoned like a child; when I became an adult, I put an end to childish ways."[2] When people depend on you to take care of them, you have to forgo the luxury of indulging yourself at their expense and pain. That's how I take Paul's meaning when he wrote, "We who are strong ought to put up with the failings of the weak, and not to please ourselves. Each of us must please our neighbor for the good purpose of building up the neighbor."[3]

That summer of 1994, I was referred a couple of clients who told me, "They say that whether you win or lose, you always take a pound of flesh." This report just flattened me. When your worst characteristics become your calling card, it is way past time for change. But how could I change what had become my very nature?

So, unfit as I was for companionship to others or myself, I retreated into the Arizona wilderness for two weeks. I would hike every morning before dawn into the woods, and I would spend the day crying out to God to change me. The Holy Spirit strongly impressed upon my heart to pray through Psalm 119. That surprised me because I knew that psalm only as the longest chapter in the Bible and an exposition of the glories of God's law. The message was clear, however, and I obeyed.

On the sixth morning, I found my way cross-country to a rocky promontory that I saw rising out of an aspen grove from the valley below. There I sat and prayed and read these words:

> May your unfailing love come to me, O LORD,
>   your salvation according to your promise;
> then I will answer the one who taunts me,
>   for I trust in your word.[4]

It was a moment of revelation. God loves me. His love is steadfast and will not fail. He will keep His promise and save me through His love. This knowledge, this truth, when transferred from my head to my heart, is salvation. The discovery then came: I will be able to answer the one who taunts me—and *the one who taunts me is me*. The answer is, "I am loved, and the Creator and Savior of the universe finds me loveable." In that moment a door opened in my heart, and I walked through to free spaces and began to love as I am loved.

I wish I could tell you that I never lost my temper again. The fact of the flesh is that it remains flesh. I am still a flawed product of my past, my environment, my temperament, my physical chemistry, my stresses, and my selfishness that comprises my flesh. What Paul says is true:

> The entire law is summed up in a single command: "Love your neighbor as yourself." If you keep on biting and devouring each other, watch out or you will be destroyed by each other.
>   So I say, live by the Spirit and you will not gratify the desires of the sinful nature. . . .
>   . . . Those who belong to Christ Jesus have crucified the sinful nature with its passions and desires. Since we live by the Spirit, let us keep in step with the Spirit. Let us not become conceited, provoking and envying each other.[5]

The simple fact of love that I've learned is this: If you belong to Christ, if you sit with Him beside His Father in His love and righteousness—then you no longer have to force the issues and people in your life to compensate for your lack of love. These words of Jesus always melt my heart: " 'I will not leave you orphaned; I am coming to you. In a little while the world will no longer see me, but you will see me; because I live, you also will live. On that day you will know that I am in my Father, and you in me, and I in you.' "[6] Accepting this promise changed everything for me. I do not have to live the way I used to live.

A year after that Arizona morning, I was driving with Patricia. I told her in amazed relief: "I'm not mad anymore. I don't know when it happened or exactly how it happened, but the rage has gone out of me rather like a forest fire must go out in the rain—slowly and gently, with steaming hisses and flare-ups—but it goes out."

This chapter was written long before I found the courage to let anyone else read it. Many persons who read my writings also work with me. There are times when I am required to take tough stands with them and set boundaries. Occasionally, someone says, "Oh that's just Kent; you know how he is," (wink, wink) instead of dealing with the issue at hand. There are persons who have never forgiven me for what I've said and done. One of them, the subject of a lawsuit I brought for a church organization, a few years ago rehashed my alleged sins in high school on a Web site complete with a photograph that had horns added to my head. There is a price to be paid for one's past.

On the other hand, while a lot is said about anger, we tend to talk about other people's rage and not our own. Angry persons have a hard time finding understanding or help. There is no loneliness like that found in the shameful silence after a rage. The fires of anger require fuel, and that fuel generally is those people closest at hand. When it's over, the ones to whom we wish to justify ourselves have gone away or are resigned to apathy against the possibility that any show of passion would draw more anger from us.

The appetite of anger is deep and intense. One psalm compares angry people to wild, hungry dogs, never satisfied:

> They return at evening,
>   snarling like dogs,
>   and prowl about the city.
> They wander about for food
>   and howl if not satisfied.[7]

There is no cure, no fulfillment, until grace is received and acknowledged.

> Let them thank the LORD for his steadfast love,
>   for his wonderful works to humankind.

For he satisfies the thirsty,
  and the hungry he fills with good things.[8]

I write my personal experience not to bare my soul, for that alone helps no one. I am telling you out of my personal knowledge about the cleansing and healing that is possible with Jesus Christ. I represent only a minuscule sample of that possibility. "The river of God is full of water."[9] There is plenty of water there to wash you clean and cool your fever. There is transforming power in the realization that you are loved unconditionally and eternally.

_____ *Questions for Reflection* _____

1. How does anger affect your prayer?
2. What does God do with your broken and sinful heart?
3. What change does the presence of Christ in your heart make in how you deal with people?

6

Jesus Stands Still for Us

With patience and compassion, Jesus Christ will stop, listen, and wait for the most broken of us.

Jesus was on His final walk to Jerusalem for the fulfillment of His destiny. No one with Him knew how the scenes would unfold when they arrived in the city, but they all seemed to understand that something world-changing would happen there. Perhaps a revolt would drive out the Romans and re-establish the throne of David, fulfilling the promise of Israel as God's light to the world. Jesus seemed to grasp the big picture, and His companions were right there with Him, waiting for the details to fill in. There was a scramble among His followers to lay claim to positions in the new order. His ministry was attracting crowds and excitement that Israel hadn't seen in a millennium. In tumult like this, fragile souls can be lost, broken, or left behind.

As Jesus approached Jericho with His retinue, a blind beggar created a sideshow by screaming, "Jesus, Son of David, have mercy on me!" The people in front of him told him to "sit down and be quiet!" Instead of complying, the blind man yelled louder. "Jesus stood still and ordered the man to be brought to him."

When they brought the man forward, Jesus asked, "What do you want me to do for you?" He said, "Lord, let me see again." Jesus said, "Receive your sight, your faith has saved you." The recovery of sight was immediate. The man followed Jesus down the road shouting "Hallelujah, Praise God!"[1]

A ways down the road, another distraction was created by a tree-climbing tax collector named Zacchaeus. Jesus stopped under the tree and called Zacchaeus down for a conversation that ended up in a leisurely dinner at Zacchaeus's home. Again those following Jesus became irritated because they resented the interruption and the fact that Jesus would spend time at the home of a person proper society considered an irredeemable gangster. "I stop for people like this," Jesus said. " 'For the Son of man came to seek and to save the lost.' "[2]

There is power in the fact that "Jesus stood still." We like to think of Jesus teaching, healing, blessing infants, calming storms, walking on water, confronting hypocrites. We see Him, as the Roman centurion saw Him, giving His subordinates a stream of unquestioned orders to "go" and "come."

It was Jesus' stopping and standing still that slowed and paced the popular, mindless drive of the crowd to Jerusalem and allowed Him to focus on His mission. That mission is centered on lost people, not dramatic events. It is the time-honored wisdom of parents of lost children that standing still and waiting is the best way to hear cries of desperation.

We all wonder at times whether Jesus hears our prayers in the midst of the competing clamors of a needy and anxious world. With so many urgent demands for His ear, how can our message get through, and why would He give it priority?

Standing still is the attitude of listening. The military calls it "standing at attention." It is the position one assumes to listen without distraction. Standing still allows assessment of course and obstacles before changing direction. It is what a parent asks a child to do so that the child can be cleaned, have clothing adjusted or shoes tied, or receive instruction.

Jesus Christ is the Creator of the universe. He is not bound by time or place. He rides "on the wings of the wind" on cloud-chariots.[3] Yet, Jesus stopped with the stillness of death itself, allowing Himself to be nailed tight to a wooden cross, so that we might "mount up with wings like eagles" and soar with Him into eternity.

After Jesus' resurrection, He went beyond standing still. He sat down at the right hand of the Father so that "we have this hope, a sure and steadfast anchor of the soul."[4] "Let us therefore approach the throne of grace with boldness, so that we may receive mercy and find grace to help in time of need."[5]

These words may reach you when you've lost your vision. The crowd around you may be blocking your access to Jesus even though you are crying out and shouting for mercy. Some may claim their spiritual position in proximity to Jesus by elbowing you back. Maybe you are desperate enough that, like Zacchaeus, your search has taken you way out on a limb. Jesus may appear to be a moving target to you—and the movement is always away from you.

I have good news for you. Your cry for mercy is not futile. Your desire to break free and regain your spiritual vision is not in vain. With "utmost patience,"[6] Jesus Christ will stand still, listen, and wait for even the most messed-up of persons.

You may be paralyzed between the conflicting demands of your friends and family wanting immediate progress and of your own fears and doubts. The impatient apostle Peter learned that Christ waits patiently for however long it takes for you to limp to the healing change of His presence. "The Lord is not slow about his promise, as some think of slowness, but is patient with you, not wanting any to perish, but all to come to repentance."[7] Peter said, "Regard the patience of our Lord *as salvation.*"[8] The very fact that Jesus Christ is waiting for you, enduring with you, hoping for you (because patience involves those things) is saving grace to you.

It is entirely possible that those who want to silence your shouts for mercy fear that their crowd-mentality might be disturbed by someone not participating in their enthusiasm and conformity. Jesus stopped still in the road to listen to the honest cry of the blind beggar in spite of the attempts of the front row to silence him. Jesus will do the same for you.

> The LORD is just in all his ways,
> and kind in all his doings.
> The LORD is near to all who call on him,
> to all who call on him in truth.
> He fulfills the desire of all who fear him;
> he also hears their cry, and saves them.[9]

Your conduct may have so shamed your community that its members resent and scorn your desire for Jesus to be a guest in your house.[10] Jesus takes your desire for His presence as all the invitation He needs, and He has a word for you, not for them. " 'Hurry and come down; for I must stay at your house today.' "[11]

Jesus Christ, the Lord of the universe, will stand still to listen to you. It is all true, and it is a grace. It is the gospel of Jesus Christ. I give you this reminder and add the prayer of the apostle Paul: "May the Lord direct your hearts to the love of God and to the steadfastness of Christ."[12]

Questions for Reflection

1. Do you picture Jesus standing still for you or on the move for you?
2. What is the effect of your crowd on your devotional life?
3. According to Hebrews 4:16, with what attitude can you approach Christ?

7

It's the Thought, Not the Words

The honest expression of a heart turned toward God is more important than knowing the right words to pray.

We need to confront the myth that God hears only prayers that use the "right" words. What I mean by the "right words" are nice, reverent, positive words and phrases. The idea that prayer requires a specific vocabulary and tone is quickly disproved by even a cursory reading of Psalms.

My friend Joyce had had enough! Years of surviving abuse, abandonment, illness, marital betrayal and divorce, bills, kids in trouble, and bad religion had taken their toll on her self-esteem and a once-vibrant relationship with God. She went home from work and climbed into the shower. There she screamed out to God, "I hate You! I hate You!" She poured out the anger and bitterness of her heart in curses as the hot water washed over her.

In the silence as she toweled off, a question rose in her soul, "You aren't dead, are You?" It surprised her. She had been taught, "If you talk that way to God, He will strike you down."

The next day her landlord was working in her backyard. He came to the back door and called to Joyce, "Come see what's out here."

She stepped out across the lawn that had been mowed just a few days before. There, rising up out of the grass was an unusual flower. It had a long stem supporting six trumpet-shaped, deep-pink-and-white blossoms with bright yellow stamens. It was perfect. The lily hadn't been there two days before when the lawn was mowed. How had it grown so fast? How did it force itself through the root thatch of the lawn? Why was there only one? So many questions—and such great beauty.

Joyce knelt beside the plant and gently cupped the blossoms in her hand. She was delighted. In that moment, God spoke to her heart: *"See, that's what I think about you. You are unique. You are beautiful in my sight. I delight in you."* Life and spirit flooded back into Joyce's heart and mind as she stood up in the restoration of the Lord.

My friend's experience is authentic grace. Even now, long after this event happened, if someone from the small group where she first told this story mentions "Joyce's flower," it brings instant smiles and tears of joy.

Crying out in pain that you hate God has this to commend it—it is honest communication. God can handle honesty.

> The LORD is near to all who call on him,
>   to all who call on him in truth.
> He fulfills the desire of all who fear him;
>   he also hears their cry, and saves them.[1]

Our cry of pain also confronts the One who has the power to do something about the pain. We project our anger and spill our angst all over people, but it only shows that misery loves company. When our children skin their knees, they insist on telling us about it. No one but Mommy or Daddy will do at such a time. No one can listen, hug, place the band-aid, and kiss the boo-boo like a parent. So our kids bite their lips and grit it out until they can dissolve their tearful anguish in our arms. We are children of a heavenly Father. It works the same way with Him. This is the premise of many of the psalms.

Some people of my acquaintance hate to read the psalms. They say that they are too full of hurt, struggle, betrayal, anger, and disappointments. "Blood-thirsty" was how one woman described them to me. The psalms are gritty because they are real prayers prayed by real people in the highs and lows of their lives.

A few years back, I was called by a friend, a long-time executive who had been devastatingly and treacherously betrayed, threatening his good reputation and career. He was upset beyond words. I suggested that he read Psalm 109 before he went to bed that night. This is a prayer of David that reads thus:

Do not be silent, O God of my praise.
For wicked and deceitful mouths are opened against me,
    speaking against me with lying tongues. . . .
In return for my love they accuse me,
    even while I make prayer for them.
So they reward me evil for good,
    and hatred for my love.

They say, "Appoint a wicked man against him;
    let an accuser stand on his right.
When he is tried, let him be found guilty;
    let his prayer be counted as sin.
May his days be few;
    may another seize his position.
May his children be orphans,
    and his wife a widow.
May his children wander about and beg;
    may they be driven out of the ruins they inhabit.
May the creditor seize all that he has;
    may strangers plunder the fruits of his toil.
May there be no one to do him a kindness,
    nor anyone to pity his orphaned children.
May his posterity be cut off;
    may his name be blotted out in the second generation.
May the iniquity of his father be remembered before the LORD,
    and do not let the sin of his mother be blotted out. . . ."

May that be the reward of my accusers from the LORD,
    of those who speak evil against my life.
But you, O sovereign LORD my Lord,
    act on my behalf for your name's sake;
    because your steadfast love is good, deliver me.
For I am poor and needy,
    and my heart is pierced within me.[2]

My friend told me the next day that this prayer helped save his spiritual life by allowing him to bring his feelings of hurt and betrayal to God. You may ask why a prayer like this is even in the Bible. It's there for two reasons. It shows us that we can pray about anything, even when we are angry, and there are texts that say we can even pray our anger and disappointment with God.[3] David did the best thing that he could do with his anger—he put the problem squarely in God's hands.

It doesn't matter that the words aren't nice. Jesus taught that greeting-card formulas for prayer are worthless. He said, " 'When you are praying, do not heap up empty phrases as the Gentiles do; for they think they will be heard because of their many words. Do not be like them, for your Father knows what you need before you ask him.' "[4]

The apostle Paul told the Romans this principle of prayer: "The Spirit helps us in our weakness. We do not know what we ought to pray for, but the Spirit Himself intercedes for us with groans that words cannot express. And he who searches our hearts knows the mind of the Spirit, because the Spirit intercedes for the saints in accordance with God's will."[5] God is so ready, willing, and able to hear and answer our prayers that He accepts the groans and sighs of an honest but desperate heart as prayer, and He has a plan for exactly the help that we need. A great writer on prayer said, "Pray as you can, don't pray as you can't."[6]

Sometimes it is impossible to pray in words at all. Seven years ago, my sister was diagnosed with pancreatic cancer, and almost immediately her body reacted with increased thrombin in her blood. This created a clot that exploded like a grenade in her brain. It deprived her of speech and the use of the left side of her body, and in three awful weeks she was dead. But at first she could recognize and respond to her loved ones.

On the third evening after the stroke, I slipped into her hospital room and sat beside her holding her hand. When the lights were turned down for the night, I began to softly sing to her the hymns and songs of our life together. She gripped my hand firmly in her right hand, and somehow she moved her limp left arm over her body and laid that hand on top of mine. I sang hymn after hymn: "Precious Lord, Take My Hand," "My Faith Looks Up to Thee," "Turn Your Eyes Upon Jesus," "Shall We Gather at the River," "In the Sweet By and By," "In a Little While We're Going Home," and more.

In between songs, I would pray aloud for our heavenly Father to hold and comfort my dear Judi and touch her with His love. I thanked Him for the many joys that we had shared. With my free hand I stroked her forehead. I thought from time to time that she was asleep, and I would start to gently pull my hand away, but her eyes would open and she would grip my hand more tightly. We were siblings in a family that loved to worship. This was the sacred threshold of eternity where life and death come together in their sunset. The songs and the touch were prayer. The hushed peace of our loving Savior enveloped us in the darkness. His presence was the answer to her speechless, waiting heart.

These words of Ole Hallesby have great meaning to me:

We will all have use for wordless prayer, if not before, when the death-struggle and the death-agony tax all our energies. That does not always take place exactly at the moment of death. The death-struggle is usually fought out some time before the end comes.

I have witnessed the death-struggle of some of my Christian friends. Pain has coursed through their bodies and souls. But this was not their worst experience. I have seen them gaze at me anxiously and ask, "What will become of me when I am no longer able to think a sustained thought—nor pray to God?"

When I stand at the bedside of friends who are struggling with death, it is blessed to be able to say to them, "Do not worry about the prayers that you cannot pray. You yourself are a prayer to God at this moment. All that is within you cries out to Him. And He hears all the pleas that your suffering soul and body are making to Him with groanings which cannot be uttered. But if you should have an occasional restful moment, thank God that you have already been reconciled to Him, and that you are now resting in the everlasting arms."[7]

Questions for Reflection

1. Why are angry psalms in the Scriptures?
2. With whom are you most likely to share your pain?
3. How have you experienced prayer without words?

8

The Sunflower Gospel, Part 1

A loving Father won't ever give His child too much to handle.
Trust God to give you what you need and the help to handle it.

My son, Andrew, and I planted a garden together when he was five. He is growing up in a southern California city, unlike my rural upbringing in the hills of coastal central California.

I wanted to teach Andrew the secrets of growing things. His grandpa and I built a box two feet by four feet by eight feet. I filled it with seventy dollars worth of compost, soil amendment, topsoil, sand, and steer manure—a suburban lawyer's and Home Depot's idea of "bottomland."

Andrew poked tiny holes with a stick, making ragged rows for lots and lots of carrots and radishes. We also planted lettuce, beets, and cabbage. He made a face at the thought of eating them. "You don't need to eat it to grow it," I told him.

The final row was devoted to heart-shaped sunflower seeds. I stuck my index finger in the soft dirt up to the first knuckle. Andrew carefully dropped in the seeds. His hands patted little mounds over them.

Two nights later I took Andrew with me on an errand. As we were driving down the freeway, he suddenly said, "Dad, we forgot rain for our garden."

"I watered it, Son."

"We need rain for our garden."

"Do you want to ask Jesus to send rain?"

He nodded.

"OK, you ask Him first, and then I'll pray."

Glancing sideways, I could glimpse his hands folded and his eyes squeezed shut in the light of the passing freeway signs.

"Dear Jesus, we need rain for our garden so that it will grow vegetables. Please send us some. I love You, Jesus. Amen."

"Dear Jesus . . ." I began.

"Dad! Don't close your eyes; you're driving," Andrew interrupted.

Two nights later it rained through the night unexpectedly. Southern California had endured a long drought between 1990 and 1992. This was a gentle rain, the first in a long time. Though it was gone by morning, it was just enough to soak the new seeds.

Through the window, I showed Andrew the wet street when he woke up. "Do you remember that you asked Jesus for rain? He sent it."

"Of course," Andrew said.

Several days later it began to rain again. The drought broke. It poured every day for nearly a month.

On the way home from preschool one afternoon, Andrew asked Patricia if he could ride his new bike when he got home.

"Not today, Sweetheart. It's raining."

"Mom," he said thoughtfully, "do you remember when I asked Jesus for rain for my garden?"

"Yes."

"I think Jesus thought I meant forever."

With that introduction of a little boy's faith in getting more from Jesus than he asked for, we examine one of the most sinister myths about prayer.

Religious cynics warn us, "Be careful about what you ask God because He might give it to you, and you wouldn't be able to handle it."

This myth about prayer is a vicious slander against God. Our Father in heaven is not some Halloween witch playing trick-or-treat with us. The ringing instruction of the apostle Paul to his protégé, Timothy, spoke of God's desire for us in this regard. "I am reminded of your sincere faith . . . [that], I am sure, lives in you. For this reason I remind you to rekindle the gift of God that is within you through the laying on of my hands; for God did not give us a spirit of cowardice, but rather a spirit of power and of love and of self-discipline."[1]

Christ will never deny heaven to someone for living too boldly the life that He gives.[2] He will deny heaven to liars and cowards who are too faithless and self-serving to commit to life and accept love and who instead try to make it up for themselves by taking life and love away from someone or something else. The apostle John wrote down this revelation from Christ: "The one who was seated on the throne said, 'See I am making all things new.' Also he said, 'Write this, for these words are trustworthy and true.' Then he said to me, 'It is done! I am the Alpha and Omega, the beginning and the end. To the thirsty I will give water as a gift from the spring of the water of life. Those who conquer will inherit these things, and I will be their God and they will be my children. But as for the cowardly, the faithless, the polluted, the murderers, the fornicators, the sorcerers, the idolaters, and all liars, their place will be in the lake that burns with fire and sulfur, which is the second death.' "[3]

Jesus told His disciples, "Don't bargain with God. Be direct. Ask for what you need. This isn't a cat-and-mouse, hide-and-seek game we're in. If your child asks for bread, do you trick him with sawdust? If he asks for fish, do you scare him with a live snake on his plate? As bad as you are, you wouldn't think of such a thing. You're at least decent to your own children. So don't you think the God who conceived you in love will be even better?"[4]

The most frequent command of Jesus recorded in the Gospels is "Do not be afraid!" A God who you never call on out of fear of disappointment is a dead god to you. James M. Scriven said it well in the memorable line from the hymn "What a Friend We Have in Jesus":

> O what peace we often forfeit,
> O what needless pain we bear,
> All because we do not carry
> Everything to God in prayer!

Jesus described God as a father who was wounded by an ungrateful son who demanded an early settlement of his inheritance, which he then squandered while partying in strip clubs and bars. The son hit rock-bottom before he finally came to his senses. When the son came home to beg for a job, the father ran to him, welcomed him, forgave him, and incredibly, threw a "welcome home" party for the boy.[5]

The apostle John defined the love of our heavenly Father this way: "God is love. . . . this is love, not that we loved God but that he loved us and sent his Son to be the atoning sacrifice for our sins."[6] We could never love God enough to earn His love—and we aren't asked to do so. Love is defined by the heavenly Father's complete, unconditional love for us. Our human love can never be anything but conditional because we are the created, not the Creator, and we are inadequate in our brokenness. That is why God bases love on what is in His heart, not in ours.

Paul fleshed out what this love originating from God is like. "Love is patient, love is kind. It does not envy, it does not boast, it is not proud. It is not rude, it is not self-seeking, it is not easily angered, it keeps no record of wrongs. Love does not delight in evil but rejoices with the truth. It always protects, always trusts, always hopes, always perseveres."[7] Because God is love, Paul has described qualities possessed by God. God is patient. God is kind. God does not envy. God does not boast. God is not proud. God is not rude. God is not self-seeking. God is not easily angered. God keeps no record of wrongs. God does not delight in evil but rejoices with the truth. God always protects. God always trusts. God always hopes. God always perseveres.

To speak of God in these terms almost seems blasphemous because our view of God has many human distortions. But these are qualities of the God who loves us and which compelled the God-man, Jesus Christ, to lay down His life on the cross to reconcile us with God. This God is not going to play cat-and-mouse with our desperate hearts. "The LORD be exalted, / who delights in the well-being of his servant."[8]

My friend Jane has undergone wearying cycles of chemotherapy in battling lymphoma for many years. After one crisis, during which she was supported by much prayer, I received a one-word e-mail from her: "REMISSION!!!!!!!!"

During the darkest days of that round of treatment, Jane sent me the following unattributed poem that speaks to God's loving will for us:

The Will of God

The Will of God will never take you,
Where the grace of God cannot keep you,
Where the arms of God cannot support you,
Where the riches of God cannot supply your needs,
Where the power of God cannot endow you.

The Will of God will never take you,
Where the Spirit of God cannot work through you,
Where the wisdom of God cannot teach you,
Where the army of God cannot protect you,
Where the hands of God cannot mold you.

The Will of God will never take you,
Where the love of God cannot enfold you,
Where the mercies of God cannot sustain you,
Where the peace of God cannot calm your fears,
Where the authority of God cannot overrule for you.

The Will of God will never take you,
Where the comfort of God cannot dry your tears,
Where the Word of God cannot feed you,
Where the miracles of God cannot be done for you,
Where the Omnipresence of God cannot find you.[9]

" 'Be still, and know that I am God!' "[10]

Questions for Reflection

1. What does fear about asking God for too much say about God and say about you?
2. What answers to prayer can you expect from a loving God?
3. Do you have doubts that God is concerned about your well-being? Why?

9

The Sunflower Gospel, Part 2

Honest prayer is the open door to God's love and healing.

I know not from what distant time Thou art ever coming nearer to meet me. Thy sun and stars can never keep Thee hidden from me for aye.

In many a morning and eve Thy footsteps have been heard and Thy messenger has come within my heart and called me in secret.

I know not why to-day my life is all astir, and a feeling of tremulous joy is passing through my heart.

It is as if the time were come to wind up my work, and I feel in the air a faint smell of Thy sweet presence.[1]

Prayer takes us to the heart of Christ. His heart is great for us. His heart longs for us. He invites us to relationship—real, honest communion through prayer. No performance, no teaching, no tradition, no doctrine, no other commitment can substitute for a relationship with Christ. The question is, Will you pray?

Real prayer begins with a longing heart and few words.

A woman dreamed she found a new shop at the mall. She entered to find God waiting on her, much to her surprise.

"What do you sell here?" she asked.

"Everything your heart desires," said God.

Overwhelmed by the possibilities of her good fortune, the woman decided to ask only for the best spiritual things she could think of. "I want peace of mind and love and happiness and wisdom and . . . freedom . . . freedom from fear," she said. Then a pang of guilt tweaked her conscience with the thought, *Oh, but all that's just for me.*

So she hurried to add, "Not just for me. For everyone on earth."

God smiled. "I think you've got Me wrong, my dear," He said. "We don't sell fruit here. Only seeds."[2]

In the previous chapter, I told about my son, Andrew, and I planting a vegetable garden when he was five years old. Jesus answered Andrew's simple prayer for rain and brought quick, luxurious growth. When the seedlings grew a bit, we thinned them out. The sunflowers needed more room in the garden box, so we took out all but two plants. Then sin and pain entered the garden.

Our backyard is unfenced. Someone stomped through the garden one afternoon. A small footprint smashed a row of carrots. A gum wrapper was tossed between the rows. One of our two sunflower plants, about three feet high and just beginning to bud, was snapped. The stalk was broken in the middle, and some of its fibers were shredded. The top half hung limp over the side of the garden box.

Andrew was upset. So was I, even more. We argued about who could have done this thing. Maybe a kid, I suggested.

"No," he declared. "A kid would never do something like that! A grown-up would."

I wasn't so sure. My anger and sadness turned to suspicion. "Did you do this?" I asked him.

Andrew was indignant. Lifting one foot up until I could see the sole of his sneaker, he demanded, "Do you see this foot?"

"Yes."

He pointed at the footprint in the garden. "Do you see that footprint?"

"Yes."

"Do you think this foot made that footprint?" The footprint was obviously larger than his foot.

"No." I averted my eyes and mumbled, "I'm sorry." The son of a lawyer had learned his lessons well. The defense rested, having destroyed the prosecution's case. Andrew huffed off across the yard.

I reached down then to pull out the broken plant, but I couldn't do it. Father and son had placed the seed tenderly in the ground and watched it grow together. We had thinned out the other plants, choosing this one to grow. We had watered it and protected it.

Now I could not kill it. I would wait until it turned brown and withered before I pulled it out. *Silly*, I thought to myself, *but I cannot destroy what I love.*

A week later I noticed a surprising thing. The plant still hung down, but its head had twisted on the stalk until its bud faced the sun. The stalk was contorted; it looked unnatural, even painful.

The broken plant continued to grow as the days passed. It reached the point where it stood straight out at a ninety-degree angle from the broken place. The torn fibers strained but held. The bud blossomed, and the warm sun drew its namesake up toward it. I marveled.

The weight of the blossom appeared too much for the broken stalk to bear. There was nothing going for the broken plant but life itself. But gradually the stalk straightened and thickened at the torn place. It actually became stronger there.

We went on vacation for ten days. I raced to see the sunflower when we came home. It bloomed full—a rich, dark chocolate face surrounded by yellow petals. It was taller than its companion plant.

The head became so heavy with seeds that I thought the stalk might break again. It held, but leaned far out of the box. The seeds filled out its heart with an intricate concave pattern. Bees fed on the sweetness of the huge flower.

Andrew took friends and visitors to see the remarkable flower. They would quiet when I told them the story of the broken plant that I couldn't bear to destroy.

We come to prayer this way, longing for life and growth and beauty as we were created to be, but broken, shredded, and limp as we really are. But this is where prayer begins its power if we know God's intentions toward us.

One afternoon the disciple Andrew brought some curious visitors to see Jesus, the full flower of God's love. Jesus used the occasion to explain the facts of life in the kingdom of God.

"The hour has come for the Son of Man to be glorified. I tell you the truth, unless a kernel of wheat falls to the ground and dies, it remains only a single seed. But if it dies, it produces many seeds. . . .

"Now my heart is troubled, and what shall I say? 'Father, save me from this hour'? No, it was for this very reason I came to this hour. . . .

". . . But I, when I am lifted up from the earth, will draw all men to myself."[3]

In our prayer a hard heart-shaped seed dies to live. Our wounds submitted to Abba in prayer become points of strength. Surprising, surpassing glory springs out of our brokenness. That glory belongs to the Father and the Son who, in their love, cannot bear to destroy what they have planted and watered.

It's true for you and me, you know. Jesus Christ will not break a bruised reed or snuff out a smoldering, flickering candle.[4] He heals with the warmth of His smile and the shelter of the hollow of His hand.

This healing is revealed in my favorite story about prayer told by Christian writer Brennan Manning.

There was an old man dying of cancer. The old man's daughter had asked the local priest to come and pray with her father. When the priest arrived, he found the man lying in bed with his head propped up on two pillows and an empty chair beside his bed. The priest assumed that the old fellow had been informed of his visit. "I guess you were expecting me," he said.

"No, who are you?"

"I'm the new associate at your parish," the priest replied. "When I saw the empty chair, I figured you knew I was going to show up."

"Oh yeah, the chair," said the bedridden man. "Would you mind closing the door?"

Puzzled, the priest shut the door.

"I've never told anyone this, not even my daughter," said the man, "but all my life I have never known how to pray. At the Sunday Mass I used to hear the pastor talk about prayer, but it always went right over my head. Finally I said to him one day in sheer frustration, 'I get nothing out of your homilies on prayer.'

" 'Here,' says my pastor reaching into the bottom drawer of his desk. 'Read this book by Hans Urs von Balthasar. He's a Swiss theologian. It's the best book on contemplative prayer written in the twentieth century.'

"Well, Father," says the man, "I took the book home and tried to read it. But in the first three pages I had to look up twelve words in the dictionary. I gave the book back to my pastor, thanked him, and under my breath whispered 'for nothin'.'

"I abandoned any attempt at prayer," he continued, "until one day about four years ago my best friend said to me, 'Joe, prayer is just a simple matter of having a conversation with Jesus. Here's what I suggest. Sit down on a chair, place an empty chair in front of you, and in faith see Jesus on the chair. It's not spooky because He promised, "I'll be with you all days." Then just speak to Him and listen in the same way you're doing with me right now.'

"So, Padre, I tried it and I've liked it so much that I do it a couple of hours every day. I'm careful though. If my daughter saw me talking to an empty chair, she'd either have a nervous breakdown or send me off to the funny farm."

The priest was deeply moved by the story and encouraged the old guy to continue on the journey. Then he prayed with him, anointed him with oil, and returned to the rectory.

Two nights later the daughter called to tell the priest that her daddy had died that afternoon.

"Did he seem to die in peace?" he asked.

"Yes, when I left the house around two o'clock, he called me over to his bedside, told me one of his corny jokes, and kissed me on the cheek. When I got back from the store an hour later, I found him dead. But there was something strange, Father. In fact beyond strange, kinda weird. Apparently just before Daddy died, he leaned over and rested his head on a chair beside his bed."[5]

Talking to Jesus as to a friend. Putting your head in His lap. That's the stuff of relationship! That's prayer! That's knowing God!

Prayer is a candid conversation with the living God. It is not pious phrases, kneeling benches, or elaborate formulas. It is planting seeds, submitting our garden of hopes to God, seeking mercy to mend and heal the broken places and the joy of Christ to fill the empty spaces, yielding our angers and suspicions and resentments so nothing wards off the transforming power of the Holy Spirit. No relationship in our lives means anything without conversation. So it is with our relationship with God.

Prayer is the point where a real life with God begins. If you don't know how to start, try telling Him what I did many years ago. "God, I want to talk to You, but I don't know how." He will come into your heart and teach you to pray.[6] Our Lord's heart desire is to be in intimate fellowship with us forever. Jesus' great prayer recorded in John 17 ended with these words:

> "Father, I want those you have given me to be with me where I am, and to see my glory, the glory you have given me because you loved me before the creation of the world.
>
> "Righteous Father, though the world does not know you, I know you, and they know that you have sent me. I have made you known to them, and will continue to make you known in order that the love you have for me may be in them and that I myself may be in them."[7]

So the Lord Jesus Christ reveals His longing for you to His Father. If you open your heart to Jesus in prayer, you become the answer to His prayer, and His presence will become your reality. This is the truth about prayer.

Questions for Reflection

1. What does the story of the sunflower bring to your mind about the character of God?
2. What happens to a relationship if there is no conversation?
3. Who will teach you to pray?

10

Without Reservation

*True intercessory prayer lays down the life of the intercessor
for friends and loved ones.*

Somewhere in boardrooms, hospital wards, jazz clubs, baseball dugouts, homes, movie theaters, and day care centers, on cruises, in hovels, in bookstores, and even occasionally—to everyone's great surprise and edification—in the pulpit, are those who feel the scars on the Fisherman's outstretched hands and are willing to forsake the crowded, beaten path for the one they can't yet see.[1]

Years ago, I stood in the driveway as a loved one who was suffering from terminal illness, laboring for oxygen with gasps that could be heard as far as the street outside her home. My companion standing with me asked, "How does one get through this?"

I thought about it for a moment, looking up to see a waxing moon keeping its faithful cycle. This question was something that I'd given a lot of thought. "I think it depends on what you believe happens after she dies," I said. "Paul wrote in 1 Corinthians 15:19, 'If for this life only we have hoped in Christ, we are of all people most to be pitied.' If it all depends exclusively on what we get here and now, then we won't get through this. We watch people we love suffer and die, and we will suffer and die, and the only difference is that some last longer than others. But if we have a life forever with the God who loves us, we can get through this because there is a lot more out there to come—and it is good."

My questioner nodded, and we did not speak of it again.

It is astonishing when it happens, but to confront suffering and death with the love of Christ shared in the prayer and comfort of one another is to demolish the walls of human limitation and enter into the spaciousness of God. Evelyn Underhill speaks of this in poetic language.

> Consider for a moment what is implied in this amazing mystery of intercession; at least in the little that we understand of it. It implies first our implicit realization of God, the infinitely loving, living and all-penetrating Spirit of Spirits, as an Ocean in which we all are bathed. And next, speaking still that spatial language to which our human thinking is tied down, that somehow through this uniting and vivifying medium we too, being one with Him in love and will, can mutually penetrate, move, and influence each other's souls in ways as yet unguessed; yet through the whole process moulded and determined by the prevenient, personal, free and ever-present God. The world He has been and is creating is a world infused through and through with Spirit; and it is partly through the prayerful and God-inspired action of men and women that the spiritual work of this world is done. When a man or woman of prayer through devoted consecration, reaches a soul in temptation and rescues it, we must surely acknowledge that this is an action of God Himself using that person as an instrument.[2]

When children, we are told cute little stories of Jesus helping to find the lost baseball in the grass and bringing lost puppies home. We graduate to prayers for convenient parking spaces, for batteries to work and start the car start even when we've let the cells go dry, and for help in finding our missing keys. Later on, the questions evolve into why won't God heal the baby? and why must such a good human being suffer so? Our concept of intercession starts going south when we are taught and teach others to pray for things, not for people, and to request gifts rather than the Giver. We want to see some magic.

The sacrament of baptism has taken on a new meaning for me in thinking of intercession. In the twenty-first century, we have vaccines to check viruses and antibiotics to destroy infections, indoor plumbing and hot-and-cold running water, air-conditioning, organ transplants, fertilizer, massive irrigation projects, refrigeration, nearly instant communication, and fast transportation. We have the illusion of well-being and know little of waiting and suffering. But here is the challenge of intercessory prayer. Do we share some tea and cookies, pray for the persons in a bad spot, and then head out to shop for groceries and pick up the dry clean-ing? Or are we willing to pray like Moses did, at Mt. Sinai, " 'Alas, this people has sinned a great sin; they have made themselves gods of gold. But now, if you will only forgive their sin—but if not, blot me out of the book that you have written.' "[3]

Consumers that we are, we want the result without the effort. If we are to intercede in the Spirit of Christ, we must be willing to relinquish our claims on life, ambitions, desires, possessions, fears, and prejudices to Christ. That is what the believer does in baptism. We pass through the water symbolizing our death to self and entry into the new life, His life, that He gives us.[4] To intercede in prayer is to sacrifice ourselves in iden-tification with the suffering of Christ and the suffering of the one for whom we pray in Christ's name. We sacrifice our time, our own desires and will, in praying, "Abba, if it is required, lay the suffering of the one I love on me and spare him from this pain." This is what Paul urged in his letter to the Philippians.

> Let each of you look not to your own interests, but to the interests
> of others. Let the same mind be in you that was in Christ Jesus,
>> who, though he was in the form of God,
>>> did not regard equality with God
>>> as something to be exploited,
>> but emptied himself,
>>> taking the form of a slave,
>>> being born in human likeness,
>> And being found in human form,
>>> he humbled himself
>>> and became obedient to the point of death—
>>> even death on a cross.[5]

Paul went on to say that he was glad to be "poured out as a libation over the sacrifice and offering of your faith" and exhorted the Philip-pians to do the same thing. When we pour out the drink intended to quench our own thirst to instead extinguish a fire, water a flower, clean a stain, or cool a raging fever, we cannot hold on to it or get it back. That's the kind of thinking behind one of Jesus' most radical teachings, " 'Love your enemies, do good, and lend, expecting nothing in return. Your reward will be great, and you will be children of the Most High; for he is kind to the ungrateful and the wicked. Be merciful, just as your Father is merciful.' "[6]

Intercessory prayer is love, it is worship, it is alignment of our will with Christ's for the perspective of heaven, and it is a willingness to sacrifice ourselves to His will, trusting in His love, even though His ways are not our ways.

> "What no eye has seen, nor ear heard,
>   nor the human heart conceived,
> what God has prepared for those who love him". . .
> "For who has known the mind of the Lord
>   so as to instruct him?"
But we have the mind of Christ.[7]

As we know, having Christ's mind means laying down our lives to save those we love. Until we make that choice in truth as well as in theory, speculations on the mechanics of God's interventions or on His reasoning behind what we think we see and know of His will have no more relationship to reality than do our guesses on how the tricks are performed in a cabaret magic show.

And so what if we knew the how's and the why's? To know the magician's craft is only to know illusion. To know God's methods is not helpful without His power. Christ is single-minded. He loves. Period. Without thought of the cost. For us to intercede is to pray and act in love regardless of cost.

But even as we choose in love to intercede, those on whose behalf we intercede make their own choices or are the victims of the choices of others. Free will is a distinct quality of love. Obviously the questions about intercessory prayer come from our desire to control the result so things come out the way we want them to. But that would not be loving and would demand for ourselves a mandate that God does not insist on for Himself. The father did not stop the prodigal from taking his inheritance and wasting it. He didn't stop his son from leaving home. Nor did he send a nutritious "care package" when the son was starving. He waited for his son to choose to come home. Neither did the father force his elder son into the house to attend the welcome-home party. He invited the son to make his choice and told him why he should forget about himself and celebrate love and life.

We can parse this out any way we like, but it is always going to end as a mystery. We have to decide whether we are willing to let God be in control. Do you and I trust God's intentions?

I learned this in a most vivid way my junior year of college. I sat in my dorm room late one night, grieving the death of my fiancée in an accident. I was confined to a wheelchair with leg injuries from the same accident. I couldn't sleep, and I sat up and demanded, "God, if You would only tell me why this has happened."

Suddenly an answer was whispered into my aching heart. *"If you knew what would happen and why, your life would be no more than a recipe on the back of a Betty Crocker cake mix—'Just add water.' That is not faith and that is not your life as it was meant to be when I created you."*

Knowing that I would receive no answer, I was set free from my questions by the knowledge that my continued life here was God's will. I could continue in that knowledge and did. This did not remove the pain of losing my loved one, but the essentials of the kingdom of God are Christ and the life that He gives—and that was what I was left with. If that isn't enough for us, nothing ever will be, and we will be ever doubtful and querulous about intercessory prayer.

Questions for Reflection

1. Why is prayer the Christian's response to suffering and death?
2. What does sacrifice have to do with intercessory prayer?
3. How is God Himself the ultimate answer to intercessory prayer?

11

Dead Trees and Impassable Mountains

Forgiveness breaks the barriers of time and place to answered prayer.

Jesus killed the tree! He was hungry. He saw the tree in green leaf and looked for some fruit to eat. It turned out to be all leaf and no fruit because it wasn't the right season.

When the Creator of the universe wants to eat, isn't He entitled to a fig from a tree He made? Jesus thought so. He talked to the tree as if it could answer Him. The disciples heard Him plainly: "May no one ever eat fruit from you again." A lot of good that did! He turned away from the tree, still hungry.

The next stop that morning was the temple. It fared no better than the tree. He drove out the salesmen, overturned the cashiers' tables, and stopped people from carrying anything through the temple. "This is supposed to be a house of prayer, but you've made it a hide-out for crooks!" Jesus thundered.

On the way back into town the next morning, they passed the fig tree, withered and drooping. It was dead. Peter called out to Jesus, "Look, the fig tree that you cursed withered."

Jesus said, "Have faith in God, will you! If you say to the Mount of Olives that we are walking up right now, 'Get lost! Throw yourself into the ocean!' and you believe in your gut without a doubt, then that will happen."

Then Jesus added a postscript, "Whenever you stand praying, forgive every grudge that you have against anyone so that your Father in heaven may also forgive you for the times you've crossed the line."[1]

This story is nearly enough to make me a card-carrying, Green-peace "tree-hugger." Here was a happy tree, going about its business to leaf out and get ready for the effort of growing fruit, and the Son of God just comes along and condemns it to firewood because He hasn't had breakfast yet and the tree can't produce the impossible for Him.

In fact, figs produce a harvest twice a year, in the late spring and early fall. The fruit grows with the leaves. Even though that tree was in full leaf, it had no fruit, meaning it wasn't going to bear that season. Its Creator was making a point.

The tree represented a creation that, like the nation of Israel and its temple, had gone terribly wrong. But still, Jesus had told a wonderful parable of mercy about a barren fig tree that the owner of the orchard wanted to cut down. His foreman convinced him to cultivate the tree, fertilize it, and give it another chance. Now, in the flesh, the Savior didn't give this barren tree a break.[2]

I've heard all kinds of apologies for this story of the withered fig tree from people who want to defend Jesus, who want to explain what He really meant so we won't be tempted to put tarps over the trees before we let Jesus into our gardens. "He didn't mean a real mountain. He was just explaining that it's possible for God to do the impossible." "That wouldn't be God's will," the apologists say. "It would only be praying our selfish motives, and God won't answer a prayer that asks for what we want instead of what He wants."

"Oh, come on! Jesus was God. It was God's will that the tree bear fruit, wasn't it? It was very possible, too, given a little time. I can read for myself, and it says plain as day that if you tell the actual mountain to go do a 'cannonball' into the bay, ask God to make it happen, and believe that it will happen, then put on a raincoat and get ready for the splash."

Sometimes, people bleed all the mystery out of the story, leaving it cut and dried. "If you are a believer who doesn't hold a grudge against another person, who doesn't pray with selfish motives, then God will give you what you want."

But, as I pointed out in an earlier chapter, Christ is the only true Intercessor because only the perfect, sinless Jesus could pray such a prayer.

That is the very point. True believers have faith in the true Intercessor when they pray. Most of us, most of the time are focusing on what we want. But this story of the fig tree and the mountain calls to us to look elsewhere.

I have come to believe that time is the theme of this story. Time is a human convention. We are born, and we start to die. We live for a while, and we die. There is a beginning and an ending for us that always comes too soon. In human time, fig trees ripen in season. In human reality, there is a time to climb a mountain and a time to hire the big Caterpillar earthmovers to level the mountain to make lots for a subdivision. Or, if our mountain is a big problem in our lives, we tend to think that there is a time to apply a spiritual, emotional, and intellectual effort that's equivalent to the earthmover leveling the mountain.

I don't think that Jesus was just having a grumpy day when He cursed that tree. Jesus existed before time, entered time as a human, growing in time from infancy to adulthood, and dying a human death by human hands on a specific date and time.[3] He was then resurrected out of time and into eternity by the Father.[4] He did all of this so that we could live with Him for eternity in heaven, a place where there won't even be the elemental time demarcation of day and night.[5]

If time is not a consideration, then a fig tree ought to bear fruit at the impulse of its Creator, and a mountain that has stood for eons can be tossed in the sea as quickly as a child tosses a penny into a fountain, and we can live forever in the love of Christ who made us, came back to save us, and will come again to take us home. When we pray to the Father in the name of Christ, we enter the throne room of God beyond time and beyond the limitations of human perception.

Prayer enters God's time and God's dimensions, leaving behind our human limitations. The deadly enemy of prayer and the chain that keeps us imprisoned in time is unforgivingness. Our resentment is a lock on a specific time, place, and person(s). The very word *resent* means to feel the grievance over and over again the way a child repeatedly flicks his tongue over the socket left by a missing baby molar.

Jesus says that we can never move into God's future if we insist on reliving our past. Unforgivingness is the one stated exception to granting the requests of the Lord's Prayer: "If you forgive others their trespasses, your heavenly Father will also forgive you; but if you do not forgive others, neither will your Father forgive your trespasses."[6]

Our thoughts of hurt and vengeance fester and seethe in our souls. Every time we think of the wrong and the one who wronged us, the chain leashing us back to them snaps taut, and the wound in our heart reopens. How dark and restricting is that prison? We gain insight into that darkness through the exclamation of the father after the prodigal had returned to the embrace of forgiveness in Jesus' parable of the waiting father. "Let us eat and celebrate; for this son of mine *was dead* and is alive again; he *was lost* and is found!"[7] Death is the absence of movement, and we end up dead to God's present and future as long as we remain in the trap of unforgivingness. Forgiveness returns the life-giving breath of the Holy Spirit into our resentment-encrusted lungs.[8]

The South African writer Laurens Van der Post tells the following story of two brothers that illustrates the point. The elder brother was strong, tall, intelligent, and an excellent athlete. Sent away to a private school in South Africa, where the family lived, he became an admired leader of the student body. His brother was some six years younger. Neither good-looking nor capable, he was also a hunchback. But he had one great gift. He had a magnificent singing voice.

Eventually the younger brother joined the older at the same boarding school. One day in a cruel outbreak of mob psychology, a group of students ganged up on the younger brother, jeered at him, and tore off his shirt to reveal his hunchback.

The older brother was aware of what was going on. He could have gone out and faced the crowd of sadistic students, acknowledged the strange hunchback as his brother, and put a stop to the cruel event. Instead, he remained in the chemistry lab completing an assignment. He betrayed his brother by what he failed to do.

The younger brother was never the same again. He returned home to his parents' farm, where he kept to himself and sang no more. Meanwhile the older brother had become a soldier in World War II, stationed in Palestine. One night, lying outdoors and gazing into the starlit sky, he realized what he had done to his younger brother in their school days. His heart told him that he would never have peace until he went home and asked his brother for forgiveness. And so he made the incredibly difficult wartime journey from Palestine to South Africa. The brothers talked long into the night, the elder one confessing his guilt and remorse. They cried together and embraced, and the breach between them was healed.

Something else happened that night. The elder brother had fallen asleep when he was startled awake by the sound of a full, rich, mellifluous voice soaring into the night. It was the beautiful voice of his younger brother, who was singing once again.[9]

This story of betrayal and confession, wounding and healing, imprisonment and release is a story of the need and the possibility of forgiveness. I think that there is no greater topic for human reflection. Forgiveness is the most significant action that a human can take or receive. Those acquainted with me will recognize my southwestern colloquialism: "Forgiveness is the whole enchilada of the gospel." I believe this with all my heart as an attorney who profits from conflict and a sinner in need of pardon.

The old saying is true, "To err is human; to forgive is divine." Only Jesus Christ possesses the power to forgive sin. Only the grace of God can empower human forgiveness for betrayal. Forgiveness is impossible without faith. Faith is impossible without forgiveness. Forgiveness, Jesus said repeatedly, is the key to answered prayer.

In Jesus' great parable of forgiveness, a CEO balanced the company books and realized that a junior executive had run up a huge debt against the company. The CEO realistically concluded that the junior executive wouldn't be able to ever pay off the debt. He called the junior executive in. The junior executive said, "Just give me time, and I'll pay." The CEO waved him away and said, "Forget it."

The junior executive walked out and encountered a day laborer who owed him repayment of a $100 advance on his paycheck. The proud junior executive was likely embarrassed by the CEO's implied acknowledgement of the junior executive's inadequacy by writing off a debt he had offered to repay. The junior executive wanted to reassert control. He demanded payment from the day laborer, who begged him for a grace period to repay. "No," snarled the junior executive. "Your time's up." He had the day laborer and his whole family locked up in debtor's prison. (This was really dumb because it wasn't going to get the subordinate's debt repaid. Vengeance is never a practical business solution.)

The unjust treatment of the day laborer so upset the other company employees that they went to the CEO and blew the whistle that the junior executive lacked the gracious spirit of the CEO and someone was being hurt as a result. The CEO called in the subordinate and told him, "I forgave you the equivalent of the national debt. Yet, you bring down the full force of the law on a guy who owes you a measly hundred bucks. This isn't right and I'm throwing you in jail where they'll torture you."[10]

Jesus' point is that unforgivingness imprisons one in the past. The injury becomes the obsession, and torment continues from the lack of resolution. Forgiveness releases the chains of the past and breaks the torment of the one who forgives and removes the guilt and shame of the one forgiven. Think of the release when Jesus told His Father from the cross,

"Forgive them, for they don't know what they are doing." He could then say, "It is finished." All the hurt and agony caused by a creation in rebellion was atoned and forgiven. Jesus was released into a new life through forgiveness, and we were released into a new life as the forgiven. By the same power, the younger brother regained his beautiful voice when he forgave his elder brother, and his elder brother could then sleep the sleep of peace.

In the freedom of forgiveness, the power of creation is restored and the eternity of God replaces our clock-watching. Fruit ripens in season, and the mountains of the past are moved like a child playing with blocks. We can enter unimpeded into the flow of God's grace, and it is in that power—the power of forgiveness—that all prayer finds its answer.

Questions for Reflection

1. How have you experienced resentment as an obstacle to prayer?
2. Have you seen prayers answered because of forgiveness?
3. Why does prayer gain power through forgiveness?

12

Enoch, Part 1—
No Excuses

Enoch was a sixty-five-year-old father when he began walking with God.
One is never too late or too busy to pray.

Enoch was sixty-five when he fathered Methuselah. He started walking with God then and kept on for another three hundred years, during which he fathered other sons and daughters.[1] This was a time when people had begun raising herds of cattle and living in communities, Jubal had commenced musical entertainment, and his brother, Tubal, had begun making tools out of bronze and iron.[2]

It's good to reflect on this. Family, work obligations, and entertainment are all commonly cited reasons for refusing or neglecting a walk with God. Scripture defines such a walk as a life of prayer and action in the faith that God lives, loves us, and has a will and a way for us.

Jesus compared the kingdom of God to a man who planned a great banquet and invited many guests. But all of them sent regrets with excuses. The first invited guest said, "I just bought property and must inspect it. Please excuse me."

Another said, "I just bought five yoke of oxen and must try them out. Please excuse me."

Another said, "I just got married, so I can't come." And so on.[3]

Property ownership, business success, marriage, family, and the arts are all things we esteem highly. Go to any bookstore, secular or religious, and you will find shelves of books on how to improve your position in all these areas. Our employers, clients, vendors, and churches hold retreats focusing on how to achieve greatness in these things. Our lives are so measured by these milestones that our first question on meeting some-one new after "What is your name?" is "What do you do?"

Jesus said the man giving the party reacted with anger at the excuses. He threw the party open to the poor, crippled, blind, and lame. In fact, anyone off the streets who could run, walk, limp, crawl, or be carried in the door of the banquet hall was welcome to enjoy the festivities. The host then said, "The original invitees won't even get a taste of my ban-quet."[4]

To hammer the point home, Jesus went on to say, "If anyone comes to me and does not hate his father and mother, his wife and children, his brothers and sisters, and yes, even his own life—he cannot be my disci-ple. . . . Any of you who does not give up everything he has cannot be my disciple."[5]

Earlier in the same evening when He told this story, Jesus had told the guests who were vying for the best seats at a dinner party that their social climbing efforts could spoil their enjoyment of the party. Now in the story of the banquet, He unleashes the radical truth about grace: Those who seek their success in wealth, business, and even, dare I say it, mar-riage and family, at the expense of their relationship with God do not get into the party at all. Only those who are hopelessly imperfect in all things human and whose only hope of making it to the party is their "yes" to God's invitation make it into the party.

Enoch began his walk with God when he became a father at sixty-five. That's a youthful age for one who will live to be 365. I began my walk with God when I was thirty-seven, having become a father just before my thirty-fourth birthday. My own experience gives me an insight into Enoch's walk and Jesus' banquet. Nothing will reveal your inadequacies like parenthood. Caring for a child will speak God's love to you as noth-ing else will.

When I walked with Andrew taking his first steps, I had to lift him up and over obstacles too large for him to master. When I held him close to my chest during night feedings and kissed the top of his sweet head, I was filled with a love that displaced all other thoughts. When he answered my call to "Come to Daddy," by toddling across my office lobby and entering my waiting arms with a smile, I came alive with delight that made all the other frictions of the work day disappear. When Andrew tried to cross busy streets by himself or climb too high to come back down, I was filled with concerned anger for his own protection against dangers he could not appreciate. When I spoke to him too quickly in judg-ment and misunderstanding or projected my own fears and insecurities in correcting his course, I realized my need for the Father's heart of wisdom and grace. How can I love my son if I do not accept that I am loved? How can I rear a son if I do not acknowledge my own childhood with God?

The excuses of work, property management, entertainment, and other relationships do not cut it against the needs of a two-year-old whose hunger will not wait, whose cleanliness and warmth is entirely dependent on your provision, and whose prayers will be learned from your words. Our God, who rules the universe and commands all things in His sovereign will, makes no excuses to us. He knows what we need and will not withhold good things from His children who ask him.[6]

Enoch faced the distractions of business, entertainment, and family and community life. Yet, somehow God reached out His hand to Enoch, and Enoch reached up and took it, and they walked together. The same hand reaches out for ours. Jesus said, " 'I'm telling you, once and for all, that unless you return to square one and start over like children, you're not even going to get a look at the kingdom, let alone get in.' "[7]

To start over as a child is to reach out and take the hand of love offered to you and to hang on in trust that the One who holds your hand knows the way and will take you there and won't let go of you during the journey. Even if you break loose and wander off, thinking you are too sophisticated to hold on, when you come to your senses and realize you're lost, you will remember that the Father's house is the place where you were loved best and most, and you will want to go home.[8] We are never too old for that desire.

Questions for Reflection

1. What tasks or appointments compete for your time with God?
2. How does a child approach a parent to spend time with him or her?
3. Are you willing to ask God to help you find the time to spend with Him?

13

Enoch, Part 2— Falling in Love

Prayer is the experience of a love affair, not the To Do list of a job.

All the things most likely to distract you and me away from God were also a danger to Enoch's relationship with God. Yet he managed three hundred years of daily devotion. We find it hard to manage fifteen minutes of spiritual reading and prayer a few days each week!

I am fifty-three years old. Since I began my career as an attorney/administrator for Christian organizations twenty-seven years ago, I have come to marvel at how many people regard business for God as an acceptable substitute for a relationship with God. Try calling some friends and colleagues together in the middle of a workday to seek God together in prayer. You will find out in a hurry that the priority is accomplishing what is in the Palm Pilot® or Day-Timer®, not in listening to God to tell us what He wants done.

Chances are that what I just said caused a pang of guilt in your soul. Each person needs to think and pray that pang through for himself or herself, but I want to make a disclaimer here. I am not writing to the single parent who can barely keep food on the table, help with homework, make school and work on time, and get the laundry done—let alone have time to read the day's devotion from *My Utmost for His Highest*. If it wasn't for prayer, you wouldn't be making it at all.

I also have assisted in firing employees who spent all their time reading the Bible at their desks and didn't get their accounting done, and I never had a twinge of conscience for doing so. I am not writing to them either.

No, I am writing for those of us who claim Christ as our leader and begin our meetings with prayer but then never give Him another thought because "we are in the Lord's work," and "we are doing God's work" whether at our desks, conference tables, PTA meetings; in the pulpit; or at the lectern. We love the label, but the actual product is more trouble than it's worth in the face of all else that we have to do.

Jesus did not mince words about what He wanted in this regard. " 'Knowing the correct password—saying "Master, Master," for instance—isn't going to get you anywhere with me. What is required is serious obedience—*doing* what my Father wills. I can see it now—at the Final Judgment thousands strutting up to me and saying, "Master, we preached the Message, we bashed the demons, our God-sponsored projects had everyone talking." And do you know what I am going to say? "You missed the boat. All you did was use me to make yourselves important. You don't impress me one bit. You're out of here." ' "[1]

More traditional versions quote Jesus as saying, " 'I will tell them plainly, "I never knew you. Away from me you, evildoers!" ' " (NIV). Have you ever really considered who these people are whom He says He never knew and whom He will condemn to an eternity of separation? They will be evangelists; preachers; battlers of evil; philanthropists; missionaries; church-going, morally upright people of all vocations; religious people taking their stands for truth, justice, and the American way; or people running homeless shelters and free clinics and demanding compassion in the form of more government support—in other words, the "best" people you and I may know. In the same discourse, Jesus said, " 'I tell you that unless your righteousness surpasses that of the Pharisees and the teachers of the law, you will certainly not enter the kingdom of heaven.' "[2]

Jesus can say that because it's His righteousness, not ours, that He is talking about. When He speaks of "knowing" us, He means the kind of intimate knowledge that comes from loving another with unrestrained and caring passion. That kind of knowledge does not occur unless the lovers yield themselves without condition, each desiring and completing the joy of the other. When I meet Patricia's or Andrew's complaints about my workaholic absences with the defense, "Why don't you understand that I am doing this for you?" I am not loving them in this intimate sense of "knowing" them. "Exactly my point!" Jesus would say. "Doing" acts of love and help is not the same as "being" in love. Without the latter state of being, the former demonstrations are meaningless. " 'This is the word of the LORD . . . : Not by might, nor by power, but by my spirit, says the LORD of hosts.' "[3]

The spirit of true love seeks out the thoughts and will of the object of its adoration. When we fall in love with Jesus Christ and know, really know, that He is in love with us, minute by minute, hour by hour, we yield ourselves to do His pleasure.

I can't tell you that this is efficient in the way that we like to measure work performance. It doesn't really fit neatly into strategic plans. But as Solomon noted, "We humans keep brainstorming options and plans, / but GOD's purpose prevails."[4] His purpose is transparent, and it isn't rocket science.

> "For God so loved the world that he gave his only Son, so that everyone who believes in him may not perish but may have eternal life.
> "Indeed, God did not send the Son into the world to condemn the world, but in order that the world might be saved through him."[5]

When we reflect on God's announced goal, we will come to the conclusion that all the rest of our due diligence in organization, improvement, and production for the sake of prestige, profit, growth, and corporate mission is only rearranging the deck chairs on the *Titanic*.

We confuse our existence with entitlement, and that confusion causes us to stray from grateful dependence on our Creator to arrogance about our own rights. The farther from the Source we move, the more power we lose. This loss is illustrated by the way the light of God's presence faded from Moses' face over time and the way that the younger son's inheritance dissipated after leaving his father's house.[6] As our resources diminish, the other stuff of materiality begins to take on appeal. Our own way is . . . well . . . our own way with all of the imperfections, limitations, and misguided perceptions of our sinful brokenness.

Some people . . . a lot of people . . . go right on pursuing their obsessions in their own strength until it runs out, and then they demand more! Why didn't Enoch do this?

Only one thing can pull us away from ourselves and the persons and things we idolize—a greater love. Enoch fell in love with God and wanted to spend the rest of eternity at His side.

How does anyone really fall in love? There is some moment, some thought, some glimpse or sound that lets you know that its source calls you to be more of your true self together than you are apart and on your own. You truly burn with desire to make that so. Your life changes from black and white to full color when that happens as it did for Dorothy when she realized she was in Oz and said, "Toto, we aren't in Kansas anymore."

It happens that way between God and us, but even more so. Your lover may send you a Valentine's Day card and a dozen roses, but God sends you a rainbow after the storm and sunlight through the forest leaves on summer mornings. He surprises you with daffodils in March and sugar maples in October. He delights you with sea foam and sounding whales. He takes your breath away with geese flying south across the harvest moon and the first grip of a tiny hand. He creates a smile out of a child's laugh and a friend's kindness.

Jesus Christ, the Lover of our souls, does not invite us to assuage our guilt by obligation. He proposes no relationship of convenience, no accommodation for sake of image, and no mutual arrangement for gain or survival. I am talking about love here—true, honest, and full-blooded "I can't live without you" passion. The kind of desire that blinds us to everything else and says, "I am going with you wherever you go because I trust that you are the right and best one for me." A love like that makes us want to walk together for three hundred years and forever, regardless of what business opportunities, entertainment, family obligations, and community service tug on your heart and call for our attention.

Who else looks you in the eye and says, "I lay down my life for you; I came that you might have life and have it abundantly"?[7] Who else takes you to meet His Father and says, " 'I ask . . . that they all may be one. . . . I in them and you in me, that they may become completely one, so that the world may know that you have sent me and have loved them even as you have loved me.' "[8]

You may fear that if you give in to a love of Christ that intense and demanding of your soul and spirit that you will not be able to meet your obligations of love and support to your family and colleagues. Be assured that God's grace is sufficient to enable you to fill all the obligations He assigns you. Loving Jesus does not mean infidelity to your spouse, your children, or your true friends. When faced with a lawyer's demand to identify the greatest commandment, Jesus responded, " ' "You shall love the Lord your God with all your heart, and with all your soul, and with all your mind." This is the greatest and first commandment. And a second is like it: "You shall love your neighbor as yourself." ' "[9]

In Jesus' teaching, "your neighbor" always means whoever needs our kindness. Obviously, Jesus taught that if we put our love and devotion into God, we are going to find that we are loving God's children as well,

"The commandment we have from him is this: those who love God must love their brothers and sisters also. Everyone who believes that Jesus is the Christ has been born of God, and everyone who loves the parent loves the child. By this we know that we love the children of God, when we love God and obey his commandments."[10] If Enoch did not care for his family, there would have been no testimony that he walked with God for three hundred years. If I don't love those whom God has put in my life, my existence is nothing more than irritating background noise.[11]

Enoch walked with God because it was the most wonderful thing he could do, and there was no excuse for not doing so. Ultimately, we, too, run out of excuses for not living and loving as we were created to do. When the Greatest Love seizes your soul, may you know the intimate companionship of the same God who loves you and waits for you to enjoy the long walk of eternity with Him. Heed the call of your Beloved to you:

> "Arise, my love, my fair one,
>   and come away;
> for now the winter is past,
>   the rain is over and gone.
> The flowers appear on the earth;
>   the time of singing has come,
> and the voice of the turtledove
>   is heard in our land.
> The fig tree puts forth its figs,
>   and the vines are in blossom;
>   they give forth fragrance.
> Arise my love, my fair one,
>   and come away."[12]

Questions for Reflection

1. What has priority in your life—what God wants from you or what you want from God?
2. How do you know when you've fallen in love?
3. What effect does a loving relationship with God have on your other relationships?

14

The Sound of a Butterfly

If you can't hear a whisper, how do you expect to hear from God?

There comes a time, sooner or later, when we have to stop talking about the need to pray and how to pray and start praying! This proposition is tougher than it seems.

There is tremendous tension inherent in these words of Matthew about Jesus: "After he had dismissed the crowds, he went up the mountain by himself to pray."[1]

The crowds had aches and pains to be healed, fears to be quieted, and hungers to be filled. Jesus had just fed more than five thousand people with five loaves of bread and two fish. Doesn't a good miracle like that beg to be repeated? The crowds tempt us to exponential goodness: more people equals more ministry.

By dismissing the crowds at a peak moment so He could go pray, the Son of God, who manifested himself to the world as a man, taught us a crucial lesson about our humanity. We are vessels made to be filled and poured out. We do not carry within ourselves an endless supply. We must go back to the Source to be filled again and again.

If we do not dismiss the crowds to go pray, they will go hungry and thirsty—and so will we. Jesus reminds us, " 'Without Me you can do nothing.' "[2]

There is a key message in Jesus' observation about the crowd of famished souls needing the redemption of God's love. " 'The harvest is plentiful, but the laborers are few; therefore ask the Lord of the harvest to send out laborers into his harvest.' "[3]

Note that Jesus didn't say, "Ride in with your sharpened gospel-scythe and start harvesting souls." He told His followers to pray for the right worker to go to the right part of the field to harvest the right crop. Seeing the need for the harvest should lead us to more conversations with the Lord of the harvest, not to our attempt to be the Lord of the harvest.

This seems counterintuitive until we think how much of the same ground is picked over by crew after crew. Like physicians who turn away from patients whom they don't have the time, energy, or skills to cure, we turn away from fields of spiritual fruit that we can't work ourselves.

We work harder and accomplish less when we don't dismiss the crowds to pray. " 'You always have the poor [with their needs], but you will not always have me,' "[4] Jesus said in calling His followers to worship Him. Through prayer, silence is transformed into more ministry.

Jesus was grief-stricken at the news that His cousin, John the Baptist, had been murdered. He tried to withdraw to solitude at that time, but the crowds followed Him to His place of retreat. Jesus' compassion was stirred when He saw the people, so He cured their sick and taught them. At the end of the day, He fed them. Between the grief and the ministry, Jesus was wrung dry. He dismissed the crowds and again headed out to be alone with His Abba.

My reaction when confronted with grief or stress is to work harder, not to retreat to pray. I have gotten in deep spiritual and emotional trouble in my life by following that instinct.

Several years ago, my barber pointed out that I had nearly rubbed off the hair behind my ears. I tend to rapidly oscillate my fingers back and forth behind my ears when I am frustrated or under extreme time demands. "Stop it," said the barber.

Easier said than done. "The problem with clients," a senior partner once told me, "is that they just won't mind." People are the wonderful thing about the practice of law. People are the aggravation inherent in the practice of law. "Hell is people," said the philosopher Jean-Paul Sartre.

Significant client issues were facing me. I found myself in prayer rising to my feet in frustration again and again, muscles tense to the point of ache, rubbing my fingers through my hair with such vigor that I was out of breath.

My time in prayer is my favorite and most important time of the day. Its invasion by the irritations of my work and my physical reaction was more than I could bear. My journal entries from that period reveal my anguish.

> I worship the Lord in the blast furnace of his holiness. There are terrible temptations to yield to the fears and demands that surround me, to chase and follow after all the competing gods who desire the sacrifice of my life to them. But there is a God, and I desperately wish to be true to Him. Jesus told Satan and so do I, "Away with you Satan! For it is written, 'Worship the Lord and serve only him'" (Matthew 4:10). Dear, Sweet Jesus, be the one desire, the one truth, the one strength of my heart. Amen.

Two weeks later, I wrote

> Another work demand pulls me to my feet from prayer, hands smashed together, wringing them, then up to rub my hair hard, breath shallow, sweat standing on my forehead, dripping all over, adrenaline pumping in toxic-sick pain to my heart.
>
> I went to the doctor yesterday. "Too much," he said. "Too many decisions. Your body can't keep up with it. Exercise one-half hour a day," he prescribed.
>
> Today, I hiked up Mount Williamson. The hiking guide says, "Mt. Williamson stands head and shoulders above other crests along Angeles Crest Highway. The 8,214-foot peak offers grand views of earthquake country—the Devil's Punchbowl, San Andreas Fault and the fractured northern edges of the San Gabriel Mountains."[5] (John McKinney, *Day Hiker's Guide to Southern California* [Santa Barbara, Calif.: Olympus Press, 1992], p. 150.) The tortured terrain expresses the condition of my soul.
>
> Standing still in the vanilla effervescence of Jeffrey pines, a whisper grabbed my attention. It was the sound of a dog-face butterfly taking flight from yellow yarrow.
>
> To hear such things is possible, but I forget this. Instead, I search for God and His meaning and purpose in the turmoil and conflicts of my days, cataclysmic events of deals and lawsuits and arguments. I am yanked to my feet out of prayer by the irritations and unrequited tensions of it all manifesting in the aforementioned symptoms. But God does not choose to speak there and then. He calls me away from the struggle for the possible to hear the impossible—the unbelievable sound of a butterfly flying.

Farther on up the trail, the northwest wind pours its scouring chill over the ridge, and my knees and feet hurt with the wear of the journey. But my mind is calmed and my heart is stilled.

There is no God like You. I thank You. I worship You. I trust You. I love You.

I write as a witness, not as a victim. After all, who victimized Elijah the day he won the argument over the priests of Baal with the help of God, the day he ran away so far and fast down the mountain in the pounding rain that, in his weariness and hunger, he forgot who he was and who had helped him? Who allowed the threat of the angry but defeated woman to spin him out of control into the wilderness of anxiety where a tornado, earthquake, and fire had no meaning beyond spectacle? Who made him retreat to the isolated darkness of his cave? "What are you doing here, Elijah?" came the question into the dark where he, and no one else, had taken himself.

It was a gentle whisper, perhaps a butterfly, that called Elijah back into living. The sound of sheer silence told him who he was, that he was not alone, and who would help him.[6] The terrors of the possible can be healed only by the revelation of the impossible.

The disciples, confronted with the impotency of material prosperity and virtuous effort to convey eternity, uttered the panicked question, "Who then can be saved?"

" 'What is impossible for humans is possible for God,' " replied Jesus.[7]

Woe is me! I am a man with a pager and a cell phone, and I dwell among a people of pagers and cell phones. We worship the urgent, terrified of its possibilities. *Do I have this covered? Have I done enough? What will happen if I fail? If I stop, nothing will get done. What if . . . ?*

The instruction is simple. " 'Be still, and know that I am God!' "[8] Jesus says the final test will be simple as well: "On that day many will say to me, 'Lord, Lord, we shared the word, and fought evil in your name, and did many powerful and good things in your name.' Then, I will tell them, 'You did do all that stuff, but you never stopped so we could get to know each other. Go away now, because you did all that stuff without me ever asking you to do it. You did it on your own, and at the end, you are all alone.' "[9]

Upon reflection, I think it's impossible to live like that, sitting still, waiting, trusting God to take care of it all without my help. The sweat from my forehead, my labored breathing, the hair behind my ears that

I've sacrificed for justice and getting things done, that pumping adrenaline must count for something!

Then, in the stillness of the mountainside, I hear the whisper of persistent love. "What are you doing, Kent?" In that question, I am both judged and assured. Finally wanting grace more than anything else, I fall to my knees and pray.

Questions for Reflection

1. What is the effect of stress and busyness on your life?
2. How have you experienced the "still, small voice" of God?
3. Where could you use help in transforming "the worship of the urgent" into waiting upon God?

Learning Prayer From Those Who Have Gone Before

15

Prayer Is
No Bargain

Whatever we are seeking through our prayers, we are never going to receive more than God. Is He enough for you?

Jacob's ambition and impatient pursuit of his destiny broke his most intimate relationships and drove him to a dark and empty place. There he lay with a rock for a pillow because daylight had faded, and he couldn't see to travel farther. During that night, God sent Jacob a dream of connection and blessing: " 'Know that I am with you and will keep you wherever you go, and will bring you back to this land; for I will not leave you until I have done what I have promised you.' Then Jacob woke from his sleep and said, 'Surely the LORD is in this place—and I did not know it!' And he was afraid, and said, 'How awesome is this place! This is none other than the house of God, and this is the gate of heaven.' "[1]

The morning light with its promise of a new day and improved security brought back Jacob's old spirit of selfishness. It was just so hard to give up on his way even when God promised that He would give him everything. *Why trust God when I can do it for myself? Doesn't the Lord help the people who help themselves? Grace? Who needs grace when you are young, quick, and clever?* So Jacob played the angles and bargained with God on the terms and conditions of his future—even after God had promised him unconditional love and grace.

" 'If God will be with me, and will keep me in this way that I go, and will give me bread to eat and clothing to wear, so that I come again to my father's house in peace, then the LORD shall be my God, and this stone, which I have set up for a pillar, shall be God's house; and of all that you give me I will surely give one tenth to you.' "[2]

It is the classic "*If* God will, *then* I will—*if* God gives me, *then* I'll give God" prayer of the unsurrendered, proud heart in crisis. It beats on defiantly even when schemes have turned to disaster and creature comforts are stripped away in a desert existence. It would not be until Jacob limped out of another night a broken man, having wrestled with God for advantage and lost, that he would understand and receive grace with open hands and heart.[3]

Isn't that just like us in our proud expectations and stubborn hearts? Tony Campolo tells a wonderful story about a little boy who begged God while saying his prayers for a new BMX bicycle. His mom told him that prayer shouldn't be used for selfish desires. Prayer was no way to get a BMX bicycle.

It was the week before Christmas. When the mom came downstairs the next morning, she was surprised to see that the figure of Mary was missing from the manger scene under the Christmas tree. In its place was a note that read, "Dear Jesus, If you ever want to see your mother again, You had better get me that BMX bicycle!"[4]

Readers send me notes about their struggles to discern God's will for their lives. That's no surprise. Christian bookstores are packed with books on how to know, how to overcome, how to accomplish, how to love, how to succeed, how to pray, how to organize, how to lose weight, how to reconcile, how to heal. . . . It is fascinating to observe that so many persons think they have just the answer—God's answer—for someone else. It sounds obnoxious put that way, but these books have a big market because so many people have questions and are looking for answers. Worse yet, we often want those answers to keep someone else in line. "Excellent sermon," said the parishioner, as she pumped the hand of the preacher. "Everything you said applies to people I know."

Several years ago, wishing to know more about God's will for my life, I spent a great deal of time reflecting on my experience in light of what Scripture says about God's will. My conclusion was that there isn't some disembodied solution out there known as "God's will." What Scripture teaches is that our lives are God's will, and He works in and through them. We are called to worship God, not seek some answer that would give us existence outside of God. In other words, we can't get the product without the process, and the process occurs when we submit ourselves to God without reservation.

The apostle Paul set out the point in his letter to the Romans: "I appeal to you therefore, brothers and sisters, by the mercies of God, to present your bodies as a living sacrifice, holy and acceptable to God, which is your spiritual worship. Do not be conformed to this world, but be transformed by the renewing of your minds, so that you may discern what is the will of God—what is good and acceptable and perfect."[5] This appeal echoes the words of Jesus when a lawyer asked Him " 'Which commandment in the law is the greatest?' He said to him, ' "You shall love the Lord your God with all your heart, and with all your soul, and with all your mind." This is the greatest and first commandment. And a second is like it: "You shall love your neighbor as yourself." On these two commandments hang all the law and the prophets.' "[6] This may not be a very Christian metaphor, but in gambling terms, we are told to "bet the farm" on God and "let it ride."

God demands everything from us. He even breaks our hard shell of pride and ambition, melts down the pieces, and re-creates us in His likeness.

> Yet, O LORD, you are our Father;
> > we are the clay, and you are our potter;
> > we are all the work of your hand.[7]

"He will transform the body of our humiliation that it may be conformed to the body of his glory, by the power that also enables him to make all things subject to himself."[8] "And all of us, with unveiled faces, seeing the glory of the Lord as though reflected in a mirror, are being transformed into the same image from one degree of glory to another; for this comes from the Lord, the Spirit."[9]

We may ask, "Does this mean that God does what He pleases with those who trust Him?" Exactly that! But we, who have formed our perceptions of authority from flawed parents and arbitrary teachers, balk at the idea of giving total control to someone who does what he or she pleases. Our cravings for security and comfort and our flammable sinful natures cause us to turn back from risking all on a holy God.

That perceived risk, however, is nonexistent with a God whose love is complete and eternal. This is what the apostle Peter came to realize near the end of his life. For a long time Peter, like Jacob, thrashed between his own ambition and Christ's contrasting instruction for his life. Jesus took this brash, blustery tough guy who thought he had it all figured out and told him that his future was to love and care for Jesus' children. This assignment took Peter past all his previous pride and prejudices to be the chosen instrument to introduce the gospel to the Gentiles.[10] In a letter to

the believers throughout the Roman Empire shortly before he was crucified by Emperor Nero, Peter gave this advice about finding God's will:

"God opposes the proud,
   but gives grace to the humble."

Humble yourselves therefore under the mighty hand of God,
so that he may exalt you in due time. Cast all your anxiety on him,
because he cares for you. Discipline yourselves, keep alert. Like a
roaring lion your adversary the devil prowls around, looking for
someone to devour. Resist him, steadfast in your faith, for you
know that your brothers and sisters in all the world are undergoing
the same kinds of suffering. And after you have suffered for a little
while, the God of all grace, who has called you to his eternal glory
in Christ, will himself restore, support, strengthen, and establish
you. To him be the power forever and ever. Amen.[11]

God is what we need. God is what we get. We are never going to get
more than God. To come to grips with this fact is to know God's will.

For God alone my soul waits in silence,
   for my hope is from him.
He alone is my rock and my salvation,
   my fortress; I shall not be shaken.
On God rests my deliverance and my honor,
   my mighty rock, my refuge is in God.[12]

It is a painful fact, but true, that if we should want more than this, we are
idol worshipers. God is enough.

Questions for Reflection

1. How have you attempted to bargain with God?
2. What are the implications for your prayer life of the metaphor of
   God as potter and you as clay?
3. Have you come to grips with God as the ultimate answer to
   prayer?

16

Steps to Discernment

Discerning the will of God is a matter of seeking God, not looking for answers. Here are seven steps for our search.

There was a rabbi who lived in a village on the Russian steppe. Every morning for twenty years he crossed the village square to pray in the synagogue, and every morning he was carefully watched by a policeman who hated Jews.

Finally one morning the policeman walked up to the rabbi and demanded to know where he was going.

"I don't know," said the rabbi.

"What do you mean you 'don't know'? For the past twenty years I have seen you go to that synagogue across the square—and now you say you don't know? I'll teach you a lesson!"

With that he grabbed the old man by his beard and dragged him off to jail. As the policeman was turning the key on the prison cell, the rabbi looked at him with a twinkle in his eye and said, "See what I meant when I said I didn't know?"[1]

In a world rebelling against God, we cannot know for a certainty the place our daily path will bring us. We can know, however, the intentions of our Creator, Redeemer, and Lord for our lives, and we can be assured that He will walk the path with us to see that we eventually make it home to His side.

Being a loving God and a parent like none other, identified in Christ as "Wonderful Counselor, Mighty God, / Everlasting Father, Prince of Peace,"[2] our heavenly Father does not leave His children without means to make right choices for their lives. Those means are identified in Scripture.

1. We have to stop what we are doing. This means a ruthless braking of our activity in order to worship God. "In the morning, while it was still very dark, he got up and went out to a deserted place, and there he prayed."[3]

> "Be still, and know that I am God!
>   I am exalted among the nations,
>   I am exalted in the earth."[4]

> For thus said the Lord GOD, the Holy One of Israel:
> In returning and rest you shall be saved;
>   in quietness and in trust shall be your strength.[5]

"Be still before the LORD, and wait patiently for him; / do not fret."[6] It is said, and I can validate this from experience, that if we simply go into the woods alone, sit down, read a passage of Scripture, and wait with open minds and open hearts, God will show us something to give us insight.

In stillness during prayer, I glimpsed the power of God this week. It is the power of the sun shining on a glacier converting it to a rock-crumbling, mountain-slashing torrent. It is the heat of the sun baking the desert into a laboratory of essential life. Night covers the land without a sound. Dawn illumines a new perspective in silence. The moon rises and sets, the tide turns, and we have nothing to do with it but to observe it and know that God is willing to use the same power on our waiting, quiet souls. "Do not pronounce judgment before the time, before the Lord comes, who will bring to light the things now hidden in darkness and will disclose the purposes of the heart."[7]

2. We have to listen. "In the day that I brought your ancestors out of the land of Egypt . . . this command I gave them, 'Obey my voice, and I will be your God, and you shall be my people; and walk only in the way that I command you, so that it may be well with you.' "[8] "Listen Israel. . . . Love the LORD your God with all your heart, with all your soul, and with all your strength. Take to heart these words that I give you today."[9] "Today, if you hear his voice, / do not harden your hearts as in the rebellion."[10] "From the cloud came a voice that said, 'This is my Son, my Chosen; listen to him!' When the voice had spoken, Jesus was found alone. And they kept silent."[11]

Mother Teresa was once asked, "When you pray, what do you say to God?"

Her answer startled the interviewer. She said, "I don't say anything. I listen!"

Not knowing what to say next, her interviewer fumbled for words and finally blurted out, "OK! When you pray what does God say to you?"

Mother Teresa answered, "He doesn't say anything. He listens. And if you don't understand that, I can't explain it to you."

3. *We must filter what we hear through Scripture.* "All scripture is inspired by God and is useful for teaching, for reproof, for correction, and for training in righteousness, so that everyone who belongs to God may be proficient, equipped for every good work."[12] " 'Let anyone who has ears to hear listen!' . . . 'hear the word and accept it and bear fruit.' "[13] "How are they to believe in one of whom they have never heard? . . . But not all have obeyed the good news; for Isaiah says, 'Lord, who has believed our message?' So faith comes from what is heard, and what is heard comes through the word of Christ."[14] "Garbage in, garbage out" is the saying of computer programmers. The same goes for those who seek God's will without Scripture as their starting and reference point.

One does not need to know Hebrew, Greek, Aramaic, or Latin to hear God speak through Scripture. It simply takes a good translation of the Bible, a concordance, and a dictionary. Using the concordance, find verses dealing with the subject of your concern. Then read those verses slowly and reflect on them, each in turn. Reflect on each verse in silence, taking note of the word or phrase that speaks to your mind. Read the verse again. Reflect on it in silence. Take note of what emotion or thought is stirred in your heart. Read the verse again followed by silent reflection. Take note of what action or direction the Scripture is calling you to take. Follow this process with each verse, writing down your thoughts and feelings in a journal.

4. *We must prayerfully submit our will to the Word of God and seek what glorifies Him, not us.* "Jesus answered them, 'My teaching is not mine but his who sent me. Anyone who resolves to do the will of God will know whether the teaching is from God or whether I am speaking on my own. Those who speak on their own seek their own glory; but the one who seeks the glory of him who sent him is true, and there is nothing false in him.' "[15] Jesus said, " 'If you believed Moses, you would believe me, for he wrote about me. But if you do not believe what he wrote, how will

you believe what I say?' "[16] In this regard, it is crucial to read and interpret verses in context and to look for two or more passages that agree with the principle under consideration. It is dishonest and manipulative to seize on a word or phrase out of context as the answer just because it agrees with our desires. It is a violation of the commandment "You shall not make wrongful use of the name of the LORD your God for the LORD will not acquit anyone who misuses his name"[17] to accept only the verses that agree with our preconceptions. The prophet Samuel condemned the selfishness of manipulating God's Word to match our stubborn wishes in the strongest of terms. "Rebellion is no less a sin than divination [superstitious rituals and occult spells], / and stubbornness is like iniquity and idolatry."[18]

5. We must obey what we learn from Scripture and prayer.

"Has the LORD as great delight in burnt offerings and sacrifices,
    as in obeying the voice of the LORD?
Surely, to obey is better than sacrifice,
    and to heed than the fat of rams."[19]

" 'Everyone then who hears these words of mine and acts on them will be like a wise man who built his house on rock. The rain fell, the floods came, and the winds blew and beat on that house, but it did not fall, because it had been founded on rock.' "[20]

6. We must not accept what someone else claims is the Word of God for us unless our own prayer and Bible study clearly lead to the same conclusion.

He will surely be gracious to you at the sound of your cry; when he hears it, he will answer you. Though the Lord may give you the bread of adversity and the water of affliction, yet your Teacher will not hide himself any more, but your eyes shall see your Teacher. And when you turn to the right or when you turn to the left, your ears shall hear a word behind you, saying, "This is the way; walk in it." Then you will defile your silver-covered idols and your gold-plated images. You will scatter them like filthy rags; you will say to them, "Away with you!"[21]

"I will put my laws in their minds,
    and write them on their hearts,
and I will be their God,
    and they shall be my people.

CLEANSING FIRE, HEALING STREAMS

And they shall not teach one another
> or say to each other, 'Know the Lord,'
for they shall all know me,
> from the least of them to the greatest.
For I will be merciful to their iniquities,
> and I will remember their sins no more."[22]

I have witnessed great damage done by self-appointed prophets who tell men and women, "I have a special word of God just for you." The message usually deals with some aspect of their love or business lives and seeks to compel action in line with the wish of the person who claims to know God's will. Scripture clearly teaches that we each have access to God, and He will speak His word to our hearts and minds. "Surely I know the plans I have for you, says the LORD, plans for your welfare and not for harm, to give you a future with hope. Then when you call upon me and come and pray to me, I will hear you. When you search for me, you will find me; if you seek me with all your heart, I will let you find me, says the LORD."[23] "Let us therefore approach the throne of grace with boldness, so that we may receive mercy and find grace to help us in time of need."[24]

7. Having received God's guidance, we must remain faithful to it regardless of who tries to change our minds. "Those who trust in the Lord are like Mount Zion, / which cannot be moved but abides forever."[25] " 'I have come in my Father's name, and you do not accept me; but if someone else comes in his own name, you will accept him. How can you believe if you accept praise from one another, yet make no effort to obtain the praise that comes from the only God?' "[26] "If any of you is lacking in wisdom, ask God, who gives to all generously and ungrudgingly, and it will be given you. But ask in faith, never doubting, for the one who doubts is like a wave of the sea, driven and tossed by the wind; for the doubter, being double-minded and unstable in every way, must not expect to receive anything from the Lord."[27]

I think there are no sadder words in Scripture than Luke's record of Pilate's surrendering Jesus to be crucified simply because he couldn't withstand public disapproval. "With loud shouts they insistently demanded that he be crucified and their shouts prevailed. So Pilate decided to grant their demand. He released the man who had been thrown into prison for insurrection and murder, the one they asked for, and surrendered Jesus to their will."[28]

These are principles that I've learned over time and through experience. They aren't the truth itself because, as I said in the previous chapter, the will of God is not an answer apart from us. Our journey of experience doesn't lead us to the truth; it teaches us how to discern the truth. The will of God is something that happens in us and to us and through us in love. "Love never ends. . . . For we know only in part, and we prophesy only in part; but when the complete comes, the partial will come to an end. . . . For now we see in a mirror, dimly, but then we will see face to face. Now I know only in part; then I will know fully, even as I have been fully known."[29]

That God loves us and won't stop loving us is the most important thing we can ever know about God's will. Why not set your plans and your anxieties aside, sit still, and yield to God's love? Allow the love of Jesus Christ to fill you with His presence. Whatever else that you may want, it doesn't get any better than being loved forever by the One who made you.

Questions for Reflection

1. Why do you suppose that God seeks our stillness through which to become known to us?
2. What would a relationship be like if each person listened carefully to the other?
3. What would it take for you to surrender yourself—body, soul, and spirit—to God?

17

The Hardest Thing About Prayer

Waiting for God's timing is the hardest thing about prayer.

Perhaps the hardest thing about prayer is waiting on God to open the door and give us the power to follow Him through it.

Jesus' last instruction to His disciples was this: " 'I am going to send you what my Father has promised; but stay in the city until you have been clothed with power from on high.' "[1]

The disciples had just been traumatized by the crucifixion and shocked by the appearance of the resurrected Christ. They also feared for their lives against the persecution of the same religious establishment that had just killed Jesus.[2] The temptation to get out of town and into the sheltering anonymity of the countryside must have been great. Instead, Jesus told the disciples to go out and preach repentance and forgiveness of sins in the name of the risen Christ to all nations beginning with Jerusalem.[3] The disciples were undoubtedly anxious to "get the show on the road."

But Jesus had said, " 'Stay in the city until you have . . . power from on high.' "

"The Lord helps those who help themselves." "When the going gets tough, the tough get going." These tapes play in our head. "We can't just sit here and do nothing," we tell ourselves. "We must do something."

So we move on out—exhorting, organizing, building, growing, maintaining, struggling, and burning out. Entire industries serve this cycle. There are motivators, strategic planners, fund-raisers on the upside, and counselors for the downside.

Observing the human tendency to leap into action, Solomon wrote,

Unless the LORD builds the house,
    its builders labor in vain.
Unless the LORD watches over the city,
    the watchmen stand guard in vain.
In vain you rise early
    and stay up late,
toiling for food to eat—
    for he grants sleep to those he loves.
Sons are a heritage from the LORD,
    children a reward from him.
Like arrows in the hands of a warrior
    are sons born in one's youth.
Blessed is the man
    whose quiver is full of them.
They will not be put to shame
    when they contend with their enemies in the gate.[4]

The "gate" is the place of trade and news. It is the place of tension on the edge between the inside and the outside. It is the place where one moves between the old and the new. Solomon's half brother Absalom stirred a revolt by standing in the gate and urging action by implying that their father David wasn't doing enough. Absalom almost brought down David by his lies and manipulations.

Contending with enemies in the gate is the human condition. We all pass through the gate, the place of trade-offs, information, enticement, and attack. We have our passages of work and relationship where we fear embarrassment and shame, loss and abandonment. The question, Solomon said, is where are your head and your heart? Do you depend on God to build and guard, or are you taking care of yourself? Do you have family relationships of intimacy gifted to you by God? Do you respect that blessing for the grace it represents? Or are you watching out for *numero uno*, anxious and tired? The persons who get through the gate safely are those who let God take care of the details. That's what Solomon was saying. It is the challenge of trust that Jesus placed before His disciples.

"After [Jesus'] suffering, he showed himself to these men and gave many convincing proofs that he was alive. . . . On one occasion, while he was eating with them, he gave them this command: 'Do not leave Jerusalem, but wait for the gift my Father promised, which you have heard me speak about. For John baptized with water, but in a few days you will be baptized with the Holy Spirit.' "[5]

Of course His listeners were still dealing with their dashed hopes and broken dreams. "They asked him, 'Lord, are you at this time going to restore the kingdom to Israel?' "[6] Ah, one of the reasons I love Scripture is it is so true to life. I've prayed prayers that asked God, "Are you going to fix what is broken and do it right now? Time is wasting! It's time to make a move, God. Restore what I've lost, and do it now, please."

"He said to them: 'It is not for you to know the times or dates the Father has set by his own authority. But you will receive power when the Holy Spirit comes on you.' "[7] It's maddening to have to wait in the place of danger and pain, not knowing when things will change, to wait on the promise of new life and power to come from Christ alone—and then to have Him vanish in a cloud and not be seen again.[8]

So we make a big deal out of trying to put things back exactly the way they were before. There were twelve disciples before; there have to be twelve disciples again. " 'It is necessary to choose one of the men.' . . . they proposed two men: Joseph called Barsabbas (also known as Justus) and Matthias. Then [and only then] they prayed . . . 'Lord. . . . Show us.' . . . Then they cast lots, and the lot fell to Matthias."[9] All seemed back in order. But they hadn't waited for the Holy Spirit, and their own solution, Matthias, was never heard from again. Meanwhile, God was preparing the fire-breathing, believer-hating Saul to be Paul, the twelfth apostle,[10] an idea that they would never have conceived in their wildest imaginings.

Where are you right now? Are you contending with your enemies in the gate, trying to make it through on your own? Are you obsessively and compulsively planning to get things back the way they were and then asking God to bless the Matthias and Justus that you've chosen as your only options? I ask because I have experienced the situation myself.

The choice between Matthias and Justus is a false dilemma arising from the false premise that it all depends on us and we have to do something. Our real choice is to stay in the promise or to attempt to go on our own compulsion. Only one of those choices leads to life.

"Unless the Lord builds the house, its builders labor in vain. . . . wait for the gift my Father promised. . . . Stay . . . until you have . . . power from on high."

Questions for Reflection

1. Why are we so easily tempted to act when we should wait?
2. How are you doing with "contending with enemies in the gate"?
3. How do you know when it's time to act after waiting on God?

18

Our Work As Prayer

It makes all the difference of eternity to think of our business in terms of obedience to Christ rather than to seek His help for our success. To think like this is to consider our work as prayer.

I am blessed to represent many Christian organizations. It is not unusual for my clients' meetings to start with prayer for God's guidance and for His will to be done.

It is tempting in the Christian organizational culture for prayer to become an end in itself, a kind of symbolic rabbit's foot to be rubbed for luck before getting to the "real business" at hand or a symbolic last rite when all other strategies have failed.

The fervent prayer and listening that led to the beginning of institutions and initiatives fade to a number on an agenda and are replaced by management principles, systems, policies, and the comfort of traditions. Somewhere along the line, regard for divine providence goes from a cherished gift to simply the ribbon on the package.

Substantive time taken for careful, deliberative corporate prayer as an approach to organizational planning and problem solving is something rare, even extinct, in my experience. "God gives us common sense and expects us to use it," I heard one leader comment about a suggestion that time be taken in a meeting for corporate prayer.

The truth is that the silence and waiting necessarily involved in honest prayer causes those who take their worth from their busyness to squirm in embarrassment. The wonderful promise " 'The LORD will fight for you, and you have only to keep still' "[1] is ignored by functional atheists in many boardrooms and around conference tables in many Christian organizations. By "functional atheists" I mean those who pay lip service to God in stating their beliefs but in practice place their reliance on human effort, performance, and approval. Lest you think that I am harsh in using this term, I give you the succinct conclusion of Jesus that those who crave recognition and acceptance from their peers more than the approval of God are unbelievers. " 'How can you believe when you accept glory from one another and do not seek the glory that comes from the one who alone is God?' "[2]

However, prayer, in and of itself and no matter how fervent, is no substitute for positive systems of quality, service, justice, and accountability that lead to effective, fair, and reproducible results.[3] Few sights are more appalling to the committed believer than to see church leaders taking enormous risks without due diligence or prudent safeguards on the presumptions that "we prayed about this," or, "God gave us the opportunity and the authority to make the most of it. Who can question us about this?" Solomon observed that "desire without knowledge is not good, / and one who moves hurriedly misses the way."[4]

It is also possible to get so wrapped up in praying that we fail to see the answer when it arrives. When King Herod went on a murderous campaign to exterminate the new church in Jerusalem, he killed James, the brother of John, and arrested Peter, intending to try him in public and execute him after the Passover. The church went into hiding and fervent prayer for Peter.

Peter was released from prison through the direct intervention of "an angel of the Lord." When Peter showed up at the home where the believers were gathered praying for him, he had a hard time convincing them he was indeed free and present with them in answer to their prayer.[5] This can be a problem with our contemporary prayer gatherings, conferences, and summits—method and fervor sometimes are emphasized over object and purpose.

Jesus prayed spare, simple prayers. He instructed His disciples to make direct, simple requests to Abba.[6] He warned against piling on words, trying to impress others with our prayers, or manipulating others to share our misery through our prayer practices.[7]

One could read what I've written thus far and ask, "Is it better to pray for organizational advancement or to keep our eyes open and work hard?" I say, Both activities are correct.

I take a hint from Jesus in the answer. He said that each of us fulfills a specific intention of God and is also invited to ask for others to do

God's work in the world. We should pray and then go out and seek the place where we find peace in serving him. We should do what needs to be done in the relationships that we currently find ourselves in, not imposing ourselves or looking around for a better deal. We are to share meals without complaint, work to heal anyone we encounter who is suffering in body and soul, and tell them that "God's kingdom is close to you because He loves you." If we are rejected or pulled into conflict, we need to leave without demanding anything for ourselves and taking nothing with us.[8]

Each one of us is an answer to prayer when we live like this. "He said to them, 'The harvest is plentiful, but the laborers are few; therefore ask the Lord of the harvest to send out laborers into his harvest.' "[9] To think of ourselves as ones sent by God to do His work and will rather than to ask what will God do for us would take a radical change of mind for many of us. This is the mindset described by Carlo Carretto, who surrendered his life as a powerful youth leader and Christian activist to live, work, and pray with the impoverished, suffering Tuareg people in the Sahara. "The first thing I must understand and believe is *that my work is of enormous value, that the duties incumbent on me as a human being are holy because they are willed by God and I fulfill them in obedience to his Law.* And if God allows me a little free time after all the work and chores, I can devote a few minutes to contemplation, enabling my life to achieve its proper balance."[10]

A crucial decision that each of us must make is whether we ask how we may be of service to God or ask God to be of service to us. It is all the difference of eternity to think of our business in terms of obedience to Christ rather than to seek His help for our success. To think like this is to consider our work as prayer.

If we are saved, we are loved. If we are loved, we are free to give ourselves in love. The early Christians called their vocations and care for each other "the grace of daily obligation." In such grace we can love each other as Christ loved us and can be the kind of beings that we were created in love to be. We find our meaning through our unique relation to our Creator, and not in competition with each other. Paul spoke of this relationship when he wrote, "Bear one another's burdens, and in this way you will fulfill the law of Christ. For if those who are nothing think they are something, they deceive themselves. All must test their own work; then that work, rather than their neighbor's work, will become a cause for pride. For all must carry their own loads."[11]

Commenting on this text, Eugene Peterson writes,

> I have listened to some . . . teachers contend, with many illustrations and arguments, that every child is a natural artist. Creativity, they say, is innate in all of us and only needs opportunity and encouragement to be expressed. But most of us have it bred out of us. If we were given the right materials and provided with the proper environment and stimulus, all of us would be artists, realizing and enjoying the energies and results of creativity.
>
> I believe that. I believe that we were not put here to copy someone else's drawing. I believe that our highest function is not to fill in the colors of someone else's outline. I believe that we are made in the image of God and that because God is a creator, we are creators.
>
> Our early experience often does not encourage that. We are instructed to stay within the line. In school and church, at home and at work, we are handed someone else's outline and told to learn, pray, play, work—whatever—within it. The intimidation is appallingly successful.
>
> In Christ we are set free to create. He sets us free to live— toward God, with people, in the world—as artists, not as copiers. He sets us free to use the stuff that God gives us to live something original.[12]

In the time when the thought of God was more pervasive in the everyday life of Western culture, the work of men and women was referred to as their "calling." We derive the word *vocation* from this idea. *Vocation* is a Latin word meaning "to listen." In the biblical narrative we find the fruits of listening in the vocations of men and women such as Noah, Abraham, Joseph, Moses, Joshua, Deborah, Gideon, Hannah, Samuel, David, Elijah, Elisha, Isaiah, Jeremiah, Daniel, Mary, Joseph, Jesus, Peter, Paul, John, Steven, and Lydia. These are men and women who, like us, entered the world made in the image of God, and who, by God's grace, resisted the evil effort to remake us in the image of someone else. This is an especially apt lesson in the current attempts to seduce us into the cult of celebrity worship. Comparison, truly, is the enemy of grace, for it focuses on the gift at the expense of gracious response to the Giver.

The Quaker sociologist Parker Palmer wrote a provocative book on the subject of vocation titled *Let Your Life Speak.* Palmer writes,

Today I understand vocation . . . not as a goal to be achieved but as a gift to be received. Discovering vocation does not mean scrambling toward some prize just beyond my reach but accepting the treasure of true self I already possess. Vocation does not come from a "voice out there" calling me to be something I am not. It comes from a voice "in here" calling me to be the person I was born to be, to fulfill the original selfhood given me at birth by God.

It is a strange gift, this birthright gift of self. Accepting it turns out to be even more demanding than attempting to become some-one else! I have sometimes responded to that demand by ignoring the gift, or hiding it, or fleeing from it, or squandering it—and I think I am not alone. There is a Hasidic tale that reveals, with amazing brevity, both the universal tendency to want to be some-one else and the ultimate importance of becoming one's self. Rabbi Zusya, when he was an old man, said, "In the coming world, they will not ask me: 'Why were you not Moses?' They will ask me: 'Why were you not Zusya?' "[13]

Our work, therefore, expresses a Creator who not only made us but also empowers us to live by the creative power implanted within us at our creation. More than that, our work demonstrates the love of our Creator through creative and redemptive service for others. Our ability to work well is not a teeth-gritting, self-propelled exercise of survival, but it is a manifestation of the gift of our life. Out of this inspiration comes the desire and the courage to do the job well. To "cut corners," lie, cheat, and steal in our work, is to deny that we have a Provider. To demand recognition for ourselves as the price of our work is to deny our Lord and Master and is the antithesis of faith.

The recognition of our work as God's gift can make all the difference of life itself as it did for Brother Lawrence, the seventeenth-century kitchen worker and commentator on prayer in everyday life. An observer said of him:

When he had filled his mind, through prayer, with great senti-ments of divine Being, he went to his appointed work in the kitchen [he was a cook in a hospital]. There he first considered carefully the things that his office required, when and how each thing was to be done. He then spent all the intervals of his time, and before and after his work, in prayer.

When he began his business he said to God, with a filial trust in Him: "Oh my God, since You are with me, and I must now, in obedience to Your commands, apply my mind to these outward things, I ask You to grant me the grace to continue in Your presence. To this end make me prosper through Your assistance. Receive all my works and possess all my affections."

He proceeded in his work each day, continuing his familiar conversation with his Maker, imploring the Lord for His grace, and offering to the Lord all his actions.

When Brother Lawrence had finished, he examined how he had discharged his duties. If he found he had done well, he returned thanks to God; if he found otherwise, he asked pardon, and without being discouraged he set his mind right again. He then continued his exercise of the presence of God as if he had never deviated from it. Brother Lawrence commented, "Thus, by rising after my falls, and by frequently renewing my acts of faith and love, I have come to a state wherein it would be as difficult for me not to think of God as it was to accustom myself to think of Him."[14]

Brother Lawrence died in 1692. Three hundred years later the words and example of this lay worker still call men and women to prayer in the midst of their busy days. His witness is simple and true: Our work is worship. Our work is prayer.

In this witness of work as prayer, Brother Lawrence is in good company. Hear the word of the apostle Paul on the same point: "So here's what I want you to do, God helping you: Take your everyday, ordinary life—your sleeping, eating, going-to-work, and walking-around life—and place it before God as an offering. Embracing what God does for you is the best thing that you can do for him."[15]

_____ *Questions for Reflection* _____

1. Does your attitude about prayer reveal you to be a "functional atheist" or a true believer in Christ?
2. What is the right balance of prayer and work?
3. How can your work be an expression of your prayer?

19

Praying for Those You Cannot See

Faith is trusting God to do what we cannot do ourselves.

A friend of mine is a teacher and coach at a Christian high school. He took a group of his students on a special trip to Hawaii. While there, they joined another youth group for a time of worship. At the conclusion of the meeting, the Hawaiian youth leader called on one of the California students to give closing prayer.

The student shook his head No.

The youth leader insisted. What he didn't know was this young man was new to the school and Christianity. He came from a dysfunctional home in which the only time God's name was mentioned was in curses.

The student vigorously declined to offer prayer.

The youth leader grew vehement in his request and stood right over the student. "Every one takes part here. It is an honor to pray. You can't refuse."

Reluctantly, hands shoved in his pockets, feet shuffling nervously. The student stood and prayed the only prayer that he knew. He had heard his smart aleck older brother say it a few times before meals at the kitchen table back home.

"Dear Pop, bless this slop, now let's dig in."

It took my friend the coach a good while to hush his students and convince the apoplectic youth leader that the young man meant no blasphemy or disrespect.

There comes a time in the experience of all Christian believers gathered around a conference table, before a campfire, in a small prayer group, or in a meeting of one sort or another when one is invited to pray for a person or family or a situation that he or she doesn't know or barely knows. The thoughtful among us have a problem with this. Does prayer for someone you don't know, with concerns of which you know nothing, mean anything?

Sometimes prayer requests for the unknown and far away are escapes from the challenge of intimacy with those sitting or standing next to us. "The grass is greener on the other side," even in prayer. We think the real dramas or opportunities for effective prayer and giving are in extreme situations in faraway places. Eugene Peterson calls this "the moral disease of Afghanistanitus."[1] Our spiritual muscles atrophy and our capacity for love and service shrinks as we ignore the challenges of relationship in our everyday lives.

But we are members of the body of Christ and brothers and sisters in the family of God. Calls to the family for help shouldn't be denied. The question is, What do we request of God in such circumstances?

I was writing a study guide on Paul's Letter to the Colossians for a workplace prayer group when I found an answer to this dilemma. Paul never visited the city of Colossae. The closest he came was the city of Ephesus, one hundred miles away, where he preached and taught for three years.[2] A resident of Colossae, Epaphras, probably became a believer in Ephesus and returned to found the church at Colossae.[3] That church met in the home of Philemon.[4]

The little church at Colossae became infected by the heresy of the Gnostics, who taught that Christ is not the only way of salvation.[5] The Gnostics claimed that acceptance by God takes special knowledge possessed by an elite spiritual few. Epaphras visited Paul in Rome and brought him news of the problem of the Colossian heresy. Paul wrote to the Colossian believers and described a prayer that he prayed for them daily ever since he first heard about their church.

Paul's prayer provides a good template for our own prayer for faraway strangers.

Paul began, "In our prayers for you we always thank God, the Father of our Lord Jesus Christ, for we have heard of your faith in Christ Jesus and of the love that you have for all the saints because of the hope laid up for you in heaven."[6]

My son is completing his junior year in high school. Recently his religion teacher and other students challenged his assertion that faith in Jesus Christ alone as our Savior and Lord is the one essential of salvation. "More than faith is required," the teacher said. "You have to do good works to prove to God He should save you."

"Yeah," some other students said, "You have to prove your worth to God."

"You don't understand," Andrew said. "We don't have to make God love us. Faith is our acceptance *that* He loves us. We love each other and do good things because we have that faith, not because we have to prove anything more."

Andrew is correct. Faith is trusting God to do what we cannot do for ourselves.[7] When I heard of his classroom exchange, I thought back to Andrew's second-grade year in church school, when he came home one day with a can decorated with a bright crepe-paper label and a slot in the top. A note to us from his teacher accompanied the can announcing a classroom fund-raising project. She wanted parents to put a nickel in the can each time their child obeyed, was courteous, told the truth, etc. We were horrified. We were raising Andrew to be a human being and a follower of Christ, not Pavlov's dog.

Andrew's uncle Terry happened to be visiting with us that evening. He came up with the winning solution, "Fill the can with nickels and return it with a note the next day saying, 'Andrew is under grace, not the law!' " Nine years later, it is gratifying to us that Andrew knows this essential truth and can stand for it.

Paul's prayer continued, "We have not ceased praying for you and asking that you may be filled with all the knowledge of God's will in all spiritual wisdom and understanding."[8]

Asking God to help His children know what He wants them to do is always appropriate. I don't know about you, but I have learned to be very skeptical of men and women who approach me with a "word from God" about what I should be doing. It may be just a coincidence, but the word always turns out to be exactly what the person telling you thinks everyone should do. Paul was explicit to the Colossians that everything they did was to be for God and their obligation was to God, not to other men and women.[9]

To have a loving, instructive relationship with our Creator and Savior is the goal of prayer for each one of us. That relationship is available to each one of us when we come into God's presence, even if we are weak, low, and despised in the eyes of the world. For God "is the source of your life in Christ Jesus, who became for us wisdom from God, and righteousness and sanctification and redemption, in order that, as it is written, 'Let the one who boasts, boast in the Lord.' "[10]

Paul said that, having begun to pray for them, he kept right on praying. "We have not ceased praying for you . . . so that you may lead lives worthy of the Lord, fully pleasing to him, as you bear fruit in every good work."[11]

Asking God to make His children live fruitful, helpful lives in His love and power is to ask for a gift that keeps on giving. Paul continued, "and as you grow in the knowledge of God." There is no better prayer than to ask God to give His children more knowledge of Himself. Take the word of Jesus on this. " 'Father, the hour has come; glorify your Son so that the Son may glorify you, since you have given him authority over all people, to give eternal life to all whom you have given him. And this is eternal life, that they may know you, the only true God, and Jesus Christ whom you have sent.' "[12]

Paul was mindful in his prayer that not all was going to be easy and peaceful for the Colossians. "May you be made strong with all the strength that comes from his glorious power, and may you be prepared to endure everything with patience."[13]

Concluding His last conversation before His arrest and execution, Jesus assured His disciples, " 'I've told you all this so that trusting me, you will be unshakeable and assured, deeply at peace. In this godless world you will continue to experience difficulties. But take heart! I've conquered the world.' "[14]

Every man, woman, and child on this planet faces problems and circumstances beyond their capability. We all need the power of the One who made us and can save us. There is never a time when this request to God is not relevant and necessary. Many mornings I wake up with the melody and words of the old hymn "I Need Thee Every Hour" going through my mind.

> I need Thee every hour,
> Most gracious Lord;
> No tender voice like Thine
> Can peace afford.
>
> I need Thee every hour,
> Stay Thou near by;
> Temptations lose their power
> When Thou art nigh.
>
> I need Thee every hour,
> In joy or pain;

Come quickly, and abide,
Or life is vain.

I need Thee every hour,
Teach me Thy will,
And Thy rich promises
In me fulfill.

I need Thee, O I need Thee;
Every hour I need Thee!
O bless me now, my Savior—
I come to Thee.[15]

Finally, Paul prayed that even while the Colossians endured trials and troubles, that they would do so "while joyfully giving thanks to the Father, who has enabled you to share in the inheritance of the saints in the light. He has rescued us from the power of darkness and transferred us into the kingdom of his beloved Son, in whom we have redemption, the forgiveness of sins."[16]

The surest sign of the presence of God in a life is joy regardless of circumstance because that's what His goodness and love evokes. No one or nothing can deny His children those blessings.

The surest sign of faith is thankfulness because it carries with it an admission that God, manifest in the person of Christ, is the one to whom we owe our very lives. It is always a good thing to pray that our brothers and sisters everywhere know the joy of the Lord's presence and give the thanks that rises out of true faith. Knowing that our brothers and sisters throughout the world have come to accept Christ as their Savior is cause for thanksgiving.

There it is, then. We can pray with assurance and specificity anytime for God's children that we don't even know. We can
- be thankful for their faith and transformed lives;
- ask God to help them know what He wants them to do;
- ask God to give them spiritual wisdom and understanding;
- ask God to help them live fruitful, pleasing lives for Him;
- ask God to give them more knowledge of Himself;
- ask God to give them strength and patience to endure the difficulties they face;
- ask God to fill them with the joy of His presence and with thankfulness for all that He has done for them.

Many times, in my early morning prayer time or driving to or from work, I think of those near and far who I know need God's help, and I turn to an old, simple prayer that I learned years ago, "Father God, and Jesus Christ whom You sent, as You know and as You will, have mercy." This prayer expresses to me the thought of David in his psalm for wisdom and forgiveness in which he struggled with God about the right thing to say and do. He came to realize that it is God alone who makes the difference, and he asks honestly, "And now, O Lord, what do I wait for? / My hope is in you."[17]

It is the reality of eternity that we hope for the help of our God, or we are hopeless.

Questions for Reflection

1. In what situations are you embarrassed to pray?
2. Can you think of situations in which prayer would be an escape from the challenge of intimacy?
3. Is prayer a matter of whom you know or what you know?

20

Learning to Pray in Afghanistan

A mission to Afghanistan teaches a lawyer that his only calling is to love, and his only resource is Jesus Christ.

I thought that my voyage had come to its end at the last limit of my power, that the path before me was closed, that provisions were exhausted and the time had come to take shelter in a silent obscurity.

But I find that Your will knows no end in me, and when old words die out on the tongue, new melodies break forth from the heart, and where the old tracks are lost, new country is revealed with its wonders.[1]

I stood in the mud of a Kabul, Afghanistan, marketplace one May afternoon. Standing beside me was Don Nicolay, a surgeon from Colorado. Other members of our team bargained in a shop nearby.

As butchers, bakers, hat makers, fruit sellers, carpet dealers, and tea vendors all hawked their goods, curious old men, teenagers, and children surrounded us. The teenage boys wanted to practice their English. One of them spoke to us with passion of the power of education to change lives and his desire to attend the university in Pakistan. His father in traditional dress came and took hold of his arm and led him away. A little boy reached out and enviously fingered the dial of my "cheap" watch that I had purchased for this trip so that my "good" watch wouldn't be a temptation to thieves.

I kept one hand on my cell phone and another in my pocket on my money clip. These items reflect my values just as the chickens, goats, bread, and simple inventory in the market stalls represent the values of the Afghans. But their possessions represent survival. My possessions reflect the cares and riches of this world. I do not live in daily fear that everything I have will be swept away. Or do I?

In fact, I do live with that fear, and I struggle every day for more while these folk battle every day to hang on to what they have. They smile easily. They keep their clothing clean and their market stalls in neat order. The familial affection between them is obvious. Their family and friendships are their "safety net" while my bank account, home-ownership, health insurance, and vehicle are mine. When Don told them, "I am a doctor," they responded with grins and words of recognition. When I told them, "I am a lawyer," the shopkeepers and their children had no clue what a lawyer is or does. I think that they settle their disputes without a civil legal system, and who is to say that they aren't happier for this.

When I asked the physicians on the negotiating team for the Ministry of Health if any of them had ever purchased or even seen a policy of medical malpractice insurance, they told me No. I would starve to death in Kabul if I had to depend on my profession for my livelihood.

When the possibility of going to Afghanistan was first broached to me, I thought it was a joke. Husband, father, suburban business lawyer from southern California—I am an unlikely candidate for a mission to a war zone. When one thinks of overseas mission and aid projects, having a lawyer along is not the first thing that comes to mind.

For more than forty years, intrepid physicians from my client Loma Linda University have worked in Afghanistan to improve medical education. After the Taliban were driven out of power in 2001, the Ministry of Health of Afghanistan and the U.S. Agency for International Development invited Loma Linda University Adventist Health Sciences Center to assume management of the two hundred–bed Wazir Akbar Khan Hospital and develop it as a model for other hospitals in the country. A contract needed to be negotiated and documented to formalize the arrangement, and the assistance of a lawyer was needed. That's what brought me onto the team of physicians, administrators, and an engineer that traveled to Kabul.

Afghanistan is a place of ancient and still-seething conflicts. It has been the crossroads of imperial ambitions for centuries. Darius the Great of Persia, Alexander the Great, Tamerlane, Genghis Khan, Great Britain, Nazi Germany, Soviet Russia, and the Taliban have all tried, with no lasting success, to hold and subdue the country.

Violence is ever present in Afghanistan. One night during our visit, a suicide bomber blew up an Internet cafe frequented by foreigners about a mile away from our compound. Three persons were killed.

A nation and a people cannot be the pawns of the ambitions of human powers without suffering. Afghanistan's people are sick. Kabul, the capital, which has a population of three million, has no municipal water or sanitation systems. The infant mortality rate is high. Women die in childbirth at an alarming rate. Between one hundred fifty and three hundred civilian casualties a month result from the five to seven million land mines left over from years of war. It is estimated that five hundred thousand persons have died from mines in the country since the war with Russia began in 1978. Average life expectancy is only forty-seven years.

Frankly, the situation is overwhelming. Doubts and discomfort over this trip plagued me with a vague oppression before I left. I wrestled with those doubts in prayer to the point that I realized that what was bothering me was a loss of control. All of my so-called advantages were neutralized in this mission. My title and position brought me to Kabul but meant little there. My license as an attorney was of no effect. My facility with the English language failed me because the official language is Farsi. My middle-class affluence and network of influential contacts bought me nothing. I was vulnerable and without influence, an alien in a land that is hostile to my people and nation. Even my Christianity and spirituality shared with my friends and family back home were considered a handicap and an offense in Afghanistan. I was far from my safe and comfortable life, where I have at least the illusion of control over my circumstances. Who am I, stripped of the props of my life and my illusions?

I have written and spoken of prayer as if I know what I am talking about. A few years ago I wrote these words: "Jesus values His life and the life that He gives you and me as a ransom. A ransom is something worth exchanging for a life. We are the currency of God. We are His to spend and His to invest. Why, indeed, are we trying to save our own lives? We were not meant to be banked and held in reserve. We are meant to be spent by God as ransom for others held captive."[2]

Noble feelings surged in my soul when I wrote those words. But beyond the finite cash in my pocket, the things that I have believed give my life value would not ransom much from the mud of the Kabul marketplace.

A young Christian woman who is a project director for the World Bank in Afghanistan told a story of one of her community organizers who hiked ten kilometers to a remote mountain village. He passed a young woman carrying an infant going the opposite direction down the trail. He did not speak to her because in that area she could be stoned to death for speaking with a strange man. That evening when he hiked back out, he met the same woman coming up the trail. She was still carrying the infant.

Because it was nearing dark and the young woman was so far from home, the man spoke to her out of concern. "Are you all right?" he asked her in Pashtun.

"My son was sick and I was taking him to the hospital in the city," she said. "But I don't need to go now because he died on the way."

I heard of that woman's unrequited pain. I saw the beggars in the streets and the traffic stirring the dust with nothing changing. I watched the Gurkha guards watching me. I looked up to the summits of the Hindu Kush towering over Kabul and desired to be alone with God in the snowy solitude. In that moment, I realized that I am insensate of the purpose of prayer.

I have been praying for escape my whole life, asking God to help me or someone I love to get by, get out, get over, get through, get more, and to get "It." I seek to meet God alone and hold him all to myself. I confess that my prayer for others at its best has been offered up in the spirit of noblesse oblige, rather than out of the heart of a servant. My prayer is directed more to a denial of my circumstances than their acceptance.

But Afghanistan is a truth that I cannot deny. It is a mother carrying her dead infant up a trail as night falls around her because the only hope of healing is too far away. It is a father pulling a son back from his effort to slake his intellectual thirst for new experience. It is foreigners buying "cheap" and bargaining for "cheaper" with Afghans while closely guarding their own possessions. My prayer of thankfulness for my blessings in this context sounds a lot like the Pharisee praying in the temple, " 'God, I thank you that I am not like other people.' "[3]

"You will be judged according to your ability to love," wrote Carlos Caretto in *Letters from the Desert*.[4] I read those words and squirm because they are true and because they render irrelevant every argument that I make to justify my life.

A lawyer once asked Jesus, " 'What must I do to inherit eternal life?' " Jesus asked him, " 'What is written in the law? What do you read there?' "

" 'You shall love the Lord your God with all your heart, and with all your soul, and with all your strength, and with all your mind; and your neighbor as yourself,' " the lawyer replied.

Jesus said that is the " 'right answer.' "

But the lawyer, seeking to justify himself, demanded to know, " 'And who is my neighbor?' "[5]

Jesus taught him that the one who needs mercy and the one who shows mercy are neighbors.[6]

What was I doing in Kabul? Do neighbors think of their visits as "mission trips," with all the judgment and condescension that implies?

The radical truth is that Jesus Christ went to extreme lengths to become our neighbor. He "pitched his tent in the neighborhood." He gave up the wealth and power of heaven to begin His life as a diapered infant, a vulnerable child dependent on the good will of other humans, in a poor family living in a captive land. He lived without permanent shelter or possessions, ministered to the shunned and dispossessed, took on our diseases and sins, and died our death in our place. He identified with us, "us" not just being the residents of Beverly Hills, 90210, but the poor in District 11 in Kabul.

Ministering the compassion and wisdom of Jesus Christ requires an intimacy and equality of relationships that are the antithesis of a focus on individual attainment and a secure retirement. The apostle Paul set aside his own considerable intellectual achievements and perceived cultural and religious superiority to bring the gospel of Christ to the diverse peoples of the Roman Empire. He offered this profound counsel for the followers of Christ.

> If then there is any encouragement in Christ, any consolation from love, any sharing in the Spirit, any compassion and sympathy, make my joy complete: be of the same mind, having the same love, being in full accord and of one mind. Do nothing from selfish ambition or conceit, but in humility regard others as better than yourselves. Let each of you look not to your own interests, but to the interests of others. Let the same mind be in you that was in Christ Jesus,
> who, though he was in the form of God,
>   did not regard equality with God as a thing to be exploited,
> but emptied himself,
>   taking the form of a slave,
>   being born in human likeness.

And being found in human form,
    he humbled himself
    and became obedient to the point of death—
even death on a cross.[7]

I completed the task that brought me to Kabul. A contract was negotiated and signed. Doctors and nurses have already begun the actual work
of healing and teaching alongside Afghan colleagues. I have returned to
the workaholic rhythms of my life in southern California. But I did not
return unchanged.

My prayers have been so focused on my anxiety of how God would
use me and whether I would measure up that I missed for too long the
obvious truth in the teaching of Jesus, "I am the Vine, you are the
branches. When you're joined with me and I with you, the relation intimate and organic, the harvest is sure to be abundant. Separated, you
can't produce a thing."[8]

Before Afghanistan, I sought God's help for increased power and
spectacular results. My experience in Kabul stripped off the veneer of the
power and privilege that have cosseted my prayer life. In the streets of
Kabul, I was confronted with an unrelenting, stony poverty of resource
and spirit and overwhelming suffering that made me realize my human
insecurity and powerlessness.

There is a refugee camp on the northern edge of Kabul. It is a squalid
tent city stretched out on the flats behind the shells of a blown-up com-
mercial complex. A Swiss physician who leads a relief effort in Afghanistan told me of going into the camp on Christmas Day last year to dis-
tribute blankets and food. They came upon a woman, squatting alone on
the frozen ground outside, giving birth to a child. The men of her family
remained in the warm tent because they believe it wrong to even acknowledge a woman's pregnancy, let alone attend to the woman's physical needs. The baby lived because of the miraculous intercession of love
in the very moment that he entered the world.

On the same day, the relief workers visited a family who had requested
blankets to keep them warm during the freezing nights. Kabul is more
than a mile high, and the winters are fierce. The refugee families heat
stones and place them in the center of the tent. They sit in a circle with
their feet toward the hot rocks, wrapped in blankets, if they have them,
to conserve the warmth from the rocks and their body heat.

The family had asked for and received four blankets to comfortably
cover the parents and children. But turning away with their treasure,

they saw another family for whom there were no blankets. The astonished relief workers watched the family with the blankets without hesitation give two of them to the other family. That family, in turn, gave one of their blankets to a family that had none.

" 'Truly I tell you,' " Christ announces, " 'just as you did it to one of the least of these who are members of my family, you did it to me.' "[9] I have been taught these words throughout my life. I'm not sure that those who taught me really believed them. Their truth was meant for the rough streets of places like Kabul, not the comfortable abstractions of a classroom, pew, or carpeted, air-conditioned office.

My experience in Kabul forces me to ask myself what I am going to do from now on because, contrary to the illusions by which I have conducted my life to date, my only calling is to love, and my only resource is Jesus Christ. Love does not appear to be a miracle when we can buy what we need. But love in the face of impossibility is the greatest miracle of all. Recognizing the finitude and the futility of human existence and despairing over my selfish, irritable nature, I come to pray to the God of love for whom life appears out of nothing and who motivates His poor, cold children to share their blankets with their freezing brothers and sisters.

"Lord, having shown me the way, please do not let me grow weary or lose heart in following You in the actions of Your grace and mercy to whomever and wherever You lead."

Questions for Reflection

1. How can your material possessions and status affect your prayer?
2. Would you characterize your prayer as a plea for an escape from your circumstances or an acceptance of God's will in all circumstances?
3. What does serving others in their need and distress teach you about prayer?

21

The Burning Bush, Part 1

The recognition of God's presence does not depend on the time or place of the encounter. It comes with the acceptance of God's eyes as our own.

Moses was keeping the flock of his father-in-law Jethro, the priest of Midian; he led his flock beyond the wilderness, and came to Horeb, the mountain of God. There the angel of the LORD appeared to him in a flame of fire out of a bush; he looked, and the bush was blazing, yet it was not consumed. Then Moses said, "I must turn aside and look at this great sight, and see why the bush is not burned up." When the LORD saw that he had turned aside to see, God called to him out of the bush, "Moses, Moses!" And he said, "Here I am." Then he said, "Come no closer! Remove the sandals from your feet, for the place on which you are standing is holy ground." He said further, "I am the God of your father, the God of Abraham, the God of Isaac, and the God of Jacob." And Moses hid his face, for he was afraid to look at God.[1]

A sheepherder would cover a lot of ground and pass by many bushes in the span of forty years. The monks of St. Catherine's monastery on Mount Sinai have claimed for sixteen hundred years that they house the burning bush on the monastery grounds. It's a brambly, fast-growing shrub from the mountains of Central Asia belonging to the species *Rubus sanctus* that is rarely found in the desert. The claim is that the red berries appeared to be flames, but the monastery's bush doesn't bear fruit. The monks argue over whether their bush sprouted from the root system of the bush that Moses saw or was replanted in the tenth century at its current location. They water and fertilize it with goat droppings to keep it alive and flourishing.

A fascinating account of the monastery's claim was written by Bruce Feiler in *Walking the Bible*.[2] Feiler describes his visit to the bush in colorful terms.

> Directly across the walkway was a rounded stone wall about ten feet high that looked as if it were made of peanut brittle. Sprouting from the top was an enormous, fountaining bush. The plant was about six feet tall, with large, dangling branches like a weeping willow that sprouted from the center like a cheap wig. A white cat with a brown splotch around one eye was perched at the base of the bush, and off to the side was a slightly out-of-date fire extinguisher. A fire extinguisher? At first I thought it was an eyesore, but then I realized the unintended humor. Was this in case the burning bush caught on fire?[3]

After thirty-one hundred years, a transplanting, and being pruned down to the roots in 1948, when the monks thought it looked sickly, one would expect to find any vestiges of the Divine Presence in the bush to be eradicated.

And who really knows if it was this bush or another long gone? The places where we find God are pretty ordinary. For me it was a window seat in economy class on an American Airlines flight between Chicago, Illinois, and Ontario, California, on a Thursday afternoon. A friend met God in a lily growing in the middle of a backyard lawn. Another friend experienced Him as a child in a Cuban pasture.

The issue isn't the place of encounter; it is the vision of the observer. Driving home from work one afternoon in the early spring, I was delighted to find the bare southern California hills clothed in emerald green with white clouds spilling over the ridgelines and running down into the canyons. I called a friend on my cell phone. "Do you see the clouds on the hills?"

"Yes."

"I think this is what David was talking about when he said, 'The mountains skipped like rams, / the hills like lambs.'[4] Do you see it?"

"No."

"Don't you see the white clouds pouring over the hills?"

"Yes."

"Doesn't it make you think of a flock of sheep running across a pasture?"

"Not really."

"Oh well, it does to me—and I think it's great."

"Well, that's nice."

Frustrated, I called another friend who was driving home. She saw the clouds on the hills but couldn't see the rams and lambs in them. I am still sad at this.

One windy afternoon, I drove to a church-league softball game. My five-year-old son was by my side. We were stopped at a red light when he said, "Look, Daddy, the trees are talking to each other."

"What do you mean?"

He pointed up to the Chinese elms, eucalyptus, pepper trees, and palms that were leaning in close to each other in the wind like friends sharing confidences.

"You're right, little man. They are talking to each other. It's like the song we sing.

> The trees are gently swaying,
> swaying, swaying;
> The trees are gently swaying,
> saying God is love."

He nodded his head yes and kept watching as we drove down the street.

In her poem *Aurora Leigh*, Elizabeth Barrett Browning famously made the point.

> Earth's crammed with heaven,
> And every common bush afire with God;
> But only he who sees, takes off his shoes,
> The rest sit around it and pluck blackberries,
> And daub their natural faces unaware
> More and more from the first similitude.[5]

When he saw the burning bush, Moses was eighty years old, approaching middle age in a time when humans lived much longer than they do today. When he had come into the desert, he was a shamed forty-year-old exile, rejected by his people after he had taken a violent stand for them and forced out of his privilege and power as a prince of Egypt.

He found work and life as a tribal sheepherder. He passed by a lot of bushes, but I doubt he noticed them. He was too focused on the raw inflammation of his loss—too consumed by the "what if's" of his dreams and ambitions denied. He had spent his life as an achiever in the most advanced society in the world to that time. His mind was filled with engineering concepts, military strategies, political intrigues, the mannered protocols of life in the Pharaoh's court, and grief over what might have been.

Forty years of watching dumb sheep during hot days and cold nights, looking for water in arid wastes, the humbling experience of parenting, and coming to treasure the precious simplicity of a spouse's smile and a child's laughter would give a person new eyes and an appreciation for the possibilities of God in an ordinary shrub.

Jesus said, " 'I came into this world for judgment so that those who do not see may see, and those who do see may become blind.' "[6] He said this to religious persons who thought they had everything figured out. Moses must have thought he had it all figured out when he killed an Egyptian for beating a Hebrew and sought to adjudicate disputes between his own people. But he became afraid of the truth of murder becoming known, and he fled from Pharaoh's retribution into the desert.[7]

Like every human, Moses would enter his alienation thinking he could see because of his fears, beliefs, and attachments. We think our fears help us see and protect us. Moses was a palace-trained individual from an urban society. There was plenty for him to fear in the desert. We know he was afraid of snakes.[8] Having committed murder, he would fear the same fate in a lawless, desolate place of nomads. He had held power and position. He would fear uselessness and oblivion. He had been fed and clothed as royalty. He would fear the lack of those things. He was born and grew up next to the greatest river in the then-known world. Now he would be driven by fear of unassuaged thirst. Having committed sin and crime, he would fear the wrath of a God whom he did not yet know well. Our fears make us alert and aware and are a gift in that respect. We think they help us see what might hurt us. But when they become our focus, we lose sight of reality and perspective in our obsession over what could or might happen.

Moses was raised in the oral tradition of the Hebrews and the complex and ritualized religion of the Egyptians. He obviously held convictions strong enough to motivate him to kill. We think our beliefs make us what we are. "Seeing is believing," the saying goes, but we think, "believing is seeing." We have a hard time accepting evidence that contradicts our beliefs. What could the desert possibly teach a man of Moses' erudition? His beliefs would color his view and obscure the possibilities of new circumstances.

We think the people and things that hold our affections make our lives exciting and meaningful. Moses had lost family, friends, power, status, and position. Attachment, like its first cousin unforgivingness, keeps us looking back. Attachment diverts the flow of grace. We think our salvation and happiness depend upon people and things. Fixation on who and what is finite and imperfect blinds us to the infinite and the holy. The stars are obscured by the artificial glow of streetlights. That's why astronomical observatories are built on desert mountaintops, away from the cities. It would take forty years of arid solitude before the false light of Moses' fears, beliefs, and attachments faded so that he could see the fire of God in an ordinary desert shrub.

I know men and women who seek to gain this vision by affinity with those who have experienced it. They diligently read spiritual classics, go on retreats and fasts, learn new methods of prayer, and seek guidance from spiritual "giants." I've done the same but have learned that the vision is not for sale. Looking for God through the thoughts of others is like reading about the sun in the light of a living-room lamp. Without coming to the place where I had exhausted my emotional resources, physical strength, intellectual abilities, and spiritual understanding in pursuit of what I had no power to change or control, I would never have gained the insight that it is only God and all God—and that must be enough or nothing ever will be. It took the genuine, natural light of God for me to obtain true vision. As David prayed to God, "For with you is the fountain of life; / in your light we see light."[9]

What spiritual disciplines I have learned and practice are an effort to realize from my brokenness that the only righteousness and healing that I will ever know comes from Jesus Christ, who has made me and bought me back with His blood from the debt and darkness of my own folly to live in the provision and light of His love. In the words of Paul, "I want to know Christ and the power of his resurrection and the sharing of his sufferings by becoming like him in his death, if somehow I may attain the resurrection from the dead. Not that I have already obtained this or I have already reached the goal; but I press on to make it my own, because Christ Jesus has made me his own."[10]

Moses would have never chosen the forty years in the desert. Neither would you or I. But without desolation—the stripping away of all that makes us comfortable and confident in ourselves—without need born from the reality of human inadequacy, we would not turn aside to see and know *Yahweh*, the God who told Moses out of the burning bush that My name is "I AM"[11] as in "I am who you need, and what you need, and all that you will ever need." He told Moses that " 'I am the God of your father [the source of your existence], the God of Abraham [who believed me, withheld nothing from me, and trusted me to be righteous for him], the God of Isaac [who received the provision of grace and lived it], and the God of Jacob [who pursued his destiny by his own strength and cleverness until he wrestled with God and lost].' "[12]

You may be in a desert right now. Have you considered that God has brought you to the place where you can see Him and renew your relationship with Him?

" . . . me she forgot,"
    declares the LORD.
"Therefore, I am now going to allure her;
    I will lead her into the desert
    and speak tenderly to her."[13]

Questions for Reflection

1. What do everyday, ordinary circumstances tell you about God?
2. How does asking "What if . . . ?" distract you from God's presence and plan?
3. What can "desert experiences" teach you about prayer?

22

The Burning Bush, Part 2

All children of God get the eyes of the Father, but they may see different things through those eyes.

Life in the desert is a matter of the here and the now. One's past is of no account, and the scarcity of resources leaves no ability to hoard for the future. I live 150 miles from Death Valley, where European tourists experience one of the harshest deserts on earth in four-star-luxury lodgings. I would not depend upon the concierge from the Furnace Creek Inn to lead me safely through that desert on foot. Instead, I would want a guide who learned to see the desert through forty years of living there. And if I am going to enter a spiritual desert, I want a guide who has found God in such a place.

The forty years before the burning bush were only prologue for Moses. He would spend the rest of his life in that desert other than the one trek back to Egypt to pick up his people. They became a nation in those empty spaces. They found their God there and learned His ways. God fed them there when they had nothing to eat. He brought water out of rock when they were thirsty. He spread a cloud over them for shade and gave them fire to light their way by night.

There is no place like a desert to learn the possibilities of the God who loves you. Those possibilities will be realized in elemental and ordinary things, such as rocks, shrubs, family,[1] and groaning prayers for relief.[2] The realization of grace will come when one has nothing more with which to bargain, nothing left to depend upon. The Lord "will regard the prayer of the destitute, / and will not despise their prayer."[3]

Not everyone sees this. Many are stubborn children wanting to do things for themselves or not do them at all. Only those who are willing to turn aside to see God's glory for themselves gain the vision.[4] Only those come to sight who consider their calling a gift, not an entitlement, who can ask God, " 'Who am I that I should go to Pharaoh, and bring the Israelites out of Egypt?' "[5] With those words of perspective, Moses revealed his vision of grace. Earlier, he had observed wrongdoing and had arrogantly taken vengeance into his own hands. Now he claimed no privilege or power for himself.

I tire of those arguments in Bible studies and discussion groups about whether the bush really burned with God and whether God actually talked to Moses or whether Moses was hallucinating in the heat and isolation or whether it was simply an unusual bush, bright with blossom or fruit. What is the point? I am general counsel for a large Christian academic health-sciences center. Every day at that center of teaching, healing, and research, problems occur that science cannot resolve and that religion cannot adequately address. Some religious fundamentalists say that scientific evidence that conflicts with their beliefs must be ignored. Some scientists equate faith with superstition and deny any phenomenon that does not have a rational explanation.

I believe that Moses saw that bush burn and heard God's voice because there is no denying the effect of God's will on Moses and His people after that. If you had known me before October 4, 1989, when God spoke to me, and have observed me since, you would have to conclude that as imperfect and volatile as I am, there is no denying that God's love has become the driving compulsion of my life. You might have been with Moses at the bush or beside me in that airplane that day and never saw or heard a thing out of the ordinary. All politics are local, and all faith is personal. The life that you receive from God is real and personal.

It would be hard to find in history a more committed rationalist than the mathematician and scientist Blaise Pascal (1623–1662). The computer owes its existence to his ideas and proofs. He pursued the truth of Jesus Christ with the same vigor. He wrestled with pride, selfishness, materialism, and suffering from his own ill health. One night he also encountered the God of the burning bush. He wrote down what happened on a scrap of paper and copied it over on parchment that he carried on his person for the rest of his life:

The year of grace, 1654. Monday, 23 November. . . . From about half past ten in the evening until half past midnight. Fire. God of

Abraham, God of Isaac, God of Jacob, not of philosophers and scholars. Certainty, certainty, heartfelt, joy, peace. God of Jesus Christ. God of Jesus Christ. My God and your God. Thy God shall be my God. The world forgotten, and everything except God. He can only be found by the ways taught in the Gospels. Greatness of the human soul.

O righteous Father, the world had not known thee, but I have known thee. Joy, joy, joy, tears of joy. I have cut myself off from him. They have forsaken me, the fountain of living waters. My God will thou forsake me? Let me not be cut off from him forever! And this is life eternal, that they might know thee, the only true God, and Jesus Christ whom thou has sent. Jesus Christ. Jesus Christ. I have cut myself off from him, shunned him, denied him, crucified him. Let me never be cut off from him! He can only be kept by the ways taught in the Gospel. Sweet and total renunciation. Total submission to Jesus Christ and my director. Everlasting joy in return for one day's effort on earth. I will not forget thy word. Amen.[6]

Commonality and conformity of view are no substitute for authenticity of experience. It is ironic that we can differ in perspective on so many things and yet demand that we all see God in the same way at the same time. That was the mistake of the Pharisees, who repeatedly demanded that Jesus give them a sign from heaven so that they could all reach objective agreement on what they saw. He "sighed deeply in his spirit and said, 'Why does this generation ask for a sign? Truly I tell you, no sign will be given to this generation.' "[7] God in person is either enough for you, or nothing ever will be. Pascal's words of testimony bring tears to my eyes and tenderness to my heart because three and one-half centuries later, I recognize the vital truth of his words even though I experienced that truth in a different time, different place, and different way—I met the same Jesus Christ that Pascal met.

I often speak or write my belief that, in spiritual terms, there are only two kinds of persons—those to whom God is an intense reality and those to whom He is not. God was an intense reality for Moses because in the middle of the desert and confined by the limits of his experience and knowledge, God met him and took him the rest of the way. God is an intense reality for me for the same reasons. He has a grip on my life, and no matter how I sometimes twist and turn, I cannot shake that Grip that shapes me in love and dispels the fears that had driven me up to this point in my life. I suspect that, if you have read this far, that either God is an intense reality for you or you have an intense longing for God to be real for you. Be assured that God will honor an honest longing for His presence.[8]

Fulfilling the human longing to regain an intimate relationship with our Creator is the mission of Jesus Christ. Every one of us has the opportunity to see the light of God in the ordinary world of human existence because Jesus is the light and brought in His person the enlightenment that Moses found in the burning bush. Moses asked, "Who am I?" God answered and said, "It is not who you are but who 'I am' that matters." The apostle John observed that with Jesus Christ, "The true light, which enlightens everyone," had come into the world.[9] He continued with the illuminating truth that regardless of the explanations of who we are and what we have done, we belong to God. "He [Jesus] was in the world, and the world came into being through him; yet the world did not know him. He came to what was his own, and his own people did not accept him. But to all who received him, who believed in his name, he gave power to become children of God, who were born, not of blood or of the will of the flesh or of the will of man, but of God."[10]

If you are struggling to see and know but can't, if a bush is a shrub is a bush to you, but you want more, I leave you with this encouragement: Each child of God gets his Father's eyes. Tell Him you want to see—and keep looking.

Questions for Reflection

1. Is your desire to do things for yourself a help or a hindrance to prayer?
2. What is the role of rational proof in your understanding of prayer?
3. Does your spiritual vision depend on God's eyes or on your own?

23

"I'm Fine"

The story of the woman of Shunem tells us that every heart needs a secret chamber and a sacred space to go to in prayer when the storm breaks over our dreams and the gift is stolen.

"How are you doing?"

"Fine, thanks."

How many times a day are you on one end or the other of that exchange? Does the questioner care or even listen to the answer? Does the respondent tell the truth? "Well, I'm glad you asked how I'm doing because my head aches, my dog died this morning, and my kid is in juvenile hall." If someone does answer this way, how quickly do we exit the conversation?

The woman told her spouse in the middle of a weekday, "I'm going to see the preacher."

"Why? It's not a day that we go to church. Are you OK?"

"I'm fine," she said.

But she wasn't fine.

Years before she had offered lunch to the preacher when he passed by their ranch. She and her husband were wealthy. The ranch and the house were large and required a lot of attention. The conversations with the preacher about spiritual things were a welcome respite from her busy routines. It gave her a lot to think about and opened up new thoughts about God that thrilled her and sustained her for days. She extended an open invitation to the preacher and his assistant to come by for a meal anytime he was in the area.

"The preacher is a godly man," she told her husband. "He's led us both to a new understanding of God and grace that changes everything for me. I'd like to do something for him. Let's build him a retreat. We can add a room to the house and furnish it for him with a bed and a desk so he can rest and pray and reflect while he's here."

It was a simple, open-windowed room with a skylight. The preacher enjoyed it there. One day, while he was resting on the bed, he instructed his assistant, "Please call our hostess in here. I want to thank her for going to so much trouble for us. Ask her what we can do for her."

The assistant told the woman, "You know, the preacher has excellent connections to the government. Is there some favor that you need? We could ask for you."

"I don't need a thing," she said.

The preacher then asked the assistant, "Can you think of anything that she needs that we can get her?"

"Well, her husband is much older than she, and she is childless."

"Call her back in here, please."

When she returned, the preacher told her an amazing thing. "Next year you are going to have a baby son to hold."

She was shocked and hurt. *Why would the preacher expose my deepest longing and toy with my emotions?* She wanted this so intensely that she had stopped asking God for a child because she was so afraid she would be disappointed. She was in love with this gracious God that the preacher had told her about, and she couldn't bear the thought that God would let her down. "No," she told the preacher in a low, even voice that said, "I mean it. Don't go there. Please don't play tricks on me."

He wasn't jesting. She conceived, and the next year she and her husband had the baby son of their dreams and prayers. It wasn't that her life was better. It was different, as if someone had opened the windows and thrown open the doors and light poured into a room that had always been darkened by drawn curtains. The child laughed and played and asked questions and enjoyed the animals and wide-open spaces of the ranch that had always seemed just a business before.

Harvest-time was exciting. Reapers came to the ranch to bring in the grain. There was noise and activity, and the boy loved to go with his father to see all of it. On this day, in the middle of the morning, the boy cried out in pain. "Daddy, my head hurts! It hurts!" He collapsed in writhing tears.

The father was not a "kid" guy. Tears and play were a mystery to the stoic man whose world was the hard work and calculated risks of agriculture. Either you get the ripe grain in before the rains come, or you don't get it in. There was no stopping now.

He called a laborer over. "Carry the boy to his mother."

She knew when she saw the boy that it was serious. There was no doctor for many miles. She held him on her lap and sang his favorite songs as he grew weaker and couldn't even muster the little smile that she adored so. She prayed, silently, desperately. *God, I didn't dare ask you for this child, but You gave him to me anyway. Now, I love him more than life itself. I couldn't bear to ask for him, and I can't bear to lose him. Don't do this to me, God. Heal him. Save my boy. Please, God. I am begging You. I'll do anything You want.*

Then, just at noon when she should have been seeing to his lunch, he was gone. His breathing stopped, and a terrible silence filled her arms.

Looking back, she didn't know why she did any of it or what she was thinking when she did it. She stood up holding the boy tight. The household servants watched in speechless grief. She walked past them, seeing everything and seeing nothing. She carried the child into the preacher's room and laid him on the bed. The room was a gift to honor the new life that she had found in God. Now it would receive the death of the precious one that represented the blessing of that life to her. What else could she do? She brushed the hair from his already-cooling forehead, so soft and smooth to her touch, as she always did at bedtime. She hadn't asked for him, but God had given him. She had held him at birth, too warm and tiny to be true, and she wondered if she dared risk loving him, but she couldn't help it. *O God, I couldn't help myself. You gave me this child and he took my whole being into himself, and now I can't stand this. I won't stand this!*

When she turned away, her heart tore in two between the little form on the bed and her chest. Her husband was waiting at the bottom of the stairs. The question in his eyes said the servants couldn't bring themselves to tell him. She couldn't either.

In the days before God, she had always turned to activity to fill the emptiness. Competence was her refuge. Now she returned to that familiar ground.

"I need transportation and a driver," she told her husband. "I'm going to see the preacher."

"Why, today? We don't go to church in the middle of the week. Is everything all right?"

"I'm fine." She just said it by rote memory. To admit anything else in this moment would reduce her to brittle fragments like glass subjected to high-frequency sound. To speak her sorrow would give it life, and it did not deserve life. Not yet, not ever.

"Drive," she ordered. "Flat out. Don't stop for anything."

The preacher's assistant spotted them coming up the mountain. He met the woman at the foot of the drive. "Are you all right? Is your husband all right? Is your child all right?"

She brushed past. "I'm fine," she said. He followed her then. She walked faster than he thought she could through the door and into the house.

The preacher was in his study. He stood in surprise when the woman rushed in. She dropped to her knees and hugged his ankles so hard that he had to grab a chair back to stop from tumbling on her. Her sobs convulsed her body in sloppy waves. The assistant grasped her shoulder to pull her off. "Leave her alone," the preacher ordered. "She is obviously in bitter distress, and I can't tell why."

"Did I ask you for a son?" she demanded. "Did I even ask God for a son? Didn't I say to you, 'Don't trick me'?"

"Listen to me," the preacher said to the assistant. "Get over to her house now. Don't stop to talk to anyone. Go to the boy and lay my walking stick on his face. I'll be praying the whole time."

"You listen to me," the woman said. "God and you caused this to happen. You deal with this. I'm not leaving without you."

The assistant went ahead of them. When they arrived, he met them and bluntly said, "The child is dead. Nothing's changed."

The preacher found the child dead on his bed. He closed the door and prayed to God to turn this thing around. The child was so little, still and cold to the touch. *Why this, God? What are You doing? If I could give this child my life, my own beating heart, I would.* He lay down on the boy as if to impress his own breath into the boy's lungs. The boy's flesh warmed under his weight, but no breath filled the child's lungs.

The preacher was in agony. He got up and paced the floor in quick, agitated steps. "Lord, You give life. This woman extended the cup of cold water to me for the refreshment of Your servant. You have promised to honor the one who does such a thing. She asked nothing in return. Please, Lord, do not make me a liar. Do not deny her the desire of her heart. Do not deny this child his life before it has really begun."

He bent over the child even as the prayer trailed from his whispering lips.

It all ended quickly, in a blur really. The child sneezed. It startled the preacher. He watched the boy. The eyes remained closed. The sneezes continued six more times. Then the preacher saw the twinkling brown of opened eyes. He called out to the assistant, "Bring the mother in here."

When she came in, the preacher left all his words behind. "Take your son," he said.

She fell again to the floor, head touching, in prostrate thanks and worship. Then she took her son and left. Now she *was* fine.

I don't make this story up. It is found in 2 Kings 4. It always reminds me that my glib "I'm fine" may only be adhesive tape seeking to hold the unraveling package of my soul together against the battering of losses, grief, disappointments, and the disinterested "How are you doing?" of strangers and those who really should know better.

The woman of Shunem—that's what she's called for all history—built a place in her home to honor God. That sacred space is where she laid her child and the deepest desire of her heart when disaster came with its broken dreams and threats of death. Having received grace, she accepted no substitute, no human convention, no mere explanations of the possible. She went straight to the source and requested grace again. Faith? Desperation? Clear thinking? Instinctual grasp in the dark? In the moment of breaking, the heart that loves is incapable of classification. "Likewise the Spirit helps us in our weakness; for we do not know how to pray as we ought, but that very Spirit intercedes with sighs too deep for words."[1]

I wish there was a preventive formula to ward off pain and loss and to magically guarantee that "I'm fine." Saying the words doesn't make it so. There is, however, a sacred chamber to be created in your heart, a room for the Word that brings you life, a place to receive God's grace and nurture it. When the storm breaks over the dreams and the gift is stolen, you can return to that place and lay down the blessing and seek the Giver. Those who know this have prepared the space and go there for their answers can say "I'm fine" and mean it.

> Through many dangers, toils, and snares,
> I have already come.
> 'Tis grace that's brought me safe thus far,
> And grace will bring me home.[2]

Questions for Reflection

1. Where is your private place to pray?
2. How can your prayer time help you to deal with the pain and grief of others?
3. Does your prayer lead to the prevention of pain, or does it help you through pain?

24

Living in the Center

The prophet Samuel is remembered for integrity and faithfulness because he lived his life out of God, the true center.

The lamp of God had not yet gone out, and Samuel was lying down in the temple of the LORD, where the ark of God was. Then the LORD called Samuel. . . .

. . . He was afraid to tell Eli the vision, but Eli called to him and said, "Samuel, my son. . . . "

"What was it he said to you? . . ." So Samuel told him everything, hiding nothing from him. . . .

. . . The LORD continued to appear at Shiloh, and there he revealed himself to Samuel through his word.[1]

"Samuel continued as judge over Israel all the days of his life. From year to year he went on a circuit from Bethel to Gilgal to Mizpah, judging Israel in all those places. But he always went back to Ramah, where his home was, and there he also judged Israel. And he built an altar there to the LORD."[2]

These few words are a biography of a life lived in the circumference of kings, high priests, corruption, ego, rebellion, war, intrigue, madness, family disappointment, and tragedy. Yet, Samuel is remembered for integrity and faithfulness because he lived out of God, the true center. His life was a series of difficult confrontations: with his mentor, Eli, who could not face the evil dysfunction of his own household; with the Philistines, who ravaged his people; with his people, who rejected their God for a human king; with that king, whom Samuel anointed for God but who failed to wait for God and disobeyed Him; with Jesse, over which of his sons would make a better king; and with a smarmy Amalekite king. Even rudely summoned from the grave, the supposed ghost of Samuel was honest to God during confrontation.[3]

It must have tempted Samuel to stay on after the battle, to hold on to what had been gained, to attempt control against further disasters and future threats. However, when he had done his duty, Samuel "always went back" to home and to the altar of his allegiance to God.

The same way one builds an altar stone by stone, one builds a life with God prayer by prayer. Some stones are kept, others are discarded in the search for the cohesive whole. Even when the altar is built, it serves only to receive the sacrifice of the best that we know and possess to the God who possesses us. As an old hymn says, "You cannot have rest, or be perfectly blessed, / until all on the altar you've laid."[4] That goes for our successes as well as our failures, and our virtues as well as our sins.

The record shows a fearful Samuel, an angry Samuel, a disappointed Samuel, a bewildered Samuel. He claimed no wisdom of his own and frequently had to wait for God to show him what to do. He had to decide all manner of disputes and issues large and small among a notoriously feuding people. Even though his personal reputation for administration and fairness was spotless, he suffered the rejection of his grand vision of a people living in radical reliance upon God.

Samuel retired without rancor. In his final address to Israel, he requested a scrutiny of his record. The people found no fault with his service. He pointed the people to the history of God's leading them in past triumph. He reminded them that when they neglected prayer as their first resort and dropped out of their singular pursuit of God as their reason for being, they fell from this grace, and their fortunes deteriorated. He reminded them that in each dark hour of their past, God had never failed to send them a leader and a solution when they had confessed their sins and their need for help. He pointed out that the people's solution—a human king similar in style and function to the rulers of their neighbors—was no substitute for obedient submission to the word of their God.

Samuel asked the people of Israel, " 'Is it not the wheat harvest today? I will call upon the LORD, that he may send thunder and rain; and you shall know and see that the wickedness you have done in the sight of the LORD is great in demanding a king for yourselves.' " The resulting cloudburst frightened the people, and they finally saw their mistake. They pleaded with Samuel, " 'Pray to the LORD your God for your servants, so that we may not die; for we have added to all our sins the evil of demanding a king for ourselves.' "

The response was a real word of grace.

" 'Do not be afraid,' " Samuel told the people. " 'You have done all this evil, yet do not turn aside from following the LORD, but serve the LORD with all your heart, and do not turn aside after useless things that cannot profit or save, for they are useless. For the LORD will not cast away his people, for his great name's sake, because it has pleased the LORD to make you a people for himself. Moreover as for me, far be it from me that I should sin against the LORD by ceasing to pray for you; and I will instruct you in the good and right way. Only fear the LORD, and serve him faithfully with all your heart; for consider what great things he has done for you. But if you still do wickedly, you shall be swept away, both you and your king.' "[5]

I read this story of Samuel during a week when I had received up to forty wireless pages each day and dozens of phone calls and had listened to people argue about security, position, and support. My days began at 6:00 A.M. and ended at 1:00 A.M. I am not Samuel, but I am inspired by his story. What spoke to me was the observation that he always returned home and built his altar there. Samuel found his center, and he stayed with it.

Every morning at first light, I read Scripture and pray, listening for the God who knows everything about me and loves me anyway. As many evenings as possible, I walk in the dark for an hour with Patricia, setting aside all other demands to be with the person who knows me best and loves me anyway. Prayer and intimate conversation are the bookends of my day that keep me upright on the shelf and available to service. Humiliating experience has taught me to remain between those bookends.

I know why Samuel "always went back to Ramah, where his home was. . . . And he built an altar there to the LORD." Samuel could speak from his heart because he lived at peace with God in his heart. I think you and I aspire to such a life.

To leave the center of God's presence is to risk the debilitation of competition, resentment, boredom, and fear. To remain outside the center is to die a lingering, graceless death of the spirit. For the past thirteen years, I have been seeking to stay connected to the life of God by reading, meditation, and prayer. I have learned that the umbilical cord of this life is prayer in the name of Jesus Christ, who came as a living bridge between the infinite Father and our finite existence in this world.

Henri J. M. Nouwen offers a perspective on this truth:

Jesus does not respond to our worry-filled way of living by saying that we should not be so busy with worldly affairs. He does not try to pull us away from the many events, activities, and people that make up our lives. He does not tell us that what we do is unimportant, valueless, or useless. Nor does he suggest that we should withdraw from our involvements and live quiet, restful lives removed from the struggles of the world.

Jesus' response to our worry-filled lives is quite different. He asks us to shift the point of gravity, to relocate the center of our attention, to change our priorities.

Jesus wants us to move from the "many things" [of our worry, felt needs, and concerns] to the "one necessary thing" [adoration of our Lord]. It is important for us to realize that Jesus in no way wants us to leave our many-faceted world. Rather, he wants us to live in it, but firmly rooted in the center of all things. Jesus does not speak about a change of activities, a change in contacts, or even a change of pace. He speaks about a change of heart. This change of heart makes everything different, even while everything appears to remain the same. This is the meaning of Jesus' words: "Do not worry; do not say, 'What are we to eat? What are we to drink? How are we to be clothed?' . . . Your heavenly Father knows you need them all. Set your hearts on his kingdom first and his righteousness and all these other things will be given you as well."[6] What counts is where our hearts are. When we worry, we have our hearts in the wrong place. Jesus asks us to move our hearts to the center, where all other things fall into place.

What is this center? Jesus calls it the kingdom, the kingdom of his Father. For us, this may not have much meaning. Kings and kingdoms do not play an important role in our daily life. But only when we understand Jesus' words as an urgent call to make the life of God's Spirit our priority can we see better what is at stake. A heart set on the Father's kingdom is also a heart set on the spiritual life. To set our hearts on the kingdom therefore means to make the life of the Spirit within and among us the center of all we think, say, or do.[7]

I write to busy people like me who are hungry for truth and starved for love. My invitation to you this day is dare to be a Samuel. Seek the Center without compromise or detour and live in the reality of God's love. Leave from that home each morning, pausing here and there during the day to phone home by prayer. Return there each evening and leave the best and worst of yourself on the altar of devotion to the God who is always there for you.

_____ *Questions for Reflection* _____

1. What would you say is your spiritual center right now?
2. How does prayer lead us to Christ as our spiritual center?
3. How does prayer help you respond to the demands on your life?

25

Take No Prisoners

Joshua's unflinching pursuit of the five kings shows us the way to defeat of our enemies and to have peace in Christ through ruthless prayer.

Watsonville, California, the town of my birth, was named for the flamboyant lawyer, jurist, and promoter Judge John H. Watson. He once defended an accused horse thief in the town of Santa Cruz, the county seat. In the American West of the mid nineteenth century, stealing a man's horse was considered a low and despicable crime, and the punishment was death by hanging.

Things were not going well for Watson's client, and Watson asked the judge for a fifteen-minute recess "so that I may advise my client as to the best course to pursue."

The recess was granted, and Watson was allowed to speak with his client in private. When he returned to the courtroom, his client was not with him.

"Counsel," asked the judge, "where is your client? I thought you were going to advise him as to the best course to pursue."

"Precisely so, your honor," said Watson. "I told him that the best course to pursue was the northeast course up the canyon, and he is pursuing it right now."

Selecting a course is an important step in any endeavor. Sometimes our options are limited by previous bad decisions. That's the situation Joshua found himself in when he was approached by the Gibeonites, a people who had tricked their way into a subservient alliance with Israel rather than being driven by force from the land of Canaan.[1]

The kings of five other cities decided to attack Gibeon because it was a large city with much spoil to be taken. In addition, it had made peace with Israel. The Gibeonites appealed to Joshua to make good on the alliance by coming to their defense. Joshua obliged with zeal, and the Lord helped out by dropping great hailstones on the retreating armies. God even made the sun stand still so that Israel could take complete vengeance on its enemies.[2]

The five kings survived and took refuge in a cave at Makkedah. Joshua, still in pursuit of the enemy armies, ordered stones to be rolled over the mouth of the cave, sealing in the kings, and placed a guard on the cave. He then continued on to attack, plunder, and destroy their cities and their armies. On his return, Joshua ordered the cave unsealed and the captive kings brought out for an object lesson. Joshua summoned all the Israelites and said to his commanders, "Come and put your feet on the necks of these kings." His commanders followed his instruction.

Joshua told the Israelites, " 'Do not be afraid or dismayed; be strong and courageous; for thus the LORD will do to all the enemies against whom you fight.' "[3] He then struck the kings down himself, put them to death, and hung them on five trees. At sunset, he had the kings taken down and their dead bodies thrown back in the cave and the stones rolled over the mouth of the cave. Joshua then totally destroyed the population of Makkedah that had given aid and support to the five kings.

You may be wondering where I could possibly be going with this story of vengeance and destruction. Well, have you ever been victimized in a transaction or arrangement or relationship that was not what it seemed at the time you entered it? It is important to keep our word. God values honesty and fidelity. Our word should never be given lightly. Those who will be welcomed into God's presence will keep their word even when it hurts them to do so.[4] It is the gracious thing to do and expected of us by the God of grace.

You may have entered arrangements that are now making demands on your material, emotional, and spiritual resources. Maybe the problem is an entangling sin or addiction that harasses, wears, and drains you. There is no choice but to pursue it to a complete resolution, seeking the guidance of the Lord as to method as Joshua did.

Perhaps on the way to resolution, concerns arise, such as the five kings in the cave, distracting you from the main challenge. It could be that these concerns are the persons who have enabled the problem that is besetting you. Maybe you lack the time, the energy, or the resources to deal with the concerns right now. Tie up those concerns and seal them off, while you continue on with the essential effort to be accomplished. Don't stop until you are finished with the issue that would destroy you and those whom you are obligated to help.

Then turn your attention back to the concerns that you contained until you could return to address them. Bring them out, put your foot on their necks, claim the strength of the Lord against the enemies you are fighting, and finish them off. Break the necks of your problems and sins. Deal with everything to the finish. Before another night falls, throw the sorry carcasses of the problems that annoy and tempt you back into the hole from which they came. Then forget about them. Take no prisoners. "So Joshua defeated the whole land, the hill country and the Negeb and the lowland and the slopes, and all their kings; he left no one remaining, but utterly destroyed all that breathed, as the LORD God of Israel commanded. . . . Joshua took all these kings and their land at one time, because the LORD God of Israel fought for Israel."[5]

The Lord God will do no less for you, that is, if you ruthlessly trust him and pursue the course He lays out for you. By "ruthless," I mean making no compromise with comfort, security, or appearance, or with approval or disapproval of others. This is the ruthlessness that Jesus showed when He healed on the Sabbath, refused to be taunted by His brothers into going to Jerusalem with them, declined to join in the shaming of the adulteress, trusted His life to no one but His Father, challenged the faith of the Canaanite woman, slept through a raging storm in an open boat, touched lepers, was silent before Herod and noncommittal to Pilate, and endured the shame of the cross.

To live ruthlessly means looking for God nowhere else but in the person and revelation of Jesus Christ,

> let[ting] the same mind be in you that was in Christ Jesus,
>> who, though he was in the form of God,
>>> did not regard equality with God
>>> as something to be exploited,
>> but emptied himself,
>>> taking the form of a slave,
>>> being born in human likeness.
>> And being found in human form,
>>> he humbled himself
>>> and became obedient to the point of death—
>>> even death on a cross.[6]

Jesus calls us to focus on Him to the exclusion of anyone else, to love Him as no other, following His instruction to the letter: " 'Whoever comes to me and does not hate father and mother, wife and children, brothers and sisters, yes, and even life itself, cannot be my disciple. Whoever does not carry the cross and follow me cannot be my disciple.' "[7]

This last verse causes many who read it to flinch, but the issue is whether we trust God with our most intimate relationships. Nothing distracts our gaze from the Giver to the gift the way family does. Of course, the gift of family is to be honored and respected, but unless we are able to yield it and all of the attachments and hopes and fears that go with it to God, we turn the gift into an idol of our worship. If we still grasp our family in our distrusting hands, seeking to be god for them or for them to be gods for us, we are not free to pick up the cross and ruthlessly follow Christ, who is the only legitimate Savior that we will ever know. The same is true of any person, possession, or habit that we feel we cannot live without. It is the essential truth of life that our Creator gives us life, along with everything that makes it desirable.

Only one response is worthy of that truth—gratitude. The grateful are honest in their acknowledgement that God is responsible for their life, liberty, and happiness and that nothing that they can do or anyone else can do for them can add or detract from who God is and what He has done for them in love. To live in that love is my fondest wish and deepest prayer. It is the course that I choose to pursue with ruthlessness, looking to kill off whatever would destroy me in my weakness or lead me away from the God I love.

—— *Questions for Reflection* ——

1. How can prayer help you deal with deceit and treachery?
2. What does it mean to be ruthless in your trust of the Lord God?
3. Why is gratitude a sign of trust in God?

26

The Most Important Thing to Do

The aftermath of Elijah's victory over the prophets of Baal shows us that the most important thing we can do in prayer is to set aside our egos and ask for help.

I listened to talk radio while driving around this week. A business consultant was asked, "What is the most important thing a person in business can do to achieve success?"

The consultant answered, "Set aside your ego and ask for help."

That rings a bell with me. In twenty-six years as a business attorney, I have counseled many clients who were in trouble because they stubbornly tried to go it alone, ignoring the advice of their bankers, accountants, salespersons, attorneys, and often their spouses, thinking that they were the only ones who understood their business and the market. It's as if Frank Sinatra is on a continuous loop in their elevators, singing, "I did it my way." They take on the added debt, buy the extra equipment, hire more employees, lease the bigger office, and develop the new product line, only to realize too late that they didn't ask if anyone wanted to buy what they are making. There are few times lonelier than the convergence of too much inventory, too few customers, and a loan coming due.

It is quite possible to get to the lonely spot by working yourself there, taking on more and more, convincing yourself that no one else can do what you do, do as much, or do it as well.

As they say, "I've been there and done that," with regard to the latter choice. Work is my addiction, my drug of choice. There are people who spurn such ideas as the self-justifications of the lazy. They should talk to my wife and son. What other word but *addiction* describes a tolerance for

138

wanting and needing more to do; the stress reaction and backlash when there isn't enough to do to feed that tolerance; the self-deception and rationalization that I'm doing good and necessary work, and one can never get too much of good and essential things; the loss of willpower to stop thinking of work even in bed, at worship, or in prayer; the attachment to my tasks that divert my attention from the God and the people who love me most; the anxiety that I will be worthless if I have nothing to do.

Elijah stood on Mount Carmel, alone but for an unseen God. He took the risk, poured out the water in drought-dusty trenches, and prayed. God sent fire, burned up his sacrifice, steamed away the water, and melted the stones of the altar to glass shards.

What does one do for an encore when that on which one has focused all thought, effort, and life itself is fulfilled, not by labor, but by grace? One can accept with gratitude the gift of a loving God, or one can run farther, work harder, and worry more about the future—all to prove worthiness to receive the gift. The conflict leading to the knowledge that one's significance rises from the creative spirit of God and not from one's productive self-sufficiency is truly the war to end wars within the heart.

Elijah ran. He ran in fear for loss of what he had gained in the threats of an enemy who just hours before had proved so powerless. He ran out of the sweet rain of grace into arid country where his only shelter was a scraggly bush shadowing an unforgiving landscape of rock. He ignored the graciousness of angels who fed and watered him. " 'Get up and eat, otherwise the journey will be too much for you' "[1] was the tender invitation of the angel of the Lord. Elijah took the strength God offered him. But on he ran, over two hundred miles into ever-rougher country.

Elijah was a man on task, a man driven to do good for God, having convinced himself that no one else believed as strongly in the work or was as willing to make the sacrifices necessary for the goal. Yes, he had seen the victory of God over his enemies back on the mountain. At God's direction, he himself had put those enemies to death. However, there were still threats and perhaps more enemies—and if he didn't deal with them, who would?

There is a point beyond which all of one's survival and self-protection skills and reactions become enemies, not friends. These responses refuse unemployment. They call us back to a battle that is over, obscuring in an adrenaline-fueled haze the truth that the only persons left to fight are the God who gave us victory and our selves re-created in God's love. Beyond that point, we are at war with love and freedom, refusing these gifts like the elder brother of the prodigal, who chose a grinding, everyday existence that he could control over the unconditional largesse of his loving father.[2] As if battered spouses and abused children, we decline to leave the cramped quarters of the one who hurts us for the open spaces where the techniques that have come to define us are no longer necessary. We choose the earth we know, in all its limitations and meanness, over the unlimited possibilities of heaven and its gracious Host.

When we are lost in that wilderness, God pleads with us to think, " 'What are you doing here, Elijah?' "[3] We tell Him, "It is worse than you could possibly know. I am looking out for Your interests, because no one else is. I'm all You have, and I'm preserving me for You."

God is patient with our thickheaded, obsessed selves. "OK, Elijah, step to the entrance of the dark hole you're living in and watch a process of elimination. So you think you're something and are saving yourself for the big deal; try a force-five tornado, splitting the very rocks of your existence, the upheaval of an 8.0 earthquake, or a firestorm. You think you are equal to a God who can do all that?"[4] In our delusion we want to contend with and for a God we think is worthy of our significance, whether positive or negative.

It isn't the twister, the quake, or the heat that pulls the incipient Elijah in us out of the dark cul-de-sacs where we have driven our lives in work and anxiety. It is "a sound of sheer silence,"[5] the soul-melting furnace of solitude, that stirs us to change. We compulsive, alienated, fearful Elijahs can't stand to be all alone. The quiet brings our adrenaline-addicted souls to crisis. Conflicted to the end, we attempt to cover our face in what's left of our defensive wrappings even as we come outside for a look.

God whispers, again, "What are you doing here, Elijah?" He asks, rather than tells us, because he really wants us to "get it."

It is so very hard for us to get it. We have only one answer: "I'm out here worrying about God-stuff, good versus evil, because I think everyone else forgot, and Your enemies are going to wipe me out, too, and then You'll have nothing to work with, God." After we have run as far as we can, stretched as far as we can reach, hidden ourselves in deep darkness—but still the wind breaks the rocks, the earth shifts under us, and the fire burns up everything around us—our assertion of self-importance seems so pathetic bouncing off the hard walls of our hollow cave.

The God of all grace wastes no time bandaging our bruised egos. "Go back," He tells us in the quiet. "I have other men and women back there who can lead and get the job done. Look for them. You help them, and they'll help you. And by the way, there are a lot of people out there devoted to me, faithful to my purpose. They have never conceded to evil. You are not a special case or a martyr or the last signal flare in the survival kit of God. What you are is a wanted, loved child in My family."[6]

I am Kent Hansen, recovering workaholic, prone to relapse when I forget to set aside my ego and ask for help. It is then that I live badly—grasping, clawing, and gasping for the dwindling resources of a self-made existence. Years into the journey, I have found no silver-bullet, no quick cure that brings me to permanent health and peace without another anxious thought.

Sometimes, in worship, in small-group settings, I play and lead this chorus:

Into my heart, into my heart,
Come into my heart, Lord Jesus;
Come in today, come in to stay,
Come in to my heart, Lord Jesus.[7]

An elderly gentleman, each time we've sung this song, has said to me, "That's a children's song; we need to move on to mature themes."

This man has anxious thoughts of his sinful past and wrestles with the worry whether God really loves and forgives him. He cannot bring himself to enjoy the childhood God offers him. He could be me. But I am coming to realize that my life and health require me to live in the childhood of my Abba, laughing and playing, with all the risks and gains of shared adventure, even if they come with some scrapes and tears, asking for help when I get in a tough spot. Children live day to day in new discoveries and fresh starts.

I've looked for other possibilities, but living as a child, starting each day by inviting my friend Jesus in to stay, is the only way I've found to live well without indulging my inflamed, "sophisticated" adult obsession and ego that it all depends on me.

Questions for Reflection

1. What gets in the way of your asking for help?
2. What is the spiritual danger to us when we cling to the human skills and reactions that we learned to help us get through the difficult battles of life?
3. What spiritual truth can you learn from children?

27

The Sophomore Year From Hell

Sometimes we can't see the end from the beginning. When God, and God alone, is our answer, we have reached true spiritual maturity.

Building a replica of one of the California missions as a social studies class assignment is a rite of passage for every fourth-grader in California. It is also a frustrating contest of endurance for their parents, who usually end up finishing the models the night before they are due. I really don't know what the project teaches about social studies, but it almost breaks up families.

The students are supposed to do all the work, but the project is fairly sophisticated, involving making a design from a picture and then building the model to scale using whatever materials are at hand. It takes a fourth-grade architectural prodigy to pull this off unaided. Kits are sold, but these are banned in most schools.

My Andrew decided to build the Mission Santa Inés, one of the more obscure missions. His mom came up with the materials of thin corkboard painted white to resemble adobe with a tile roof made from manicotti pasta painted red. He need to build a church with wings for living quarters and a chapel.

On the day the project was due, cars rolled up to the front of the school, and children emerged with models that looked like finalists in an *Architectural Digest* contest. We parents hovered right behind, glancing around at our competition, and making sure that our midnight final touches weren't dropped before making it into the classroom.

When Andrew brought his mission home from school, I had a great idea. "Let's blow up your mission," I said.

"How?" he asked.

"Daddy has some firecrackers, bottle rockets, and smoke bombs that he's been 'saving' in his desk for a special occasion. This seems like a good time. After all, the Indians burned down the Mission Inés during their 1824 revolt, so we would be historically correct. Do you want to blow it up and burn it down, Son?"

"Sure," he said.

My wife Patricia asks me sometimes, "You know that social contract, the one that everybody signs to get along with each other and stay safe and do the sensible thing?"

"Yeah, I guess so," I say.

"Well, I think you forgot your pen the day they brought it around—'cause, Kent, you never signed it!"

Andrew and I took his carefully constructed and painted mission into the backyard. I lit a smoke bomb and dropped it in the window of the upper-story chapel. I carefully aimed a bottle rocket, lit the fuse, and shot it into the wall of the church. The eaves begin to smoke and flames licked at the window. The effects were most satisfying. About the time the chapel roof began to sag and collapse, I told Andrew, "I need to get a camera and take some pictures. Stand back and wait here for me."

I went in the house, got the camera, and came out the back door to see Patricia running around the garage with a hose. "What are you doing?" I asked.

"I'm putting out the fire," she yelled over her shoulder.

I followed her, and when I turned the corner, I saw flames leaping about six feet into the air from the conflagration. The neighbors were lining the alley in mixed delight and horror watching the spectacle. Andrew was delivering a running commentary about his "fire-bug" dad. I got some pictures before Patricia drenched the fun. The spot on the lawn eventually recovered. Andrew and his pictures were the envy of his classmates, but some parents wouldn't send their kids over to our house to play for a while after that.

That was the spring of 1997. Blowing up stuff in the backyard seemed innocent back then.

The morning of September 11, 2001, witnessed a structural engineer's worst nightmare. The burning jet fuel in the World Trade Center towers was hot enough to melt the steel girders supporting the flooring, and as the top floors dropped, they took with them each successive floor into the ground. The integrity of the structure, once compromised, dramatically failed.

The concept of integrity is often minimized to mean mere honesty. But truthfulness is only part of integrity. It actually includes a completeness and unity that is sound and reliable. Integrity means the core infrastructure of a building, a community, an organization, a system, a thought, or a soul. To the believing follower of Christ, integrity means obedient reliance on the indwelling, empowering presence of God. Paul was seeking this integrity for the Ephesians when he wrote the following to them in a letter:

> For this reason I bow my knees before the Father, from whom every family in heaven and on earth takes its name. I pray that, according to the riches of his glory, he may grant that you may be strengthened in your inner being with power through his Spirit, and that Christ may dwell in your hearts through faith, as you are rooted and grounded in love. I pray that you may have the power to comprehend, with all the saints, what is the breadth and length and height and depth, and to know the love of Christ that surpasses knowledge, so that you may be filled with the fullness of God.
>
> Now to him who by the power at work in us is able to accomplish abundantly far more than all we can ask or imagine, to him be glory in the church and in Christ Jesus to all generations, forever, and ever, Amen.[1]

The question of integrity always is, What will happen when the pressure is on and the stress builds? There are times of storms and conflict when the winds are so adverse and incessant, the clouds are so dark, and the waters are rising so quickly that careful plans of calmer times are forgotten, and the outcome is truly in doubt. Perhaps a fire is burning ever closer, its heat consuming everything in its path, moving so fast that it is impossible to get out of its way. In those moments, one may simply have to stand against the blasts and take what comes without a glimpse of the bigger picture or assurance of what will be left. It is easy to become disoriented at such times when God's providence seems to be in storage, when pain distracts, confusion swirls, and waiting without alternative seems so futile.

One reaches the crossroads of faith in the darkest hour of struggle when the end cannot be seen from the beginning. More likely than not, integrity is all one has to go on at that point. David recognized this when he prayed,

Consider how many are my foes,
>and with what violent hatred they hate me.
O guard my life, and deliver me;
>do not let me be put to shame, for I take refuge in you.
May integrity and uprightness preserve me,
>for I wait for you.[2]

I am a veteran lawyer. I have been through too many battles to think one can rely on other people in such moments. Job's wry observation about the fickleness of his companions always makes me smile from experience:

" . . . My brothers are as undependable as intermittent streams,
>as the streams that overflow
when darkened by thawing ice
>and swollen with melting snow,
but that cease to flow in the dry season,
>and in the heat vanish from their channels."[3]

I have learned that misery loves company but rarely receives it in a helpful way.

No, there is no passing of responsibility when you know you are in the fight but you cannot see the end from the beginning. What is called for are watchfulness and trust, which sound like contradictory concepts but are really compatible. Watchfulness and trust are essential elements of spiritual integrity. The watching is for the answer of God to the cry of the desperate heart. The trust is in God, period, answered or not. Jesus, His heart broken on the cross, shamed and in pain, cried out, " 'My God, my God, why have you forsaken me?' "[4] He was stripped of all human comfort and approval, cut off from the view of His Father by the guilt of all the sins He was carrying to His death, feeling lost and alone and questioning, "Why?" Yet His dying thought was that He had a God, and there flows the answer—He was not abandoned, He was not alone, He still had a God who could call Him beyond the pain and the shame to a new life of glory. Jesus could surrender safely in that knowledge. His final words were a shout, " 'Father, into your hands I commit my spirit.' When he had said this, he breathed his last."[5]

When God, and God alone, is our answer, we have obtained spiritual integrity. At this point, prayer reaches the limits of telling, asking, and demanding, and it crosses the border to listening. That's the point where a betrayed and agonizing David prayed in the midst of dangerous conflict, " 'But now, Lord, what do I look for? / My hope is in you.' "[6]

The times that I am talking about are like a sophomore year from hell. You remember the freshman year, whether of high school or college, and the excitement of new beginnings. Junior year brought a glimpse of the end, and the senior year brought the end with a sense of accomplishment and new hope, but the sophomore year . . . In the winter of that second year you lose sight of where you came from and where you are going, and hope drifts just out of reach. It is then when you are tempted to do something that will get you in trouble. It is then that integrity must meet the demand of circumstances.

When I feel as if I'm repeating my sophomore year in matters of faith, I take a hint from the prophet Habakkuk, who prayed thus:

> How long, O LORD, must I call for help,
>   but you do not listen?
> Or cry out to you, "Violence!"
>   but you do not save?
> Why do you make me look at injustice?
>   Why do you tolerate wrong?
> Destruction and violence are before me;
>   there is strife, and conflict abounds.
> Therefore the law is paralyzed,
>   and justice never prevails.
> The wicked hem in the righteous
>   so that justice is perverted. . . .
> Your eyes are too pure to look on evil;
>   you cannot tolerate wrong.
> Why then do you tolerate the treacherous?
>   Why are you silent while the wicked
>   swallow up those more righteous than themselves?[7]

Habakkuk says,

> I will stand at my watch
>   and station myself on the ramparts;
> I will look to see what he will say to me,
>   and what answer he will give to my complaint.[8]

God answers, "The righteous shall live by faith," even as He condemns those who seek to have their way by bloodshed, unjust gain, debauchery, exploitation of the environment, and idolatry. He concludes with an admonishment that He remains in control, " 'The LORD is in his holy temple; / let all the earth keep silence before him!' "[9]

Habakkuk is filled with reverence by this answer and asks the Lord to do His work and render mercy. He voices his renewed understanding that oppressive human schemes will end in ruin, and then he prays these wondrous words of integrity in the face of disaster:

> Though the fig tree does not bud
> > and there are no grapes on the vines;
> though the olive crop fails
> > and the fields produce no food;
> though there are no sheep in the pen
> > and no cattle in the stalls,
> yet I will rejoice in the LORD;
> > I will be joyful in God my Savior.
>
> The Sovereign LORD is my strength;
> > he makes my feet like the feet of a deer,
> > he enables me to go on the heights.[10]

The watchfulness and trust displayed by Habakkuk are antidotes to the poisonous pretense that we command our own destiny. When we acknowledge our need for God, we become men and women of integrity, which is more important than achieving our desires. Watching and trusting God, we can walk though wind and waves that would sink those watching only themselves or others. The July 28 entry in Oswald Chamber's *My Utmost for His Highest* contains the following exposition of Jesus walking on the water:

> What is my vision of God's purpose for me? Whatever it may be, His purpose is for me to depend on Him and on His power now. If I can stay calm, faithful, and unconfused while in the middle of the turmoil of life, the goal of the purpose of God is being accomplished in me. God is not working toward a particular finish—His purpose is the process itself. What He desires for me is that I see "Him walking on the sea" with no shore, no success, nor goal in sight, but simply having the absolute certainty that

everything is all right because I see "Him walking on the sea" (Mk. 6:49). It is the process, not the outcome, that is glorifying to God.[11]

To underscore the grace of integrity in a time of trouble, I ask you this question: If you were cast adrift in the middle of the ocean, would your anxiety that you could not spot an island on the horizon overwhelm your gratitude that your life raft didn't have a hole in it?

Hear Job's prayer of revelation that the life raft carrying you in the currents is more important than the shore you cannot see:

"God, you've made me the talk of the town—
    people spit in my face;
I can hardly see from crying so much;
    I'm nothing but skin and bones.
Decent people can't believe what they're seeing;
    the good-hearted wake up and insist I've given up on God.

"But principled people hold tight, keep a firm grip on life,
    sure that their clean, pure hands will get stronger and stronger!"[12]

Not just the outcome, but the process itself is glorifying to God. At times our only hope is our honest submission to the process itself.

With the most powerful army of the world advancing behind the children of Israel and the hopeless depths of the Red Sea in front of them, God called Moses to the integrity of watchfulness and trust. Moses told the people this byword of spiritual integrity: " 'The LORD will fight for you, and you have only to keep still.' "[13]

Child of grace, carry this gracious word of God's truth as your lode-stone of integrity in the midst of your trial. Staying still while watching for and trusting God is the easiest thing, yet, in our anxious humanity, it is the hardest thing. For men and women of integrity, it is the only thing to do during the sophomore year from hell.

Questions for Reflection

1. What words come to mind when you think of *integrity*?
2. What does *integrity* mean in times of crisis?
3. How does prayer help you achieve integrity?

28

The Floating Ax

There is no substitute for putting God first in our prayers and our plans.

Crisis comes to every organization in the process of leadership succession and in the challenges of new markets and technologies.

Perhaps the greatest successor in all of Scripture was Elisha. His predecessor and mentor, Elijah, confronted idolatry and tyranny. Elijah led Israel back to its mission by opening an environment in which the people were free to worship God in public.

Elisha then came on the scene to demonstrate God's power and compassion to those in need. Where Elijah's ministry focused on addressing wrong and introducing reform, Elisha's provided compassionate care to marginalized, hurting, and distressed people. No person in Scripture, outside of the man Jesus Christ, was the instrument of more miracles. Like Christ, Elisha's miracles fed and healed and rescued people and put them in direct touch with the personal and all-powerful God.

Scripture records eighteen encounters between Elisha and needy people. He was a man of integrity who lived a life of self-sacrifice. He never sought to enrich himself at the expense of others.

Elijah and Elisha demonstrate that different times and circumstances call for various gifts. Some are called by God to battle for His cause. Others are called to care compassionately for His children.

Many of us encountered the story of Elisha during childhood as an almost magical account of God's power, but we may not have given it much thought since. I believe the portion of his story found in 2 Kings 6:1–7 speaks to profound issues of organizational change.

The prophets of Israel lived together in the same institution under the leadership of Elisha. They were feeling stifled and restless, and they blamed Elisha's leadership. They told him, " 'You can see that this place where we're living under your leadership is getting cramped—we have no elbow room. Give us permission to go down to the Jordan where each of us will get a log. We'll build a roomier place.' "[1] How many times are those of you in leadership approached with proposals for expansion, for increased freedom of choice and benefits, for less restraint on programs and expenses? How many implied insults have you heard such as, "This place where we are working under your leadership is too small for our capabilities and needs"?

Elisha did not take it personally. He gave them permission. "Elisha said, 'Go ahead.' "[2]

"One of them then said, 'Please! Come along with us!' "[3]

Why this request? Elisha represented spiritual authority. We often invite religion along in our schemes. Bringing religion along helps the endeavors of institutions through tax exemption, fund raising, rights of employment preference, or constituent relations. As valuable as those things are, it is always a warning sign when we already have our goal in mind before we seek our spiritual connection. We begin to lose our way when God becomes a means for us rather than an end.

But God is gracious even when we are not. Elisha responded to the request in the affirmative. "He said, 'Certainly.' "[4]

"He went with them. They came to the Jordan and started chopping down trees. As one of them was felling a timber, his ax head flew off and sank in the river.

" 'Oh no, master!' he cried out. 'And it was borrowed.' "[5]

The ax head was technology. Before the time of David, Israel lacked iron-working capability. The nation gained it by conquering the Philistines. Several generations later, iron implements were still relatively precious. The man had borrowed the ax head in pursuit of the expansion scheme, taking on an added risk. There is no grace in borrowing to achieve the goal.

But there is grace in the providence of God. The writer of Kings changed the reference to Elisha at this point in the narrative, calling him "man of God," or "Holy Man," for emphasis on the priority of the power of the Spirit in meeting the crisis of the material.

"The Holy Man said, 'Where did it sink?'

"The man showed him the place.

"He cut off a branch and tossed it at the spot. The ax head floated up.

" 'Grab it,' he said. The man reached out and took it."[6]

Iron molecules are denser than water. Ax heads don't float. We all know that. However, what do we really know about floating ax heads?

This miracle occurred during a time of scheming, when institutions and politics dominated the society, and the School of the Prophets longed for a larger facility. The faculty was willing to borrow to achieve that goal. It was a time when the God-designated ways of leadership were challenged and spiritual authority was seen as no more than "window dressing" and an insurance policy. God broke into the time and its conventions with an unmistakable sign that He was still in control.

Elisha's contribution, an act that transcended strategic planning to sacred purpose and that is remembered long after the School of the Prophets faded away, was the restoration of God's will and power as the first considerations of the enterprise.

Our God refuses to be constrained by the limitations and the enthusiasms of our human ambitions.

My thoughts are not your thoughts,
     nor are your ways my ways, says the LORD.
For as the heavens are higher than the earth,
     so are my ways higher than your ways
and my thoughts than your thoughts.[7]

We might want to relegate this mystical defiance of the laws of physics to an ancient time of myth. We may trust our own intelligence and experience more than the miraculous grace of God. We may believe that we face the crisis of leadership and growth without resources. We may give in to the purveyors of conventional wisdom who say, "You are doing it all wrong because you aren't doing it the way we are." We would be wrong on all accounts.

If we step back and look at the miracles of new mercies every morning, faith thriving amidst unbelief, ministry prospering through sacrifice, and institutions successfully pursuing their missions without substantial endowments and the things the world insists are essential, we should not cry out in dismay, "Oh no, master! . . . And it was borrowed!" Because if we have learned anything in following Christ in a community of faith, it is that ax heads float, and we serve a God who makes such things happen.

"The human mind may devise many plans, but it is the purpose of the Lord that will be established."[8]

Blessed be His name. We must encourage ourselves in this knowledge and allow it to inform our prayers.

Questions for Reflection

1. How is religion "useful" to human ambitions?
2. What is the problem with having your desired result in mind before you pray?
3. Will God answer your prayers with your desires or with His purposes?

29

The Water Jar

The Samaritan woman's encounter with Jesus at the well opened up issues long bottled up.

She takes one look at her boyfriend sleeping in the corner before slipping out the door into blinding light.

Noon in a desert town. Buildings and streets flicker and blur in radiated light. Nothing else moves. Dogs don't bark.

Her sandals provide little insulation from the hot sand. The relentless sunshine glints off the glaze of the water jar under her arm and magnifies its heat on her face.

There is no shade at midday. One either stays inside or moves quickly out to their task and back inside.

She prefers this time to get the water. The other women do this chore before the day is an hour old. She wakes late to their banter and lies still to wait for the sound to drop to murmurs as they pass her house. It's a grim game she plays with herself each morning, knowing they are talking about her, imagining the insults.

The cool of daybreak is comfortable neither for them nor for her when she joins them on their errand. She learned that in one attempt carried out in awkward silence. It was the first and last time. Sychar is too small a town to offer social alternatives. The well is pretty much it for entertainment.

As she walks, she thinks about the well and imagines how it used to be. No water bubbles up in it. It is a cistern, hacked out of the hard ground and reinforced with stone walls to catch the runoff. The well permits people and livestock to exist in a dry place.

Jacob dug the well on the first piece of real estate he bought after he returned to Canaan and settled things with his brother, Esau. He bought the property from the children of Hamor the Hivite, the local sheikh.[1] The day they sealed the deal was the last good day that Sychar had known.

Shechem, Hamor's son, waylaid and forced himself on Jacob's daughter Dinah while she was visiting the neighbor women. Shechem, the lout, thought it was an introduction and courtship. Hamor himself made the approach to Jacob for Dinah's hand in marriage. He and Shechem said it would be a good deal for all concerned, uniting their families in trade and benefit.

Jacob and his sons knew it was rape, pure and simple. Dinah was now unfit for decent marriage. The family was disgraced. Their thoughts turned to revenge, but they were new in the land and would have to wait for strength or move in trickery.

The brothers told Shechem and his brothers that they couldn't consent to marriage unless the males in Hamor's household were circumcised. Shechem, anxious to gain Dinah and the favor of her wealthy family, agreed. As the males in Hamor's family lay down in recovery from the painful procedure, Dinah's brothers broke in and killed them all. This set off a blood feud that deepened as Esau and his descendants intermarried with the Hivites.

The entire scenario of sex and violence plays through her mind. She imagines what it was like for Dinah. She wasn't the first fallen woman to drink from Jacob's well.

That she isn't alone occurs to her before she even sees the man sitting on the stone lip of the well. A woman living on the edge senses these things because survival depends on seeing before you are seen.

Is he asleep or praying? She slows her approach in the shade of the sycamore trees. He raises his head and looks straight into her eyes.

Afterward, she will not remember what He looks like. She knows how to appraise men—their looks, their attitudes, what they think about her—all in a second. But this one is a book she hasn't read.

He's a Jew. She can see that and hear it too when He speaks.

"Give me a drink." She can't tell whether it is a question or an order. His voice is just soft enough to make her listen.

This she knows: His kind didn't ask her kind for anything. She says so.

"How is it that you, a Jew, ask a drink of me, a Samaritan woman?"

He never drops His gaze from her eyes or hesitates before answering. "If you knew the gift of God, and who it is that is saying to you, 'Give me a drink,' you would have asked him and he would have given you living water."

Her eyes flicker over His face. Who really talks like this? She thinks she's heard every line there is. Is He flirting?

She sees nothing in His eyes except kindness. That's a surprise. She used to expect a lot from men and now not so much. But kindness? A man who would be kind to her is either a fool or a con man. A Jewish man who would talk to a strange, foreign woman at a public place in broad daylight can't be up to anything decent.

I'll play it straight and smoke out His intentions, she thinks.

"Sir, you don't have a bucket. The well is deep. Where do you think you'll get that living water you're talking about? Do you know more than our ancestor Jacob who dug this well and drank from it along with his sons and his sheep and cattle?"

The history lesson is a nice twist, she thinks.

There was a time when she thought there would be magic. Eyes would lock across a room, and she would know that here was the mate who would share all the love she had welling up inside her soul. She caught looks all right, and she heard words that made her think this was it, but there was no sharing, only taking. She tried again and again, and always the story had the same ending.

Her feelings had long since been folded and put away. Her existence was reduced to the semblance of affection that came her way in the dark and whatever she could dip out of a muddy cistern in the silence of a desert noon. She hadn't thought of it that way yet, but later she would remember that's exactly the way it was.

He answers her, "Everyone who drinks the water from this well will be thirsty again, but those who drink the water I give them will never be thirsty. The water that I give them will become a spring of water in them gushing up and bubbling over so they can live forever."

It is the most incredible thing she has heard in a lifetime of lies. It is time to end the game.

"Sir, give me this water you're talking about so I'll never be thirsty or have to keep coming back out here to draw water."

"Go, get your husband, and come back."

It is an odd thing to say, from a very odd man, who has never once taken His eyes from hers. She is beyond caring, beyond pretense. "I have no husband."

"You're right," He says. "Because you've had five husbands, and the man you're living with now is not your husband. What you've told me is true."

Hot as it is, she can still feel the flush of shame in her cheeks. She thought she was long since past that. This must be one of those wild holy men who roam the deserts, she guesses. Is He dangerous? She hasn't thought about that.

She's learned some religion along the way. She's spent some time in the company of "spiritual" men. She is a good listener, and they liked to think they were making an "honest" woman out of her. Is this His angle? It is time to change the subject with some flattery.

"Sir, you're a prophet, I see. Our Samaritan ancestors worshiped on this very mountain, but you Jews say the only legitimate place to worship is Jerusalem."

"Woman," He says, smiling, "believe me when I tell you that the time is coming when it won't matter where you worship our Father, on this mountain or in Jerusalem. Now you worship gods you don't even understand, and we worship what we understand, for the prophet Isaiah wrote that salvation comes through the Jews. But the hour is coming, in fact it's arrived, when true worshipers will worship the Father in spirit and truth, because that's the kind of people the Father is looking for to worship him. You can't limit worship to a place. God is spirit, and those who worship him must worship in spirit and truth."

The thought drifts through her mind again, but slower; more a prayer, actually, than a thought. *Who would talk to me like this?*

The flush rises once more in her. This time it is a mellow glow like candlelight, not the burn of shame. She's been standing all the while. Now she sits down beside Him on the stone wall and sets the water jar between them.

"I know that Messiah is coming," she tells Him, pensively. "When he comes, he will make all of this clear for us."

In the next moment she knows that wherever she's been going her whole life, under every rising dream and setting hope, each commitment and each rejection, she has reached the place.

"I am He," He says without inflection, "the One who is speaking to you."

She was wrong before. This, this is the most incredible thing she has ever heard in a lifetime of lies, because she believes Him.

They are turned toward each other, gazes holding, nothing further to be said.

More Jewish men show up, picking their way through the rocks, around the sycamores. They form a semicircle in front of the well. They seem to know the man. They are obviously surprised by her presence.

Their conversation stills to the same silence she knew from her early morning visit to the well with the women from town, but it doesn't matter anymore.

Everyone waits.

She knows she has to move. Not because of the staring men. Because for the first time in a long time she feels excitement and, well . . . she has to tell someone. It doesn't occur to her that no one in town has wanted to talk to her for as long as she's lived there.

She rises, turns, and walks away from the well and the men. They watch her out of sight, hearing her break into a run over the crackling sycamore twigs and leaves. The men turn back to look at their leader and offer Him something to eat. No one mentions the woman or asks what she was doing there.

One of them, a fisherman named John, far from the water but never from thoughts of it, notices the woman's water jar, left behind on the stone wall next to Jesus. He takes it all in—the well, the abandoned jar, Jesus, the Samaritan woman walking away—all set in soft, shaded light under the trees. *Something happened here just now,* he muses to himself. He will think about it, ask questions. It will take him nearly sixty years to figure it all out before he writes it down.

The woman rushes on. Afterward she won't remember how she moved between the well and town so quickly. She must have run, crunched across gravel, breathed hard, because something brought the townspeople from their midday torpor to their doorways. "What's the matter?" calls out a tall, dark woman.

"Come and see," her voice is high-pitched from the strain of heavy breathing. She raises it so all can hear.

"Come and see what?" The questions are terse and impatient. "Where's your water jar?" All of her neighbors know she ventures to the well in the noonday heat. "She's not fit for polite company," someone says.

"Shush," the tall, dark woman says, "Call her what you will, she's never lied to us."

"Come and see a man who told me everything I have ever done!" the woman pleads.

At these words, heads poked out of doorways into the sun like marmots in their holes up on the mountain. The thought of dark and sordid things drew them.

"He knows everything I have ever done, things that you only suspect that I've done. He cannot be the Messiah, can He?" Talk of sensational religion and sex! Here in their sleepy desert town! They were streaming

157

out of their homes before she spoke the last word of the question. She turned ahead of them and led them out to the well.

The townspeople bring Jesus and His disciples back to the square. They pepper Him with questions, first about the woman. He acknowledges He knows everything about her past, but he shares no details. "How do you know?" they ask Him.

"Are you a prophet?"

"Are you the Messiah?"

The woman calls out to Him. "Tell them what you told me about worship."

So it goes late into the night and starts again the next day. He answers everything. Jews and Samaritans eat together, pray together, sleep under the same roof. In turn, one after another of the townspeople stopped questioning. "I believe You," each says, falling silent, but staying close to Him.

In the late afternoon of the second day, when the questions and answers slow to a trickle, one of the townspeople turns to the woman and says, "We believed that he was something special when you told us 'He told me everything I have ever done.' You had a lot to lose by telling the truth. It's a lot more than that now. We've heard for ourselves, and we know that this is truly the Savior of the whole world."

People speak up with variations of the same reaction. Others murmur their assents and "thank-yous."

The tall, dark woman stands and says, "You forgot something." She hands her the water jar.

The woman takes the jar in both hands. It is heavy. She looks inside to see that it is full of water.

She stares into the jar for a moment as the truth sinks in to the last, dry, untouched place of safe-keeping in her heart. At contact, something molten and new springs up deep from that very place, rises with surprising pressure, spills out across her cheek, and splashes through the neck of the water jar.[2]

Questions for Reflection

1. Why is praying a good thing to do with your shame and disgrace?
2. What is more important in worship—the place, the style, or the heart of the worshiper?
3. What effect does time spent with Jesus Christ have on your doubts and fears?

30

What Do You Remember?

Jesus' question to the bickering disciples about the grace they had witnessed and so quickly forgotten calls us to remember what is truly important.

Do you ever have moments of reflection when you realize your puzzle is missing a few pieces? Maybe it's the relationship that hasn't lived up to expectations. How about the income that can't meet the debt? Perhaps your spirit is willing and optimistic, but your body fails the demand you place on it. Then again, you may have committed every resource of intellect, emotion, physical strength, and spiritual knowledge only to find you lack what it takes to meet your goal. You may have many more blanks on your test sheet than answers, and you are reduced to chewing on your pencil, paralyzed by fear of the unknown.

What do you remember in those moments of reflection?

Jesus took five loaves of bread and two fish, prayed over them, broke them, and fed a crowd of more than five thousand. And twelve baskets of bread and fish were left over.[1] Later, He took seven loaves and a few fish, blessed them, and fed a crowd of more than four thousand, and seven baskets were left over.[2]

The Pharisees saw it all and argued with Him about it. "Show us a sign from heaven," they said, trying to test him.

"Nothing doing," Jesus replied with a sigh. " 'Why does this generation ask for a sign? Truly I tell you, no sign will be given to this generation.' "[3]

The Son of man had nothing to prove. He got into a boat with His disciples and sailed away.

What do you remember when you can't see Jesus on the horizon?

There were thirteen hungry men in the boat that day, and they had one loaf of bread among them. Even though the disciples were responsible for collecting the leftovers of the miracle meals, filling nineteen baskets, they had already forgotten them.[4]

Jesus' mind was on the relentlessly obtuse Pharisees. There was no faith, no wonder at the mystery of life and love with them. They answered every question and addressed every issue with a rule or a penumbra of a rule. Instead of faith, they lived by guilt—and spread it to everyone they could. There is no practical difference between a religion of legalism and superstition. Either way, the grip on the soul is terror—terror that you'll do the wrong thing; terror that you will say the wrong words, terror that you will take your cue from the wrong event; terror that you won't measure up to others; terror that you won't know what you are supposed to know. Trying to please God by rule-keeping is to enter the spelling bee as a dyslexic.

What do you remember when there are more rules than you can keep?

Jesus pondered the other group dominating His people, the Herodians. They were a party of compromise, blending church and state, looking for power, looking for spectacular accomplishments of the elite to dazzle the masses. Herod reigned by appeasing both secular Rome and the religious establishment. He rebuilt the Jerusalem temple in great style. He built an entire city and named it after Caesar. In trade for unquestioning allegiance, Herod and his followers offered the solutions of big government, big development, and technology to an oppressed and depressed people. Their strategy was to keep the rabble preoccupied with the show and to enjoy the privilege and profit that comes to those who pull the strings and sell the tickets. Bigger is always better to Herodians, and the announced goal of public welfare is worth any compromise of personal virtue and conviction.

What do you remember when you've tried to please everyone, but they are still asking, "What have you done for me lately?"

Jesus spoke out to His companions in the boat, " 'Watch out—beware of the yeast of the Pharisees and the yeast of Herod.' "[5]

The disciples didn't get it. "Yeast—yeast? What is He talking about? It must be the bread we left behind. There must have been something special about the leftovers, and we didn't hang on to them and bring them with us. We forgot the miracle bread, and He's caught us."[6] "There will be hell to pay now!"

What do you remember when you can't reach back far enough to grab hold of what's worked for you in the past?

Their whining and finger pointing about the forgotten bread broke through Jesus' contemplations. He became aware of their obsession with what they had forgotten and what they lacked, and He had to ask them, "Why are you talking about having no bread? Don't you get it? Don't you understand what is going on here? Are your arteries so clogged and hard that it's cut off the blood flow to your brain? Do you have eyes that see anything? Do you have ears that hear a sound? AND DO YOU NOT REMEMBER?"[7]

The disciples were listening now. The only other sounds were the waves splashing on the hull, the flap of the sail, and the creak of the mast.

" 'When I broke the five loaves for five thousand, how many baskets full of leftovers did you collect?'

"They said to him, 'Twelve.'

" 'And the seven for the four thousand, how many baskets full of broken pieces did you collect?'

"And they said to him, 'Seven.'

"Then he said to them, 'DO YOU NOT YET UNDERSTAND?' "[8]

A beloved client of mine has recently been attacked by a party that thinks technology can solve most everything, and what technology can't solve, the law will intimidate. I was praying for wisdom for the defense on the morning I read this verse, and the Holy Spirit transformed these words into peace for my heart and mind.

It is easy in the pressure of catching the boat to forget what is necessary and what has sustained us in the past. It is tempting to say, "If I only had a set of rules to go by, a formula to follow, then it would come out all right." It is seductive to read the motivational and management books and think, "The secret is to keep making deals, achieving bigger scores, and undertaking larger projects. If I stop, I'll drop."

We pursue what we lack in obsessed fury. "If we only had the right consultant, the right balance of equity and venture capital, favorable legislation, or the right connection, no one could stop us." Or, "If we only followed the 'blueprint' perfectly, knew the right thing to do and always did it, could pull ourselves together to look good even when we don't feel good—then we would make it."

We rationalize, "Why be concerned with what ingredient makes the bread rise as long as we always have more bread? Success is memorizing the recipe, kneading harder, buying a better mixer, installing a bigger oven."

We succumb to spiritual anorexia and resist breaking apart the golden symmetry of our hoarded whole loaves even when we are starving.

We pray, "Jesus, I forgot the bread. Just tell me the recipe and I'll make more." Or, "Jesus, just give me a sign, fire from heaven, a crack in the ground straight through to the middle of the earth, a wet chamois on a dry lawn, a bank error in my favor—anything to tell me you are there and will give me what I need."

He doesn't respond with an answer; he responds with tough questions. "Why are you talking about having no bread? Why are you focused on what you are missing or have left behind? And do you not remember what I did for you before? Do you really think the secret of the miracle is in the bread and not the Baker? Have you forgotten not only the bread, but that I am right here in the same boat with you? Every time I filled your need before, wasn't there more than enough? Don't you understand that I can do it again? Do you understand who I am?"

I ask you again. What do you remember when you contemplate your broken heart and failed dreams?

Hear the remembrance of David:

I have been young, and now am old,
> yet I have not seen the righteous forsaken
> or their children begging bread.
They are ever giving liberally and lending,
> and their children become a blessing.[9]

It's all God, and it's all grace!

Questions for Reflection

1. What is important to remember when you are exhausted and confused?
2. Why is having a set of rules or a formula for living attractive to you?
3. What is Jesus seeking from you if He answers your prayer with a question?

31

Praying the Psalms

The psalms are a manual on how and what to pray in every circumstance of life.

The roots of my understanding of God and grace came from the family worships of my early childhood. My dad's favorite scripture was the Gospel of John, and my Mom loved the psalms and read them to us frequently. Music was a big part of our home life. There were four children, and we all played an instrument and sang. Many of the songs had words from the psalms that, over time, became inscribed on my heart. Prayer was a natural and constant occurrence for us. Our home was not perfect. Whose is? But prayer was a lubricant for the frictions and an entry to the throne of God who, I believed then and now, has the absolute best in mind for His children.

In the summer of 1974, I was working as the resident assistant in a dormitory at La Sierra University. My soul and body were recovering from a tragic accident that had taken the life of my childhood sweetheart some months before. As I grappled with my own grief and the destruction of my dreams, I began reading the psalms in the New English Bible. The prayers and thoughts that I read there were the heart cries of real people dealing with the heartaches, triumphs, and ambiguities of life. It was a great revelation and comfort to know that I was not alone. I began then to memorize and pray passages of the psalms as my own prayers. I've used different translations of them over the years, but these memorized passages remain the deepest fiber of my devotion to God.

Patricia loves the psalms also, and that is a special grace in itself. We spoke Psalm 139 to each other, alternating stanzas, during our wedding.

I have known men and women who flinched from the psalms. "They're too hard and rough," they tell me. Hogwash! Prayer that means something speaks to our reality, not to our fantasies. Eugene Peterson writes that the psalms train us in prayer, beginning with what we see all around us. "Abstraction is an enemy to prayer. Beautiful ideas are an enemy to prayer. Fine thoughts are an enemy to prayer. Authentic prayer begins when we stub our toes on a rock, get drenched in a rainstorm, get slapped in the face by an enemy—or run into the tree that has been in our path for so long that we have ceased to see it, and now stand back, in bruised and wondering awe before it."[1]

From the reality of my experience with God, I share with you some prayers from the psalms with commentary on what they mean to me. Your path may not be the same as mine, but our God is the same. There is plenty of room in the psalms for you to find your own trails to the heart of God. Come along with me then and sees what stirs in your heart.

> Hasten, O God, to save me;
>   O LORD, come quickly to help me.[2]

This is a favorite prayer. It only takes one step for me to wander off the path, and I can't seem to find my way back. In my human condition, this straying begins with the first step I take from the bed in the morning. There isn't a minute in the day that I don't need this prayer. I don't believe in the myth that I must do my part, and then God will do His. I am incompetent on my own. David must have known that about himself because he repeated this prayer in several other psalms.

> May your unfailing love come to me, O LORD,
>   your salvation according to your promise;
> then I will answer the one who taunts me,
>   for I trust in your word.[3]

This prayer changed my life one dawn when I was alone on an Arizona mountaintop. The Holy Spirit breathed the truth into my angry heart that Abba loves me and wouldn't stop loving me—ever. That answered the self-critic in my soul who taunted me that I was neither loved nor love-able. That morning marked my healing from the raging self-defensiveness I had acquired in childhood to protect against verbal and emotional abuse. I return to this prayer often as one returns to a favorite spot in the forest.

> The LORD will fulfill his purpose for me;
>> your love, O LORD, endures forever—
>> do not abandon the works of your hands.[4]

All of us have times when we find ourselves far out at sea, unable to see the shore we left or the landfall of our goal. It can be a lonely and frightening place, and I find this prayer to be a great comfort as I approach the point of no return.

> Hear my cry, O God;
>> listen to my prayer.

> From the ends of the earth I call to you,
>> I call as my heart grows faint;
>> lead me to the rock that is higher than I.[5]

In the course of a day's frictions and challenges, I puff up with pride and enlarge myself with bluster and irritation. Even on a good day, I tend to think the peace and the successes are due to my sensitive and insight-ful efforts. Then something or someone comes along that pokes a hole in my illusions and delusions, and I deflate. I have to come to grips with my lack and regain perspective on who really is in charge all the time. This prayer is an old and trusted path for me to regain my bearings on the sure landmark that is Christ.

> My heart is steadfast, O God,
>> my heart is steadfast;
>> I will sing and make music.
> Awake, my soul!
>> Awake, harp and lyre!
>> I will awaken the dawn.[6]

Each morning I awaken with a song of praise or prayer to my God singing in my heart. This is true every morning, and I never know in advance what song it will be. The day that I wrote these words, I heard this old hymn:

> Come, Thou Fount of every blessing,
> Tune my heart to sing Thy grace;
> Streams of mercy, never ceasing,
> Call for songs of loudest praise.
> Teach me ever to adore Thee,
> May I still Thy goodness prove,
> While the hope of endless glory
> Fills my heart with joy and love.[7]

Hearing these hymns in my heart is the result of years of corporate and family worship. Much of the theology that I know was learned from a hymnbook. Music is a precious treasure to me to share with those I love most. The first thing in the morning, my heart shares music with Abba and Jesus Christ whom He sent for me.

> By day the LORD directs his love,
>   at night his song is with me—
>   a prayer to the God of my life.[8]

> I am in pain and distress;
>   may your salvation, O God, protect me.[9]

The receipt of abrasions and lacerations of the soul is a consequence of living in a broken world with jagged edges and toxic evil. There is no antidote but the blood of Jesus Christ shed for you and me. I need frequent transfusions.

> Whom have I in heaven but you?
>   And earth has nothing I desire other than you.
> My flesh and my heart may fail,
>   but God is the strength of my heart
>   and my portion forever.[10]

I try hard, but I don't measure up. I envy those who are more successful than me, who take my dreams. But behind my fantasies is this truth: God is the real deal. God is the only deal. God is the good deal. No one but God can satisfy my longing heart. The truth of this prayer is ever green.

Set a guard over my mouth, O Lord;
> keep watch over the door of my lips.[11]

Kathleen Norris somewhere quotes a Benedictine monk who told her, "Say nothing unless it improves on silence." This is a good idea, but I find that it takes God's strength to accomplish it. James 3 is a good explanation of the reasons for this prayer. I should pray it a lot more than I do.

The Lord is my shepherd, I shall not want;
> he makes me lie down in green pastures.
He leads me beside the still waters;
> he restores my soul.
He leads me in paths of righteousness
> for his name's sake.

Even though I walk through the valley of the shadow of death,
> I fear no evil;
for thou art with me. . . .

Thou preparest a table before me
> in the presence of my enemies;
Thou anointest my head with oil,
> my cup overflows.
Surely goodness and mercy shall follow me
> all the days of my life;
and I shall dwell in the house of the Lord
> for ever." [12]

This psalm is my earliest memory of Scripture. My Mom gave me a new toy cattle truck filled with rubber livestock for reciting this prayer of David's in front of our congregation when I was four years old. This wondrous description of God's loving care and lavish provision turns into a prayer about a third of the way through. It is the source text for my understanding of grace. Every action in this psalm is God's except for my walk through the valley of the shadow of death, and He walks right through that with me. This prayer occupies a place in my heart to which I return over and over again at night when I can't sleep, in the cramped quarters of an overly long business flight, in the comfort of a grieving friend, in the healing of my own broken heart. God is good all the time!

Will you not revive us again,
    so that your people may rejoice in you?[13]

There is no life unless God gives it. I cannot pray unless God stirs my soul to prayer. To praise requires the pulse of the living God. This is a prayer for a time of spiritual drought.

O God, you know my folly;
    the wrongs I have done are not hidden from you.

Do not let those who hope in you be put to shame because of me,
    O Lord God of hosts;
do not let those who seek you be dishonored because of me.[14]

Psalm 69 is a blues song of a prayer. David was evidently down so far that he could see only stars overhead at noon when he wrote this. After one of my management disasters in assertive leadership years ago, the office manager told me, "Well, you made your point, but how many lambs did you slaughter?" This is a prayer for those not infrequent times when I am out on a limb that is cracking behind me, endangering those who are depending on me to do the right thing. " 'Apart from me you can do nothing,' " said Jesus.[15] That's true, but unfortunately it hasn't stopped me from trying repeatedly to take things into my own hands. I need God to protect those I love and serve from the collateral damage of my ineptness.

Because your love is better than life,
    my lips will glorify you.
I will praise you as long as I live,
    and in your name I will lift up my hands. . . .
Because you are my help,
    I sing in the shadow of your wings.
My soul clings to you;
    your right hand upholds me.[16]

Gratitude is the surest sign of faith. When I am thankful, I admit that someone else is responsible for the life that I enjoy. Saying "Thanks" to God says, "It's not about me. It's all about God who loves me. Jesus Christ proved that by saving me." "For to me, to live is Christ."[17] This is as good as it gets, and it is wonderful.

Gladden the soul of your servant,
  for to you, O Lord, I lift up my soul.
For you, O Lord, are good and forgiving,
  abounding in steadfast love to all who call on you.[18]

There is absolutely no power comparable to knowing with assurance that you are loved and forgiven. To know God is to know both belonging and freedom. That's the memory that brought the starving, lonely prodigal to his senses and caused him to say, "I will arise and go to my father."[19] There are times when each of us is the starving, lonely prodigal.

Vindicate me in your righteousness, O LORD my God; . . .
Do not let them think, "Aha, just what we wanted!"
  or say, "We have swallowed him up."

May all who gloat over my distress
  be put to shame and confusion;
may all who exalt themselves over me
  be clothed with shame and disgrace.[20]

I don't remember where I first learned the prayer that arises from this psalm, "Lord, confuse the speech of those who would attack me with words. Disorder their thoughts and turn their thinking into disarray" or other words to that effect. It is a prayer that I have prayed to powerful result before entering a verbal conflict with those who would injure my clients, friends, or me for their own gain. However, it cannot be prayed with anything but total reliance on God with no reservation of malice or self-justification in my heart. In fact, I fast before praying this prayer and call on the Lord to purify and soften my heart and lead me to make right where I am wrong.

But now, Lord, what do I look for?
  My hope is in you.[21]

Figuring out the next step sometimes seems as if I'm playing Where's Waldo? as a blind man. The further I go in the Christian life, I learn that I don't get a technique or a sure-fire formula for salvation. I get a Savior. I don't receive healing. I'm given the Healer. This prayer "cuts to the chase" and brings me to the One who can do something about the problem.

Create in me a pure heart, O God,
    and renew a steadfast spirit within me.[22]

What's impossible for me is possible with God. Only the One who made me can restore me. There is no limit to his power to redeem and renew. That's a great thing because I have to daily return to Him with this prayer.

Search me, O God, and know my heart;
    test me and know my anxious thoughts.
See if there is any offensive way in me,
    and lead me in the way everlasting.[23]

I tinker with my soul. I am hot and bothered about my future. I deny my shortcomings. "The heart is deceitful above all things," noted Jeremiah.[24] Even if I could identify the depths of what's wrong with me, I am incompetent to repair my soul. That's a job for God alone.

Teach me your way, O LORD,
    that I may walk in your truth;
        give me an undivided heart to revere your name.[25]

I find it impossible to get through a day on my own without the soiling of selfishness. I crave approval, and I'm not above pretense to try to obtain it. It is, however, impossible to serve two masters.[26] My soul needs a shower of truth. My heart, divided by my penchant for servile compromise with idolatry, needs the repair of the Master and a recalibration to worship my Savior and my Lord. This is a prayer for peace.

May integrity and uprightness preserve me,
    for I wait for you.[27]

It is a fast-food world. There is a temptation to demand instant gratification or to cut and run before God acts. God gives His Word to guide me through the moments when I can't feel His presence or see His plan. I've learned that the moment of darkness is always a call to stick to the Word and wait for the light.

Teach me to do your will,
    for you are my God;

may your good Spirit
    lead me on level ground.[28]

I don't want my life to climb and sink, twist and turn, like the plot of a soap opera. If my call is to run and not grow weary, and walk and not be faint,[29] then I need level ground. Praise God that He is faithful to supply what He requests.

Listen to my cry,
    for I am in desperate need;
rescue me from those who pursue me,
    for they are too strong for me.
Set me free from my prison,
    that I may praise your name.

Then the righteous will gather about me
    because of your goodness to me.[30]

I attach myself to the idols of work and pride, but I can't make enough sacrifices to appease them. I am trapped by my shortsighted strategies and have no strength or plan to break out of the prison of my futility. But I have a Savior anointed to preach good news to the poor, sent to proclaim freedom for the prisoners, to recover sight for the blind, and to release the oppressed.[31] I get one call from jail, and this is the call I make. This is a prayer I often share with others in the imprisonment and torment of bitterness and unforgivingness. The entire psalm is a sure path from the lonely alienation of folly, sin, and resentment back to the life of community.

My heart is not proud, O LORD,
    my eyes are not haughty.
I do not concern myself with great matters
    or things too wonderful for me.
But I have stilled and quieted my soul;
    like a weaned child with its mother,
    like a weaned child is my soul within me.

O Israel, put your hope in the LORD
    both now and forevermore.[32]

This is a favorite prayer—a when-I-get-too-big-for-my-britches prayer.

I memorized it some years ago during a silent retreat. It reflects a maturing relationship with God. If I have a proud heart and haughty eyes, I'm refusing to accept reality on anything but my own terms just like an overly tired, irritable child who refuses sleep. I need to surrender my demands and let go to the wiser thoughts and stronger hands of God. A weaned child no longer desperately needs its mother to be fed but comes to the mother by choice in peaceful acceptance of the love to be found at her side. The Triune God is both father and mother to us. I like to substitute my own name for "Israel" in the last line to personalize the hope.

> I will both lie down and sleep in peace,
>   for you alone, O LORD, make me lie down in safety.[33]

There is no moment when we are more vulnerable than when we lie down to sleep. A person who can lie down and sleep in peace is a person who trusts. If I thought about everything that is wrong in the world and everything that I believe I need to do, I would never sleep. Even if I do lie down, it's hard to sleep when I think about what I should have, could have, would have done and grit my teeth. Fortunately, that is God's problem. The government is on His shoulders. He makes it possible to lie down and sleep in peace. I am a man who is grateful for the "love that will not let me go."

I invite you to read and pray the psalms for yourself. Don't just take my word for it. Find your own prayer paths to God. He's waiting to guide you.

Questions for Reflection

1. How does remembered Scripture assist your prayer?
2. What is your favorite psalm? Pick a quiet place and read it throughout as a prayer. Tell God why it is your favorite and give thanks to Him.
3. Write out your own psalm to God, praising His works and thanking Him for His specific mercy to you.

32

Acts of God

People that we count on may leave us, or we may have to leave them. Change is hard but necessary. Trust in God expressed in our prayers is the only sure way through.

I don't know about you, but I don't like change. It generally costs too much in people and things that are dear to me.

There is no gambler in me. To risk the known for the unknown seems foolish.

The hard effort that I expend to order my affairs is devalued by the vagaries of accident, illness, storm, flood, rebellion, crime, war, and, yes, growth.

I went to the beach most summer days as a boy. It was fun to play in the great blue-green waves of the Pacific. I never spent much time building sandcastles, however, because those same waves would turn them to grainy gruel at the next tide. What was the point?

Perhaps this looking for the permanent led me into a career in the law. The ordering of responsibility and obligation in a business transaction appeals to me. "The party of the first part will do this and that, and the party of the second part will pay this much when that happens; and if it doesn't work out the matter will be resolved by the process set forth herein." A place for everything and everything in its place, neatly initialed, of course. A good contract keeps the peace.

A good lawyer can't control everything and, oh, does this ever tick us off! If something unexpected blows the deal after we make it, we like to blame God. We call such occurrences "acts of God" because we like to think God's the only one big enough to override and "wash out" our best-laid plans. We reduce uncontrollable change to a "boilerplate" excuse: "The client's failure to perform its obligations will be excused for wars, riots, insurrections, labor strife, strikes, transportation delays, and acts of God."

Here is a legal definition of "act of God":

> Any misadventure or casualty is said to be caused by an "act of God" when it happens by the direct, immediate, and exclusive operation of the forces of nature, uncontrolled or uninfluenced by the power of man and without human intervention, and is of such character that it could not have been prevented or escaped by any amount of foresight or prudence, or by any reasonable degree of care or diligence, or by the aid of any appliances which the situation of the party might reasonably require him or her to use. Inevitable accident, or casualty; any accident produced by any physical cause which is irresistible, such as lightning; tempests, perils of the seas, an inundation, or earthquake; and also the sudden illness or death of persons.[1]

So it was with all the prejudice of an experienced business attorney that I read these words from the opening of the Book of Joshua. "After the death of Moses the servant of the LORD, the LORD spoke to Joshua son of Nun, Moses' assistant, saying, 'My servant Moses is dead. Now proceed to cross the Jordan, you and all this people, into the land that I am giving to them, to the Israelites.' "[2]

This was a real dinger of a change. Forty years Moses led the Israelites, communicating the will and way of God. They had developed a rhythm—manna to eat six days of the week and more manna for the seventh, cloud by day and fire by night, personal and public hygiene, worship, water from the rock—even the miracles became routine. Now, Moses was dead, in fact, but Joshua had to be told that it was true and it was time to move on.

Who was Moses? The name means "to draw out." He pointed out that the Israelites were in bondage and told them what they could do to be free. He helped them, confronting their enemy Pharaoh and risking himself in the effort. He had a direct connection with God and conversed with him as a friend. More than once, Moses saved the Israelites from death. He told them how to live as free men and women. He was crotchety and angry at their stubbornness and whining, but he stuck with them through their most stupidly fearful moments.

Moses was the only leader that an entire generation had known. He had failings (don't we all?), but they were the failings of passion, of a heart in the right place even when his actions didn't show it. He promised them better things—a better place to live, prosperity, health, and peace—and now he was dead, and his assistant got the word to move on. That's real change!

Businesses are often valued on the basis of their leadership. What was Jack Welch to General Electric, Thomas Watson to IBM, Lee Iacocca to Chrysler, Steve Jobs to Apple, Bill Gates to Microsoft, John D. Rockefeller to Standard Oil? Nations are identified throughout history for particular defining leadership, such as France with Napoleon, Britain with Churchill, Germany with Bismarck, China with Mao Tse-Tung, the United States with Washington and Lincoln. What was Israel without Moses? This was the challenge for Joshua.

This is also a challenge that each of us faces sooner or later. Who is your Moses? Who helped you out of the pit of bondage, took your side, and shook you out of your slumber? Who showed you the way to better things? Who has meant survival to you, and who is going to get you through now that your Moses is dead and gone?

Oh. I see, you hate change also, notwithstanding all those wonderful books, articles, seminars, tapes, refrigerator magnets, and cute calendars urging you on to new and better things. In fact, to be honest, even when our Moses tried to take us through the discomfort of change, we rebelled and tried to kill the messenger.[3] I may have my bad times right here, but I am making it with the help of my Moses, aren't I? Why do I need to move on if it means trading off the known for the unknown? "A bird in the hand is worth two in the bush," isn't it?

As good as the Promised Land sounds, there are reports of hostile giants there.[4] There are so many questions and uncontrollable circumstances. We are tempted to play it safe with what we have right here and right now. We are angry at the act of God. Why did God take our Moses?

"My servant Moses is dead," God says. "Now proceed to cross the Jordan, you and all this people, into the land that I am giving them."

Two things about the verse reorient the priorities of Joshua—or us. "My servant Moses," God said. You thought this was all about you. You trusted the operating instructions that Moses gave you. You thought your life depended on your perfection in following the formula. Now you find out who your Moses was really working for. If your Moses was following God's instruction when he brought you to this place, it must have been in God's plan. It follows that the death of your Moses must be in God's plan. Your moving on must be in God's plan. You are not at the mercy of acts of God. You are an act of God and that act is no misadventure, no accident, no excuse; your life is an act of grace.

Because the other thing is that God says the place where He is sending you is His gift to you. You thought achieving the goal depended on your Moses and you. You find out that it is all in God's grace. Your Moses is gone, but God's grace continues. God told Joshua in the next verses, " 'Every place that the sole of your foot will tread upon I have given to you, as I promised to Moses. . . . No one shall be able to stand against you all the days of your life. As I was with Moses, so I will be with you; I will not fail you or forsake you. . . . I hereby command you: Be strong and courageous; do not be frightened or dismayed, for the LORD your God is with you wherever you go.' "5 You can't ask for more than this. Proceed with assurance.

I read a passage from the seventeenth-century archbishop Fenelon that puts all of this in perspective:

> The best place to be is where God puts you. Any other place is undesirable because you chose it for yourself. Do not think too much about the future. Worrying about things that haven't happened yet is unhealthy for you. God Himself will help you, day by day. There is no need to store things up for the future. Don't you believe that God will take care of you?
>
> A life of faith does two things: Faith helps you see God behind everything that He uses. And faith also keeps you in a place where you are not sure what will happen next. To have faith you cannot always want to know what is happening or going to happen. God wants you to trust him alone from minute to minute. The strength He gives you in one minute is not intended to carry you through the next. Let God take care of His business. Just be faithful to what God asks of you. To depend on God from moment to moment—especially when all is dark and uncertain—is a true dying to your old self. This process is so slow and inward that it is often hidden from you as well as others.
>
> When God takes something away from you, you can be sure He knows how to replace it. . . . Eat in peace what God gives you. "Tomorrow will take care of itself" (Matthew 6:34). The One who feeds you today will surely feed you tomorrow.6

_____ *Questions for Reflection* _____

1. Why do you fear change?
2. How do you feel when you are not in control?
3. Why is dying to self essential to accepting the changes that God brings to you?

33

Praying Through a Drought

Elijah's experience beside an evaporating stream guides us to prayer in times of vanishing resources.

It is my lifelong ambition to live beside a stream, but I dwell in dry country.

Valencia Creek runs from the foothills of the Santa Cruz Mountains toward the Monterey Bay. It has a deep, well-defined channel lined with century-old, second growth redwoods. I played there as a child.

The creek courses cold and clear over a gravel bottom from November to June. Then it just dribbles away to nothing.

The vanishing water always disappoints me. The forces that carve the steep banks and feed the big trees seem fraudulent. My winter hopes of source and terminus are empty speculations. Flood is always followed by drought. Similarly, the soul struggles when loss is inevitable and dryness is predictable. Somehow the thought of next winter's rains does not compensate for a stream that will not flow in summer.

"Now Elijah the Tishbite, of Tishbe in Gilead, said to Ahab, 'As the LORD the God of Israel lives, before whom I stand, there shall be neither dew nor rain these years, except by my word.' The word of the LORD came to him, saying, 'Go from here and turn eastward, and hide yourself by the Wadi Cherith, which is east of the Jordan. You shall drink from the wadi, and I have commanded the ravens to feed you there.' So he went and did according to the word of the LORD; he went and lived by the Wadi Cherith, which is east of the Jordan. The ravens brought him bread and meat in the morning, and bread and meat in the evening; and

177

he drank from the wadi. But after a while the wadi dried up, because there was no rain in the land."[1]

The man was a settler (that's what *Tishbite* means) from the mountains of Gilead, east of the Jordan. This was a well-watered highland split by the Jabbok River. It was a place of springs and forests with a heavier rainfall than other areas. It was also the eastern frontier of Israel, and Elijah was a frontiersman. Mountain dwellers throughout history have cherished freedom and prized purity. The influence of life lived on rugged slopes gives them a love of independence and a willingness to sacrifice for a worthy goal. Truths learned in solitude give them a plainspoken expression and an enthusiasm for reform.

Elijah came out of the mountains to confront the sophisticated, compromised monarch. His focus was clear and courageous. Elijah acknowledged his standing with God, but not with Ahab. His words were few. God was going to send a drought of long duration. No breath was wasted on telling Ahab why this would be. The principle was fundamental in the history of the nation—Yahweh, the God of Israel, was supreme. The point was the doer, not the deed. Ahab was a Baal worshiper who erected shrines and totems in offense to Yahweh who had given the land to Israel. When making the gift, God spoke these words to the Israelites through Moses:

> [T]he land that you are crossing over to occupy is a land of hills and valleys, watered by rain from the sky, a land that the LORD your God looks after. . . .
>
> If you will only heed his every commandment . . . loving the LORD your God, and serving him with all your heart and soul— then he will give the rain for your land in its season. . . . Take care, or you will be seduced into turning away, serving other gods and worshiping them, for then the anger of the LORD will be kindled against you and he will shut up the heavens, so that there will be no rain and the land will yield no fruit; then you will perish quickly off the good land that the LORD is giving you.[2]

Elijah spoke the word of God who gave Israel the land and watered it. Elijah spoke that word without bluff or condition and left it at that.

Elijah lived without back-up plans. The one time he yielded to self-preservation, he sidetracked the cause of God and experienced alienation and loneliness.[3] God's instruction to him had no contingency.

The story would probably go down easier with us if God had rewarded Elijah's courage by sending him back to Gilead to wait out the dry spell beside a gushing spring in a lush mountain valley. But that isn't God's way.

God told Elijah an unbelievable thing. A *wadi* is a valley, gully, or riverbed that remains dry except during a rainy season. On a topographical map, the Wadi Cherith would look like Valencia Creek, brown lines spaced with dots denoting an intermittent, undependable water source, instead of the solid blue line of a perennial stream. God said, "Go hide beside a stream that will evaporate in a dry-bones desert in a time of drought. You can drink the water, and birds will bring you sandwiches."

Would you trek into the wilderness on guidance like this? Elijah did. God sent the man of the mountains to a low place. He sent the man from a land of forest and springs to live in a desert. The man who settled the land to tame it was instead fed by uncontrollable wild creatures. God caused the man who courageously proclaimed God's message of the drought to live in dryness.

Again it would be a wondrous story if water had flowed through the dry creek all through the drought or if God had given Elijah the vision for an ingenious dam or cistern to conserve the water. Those things didn't happen. Eventually the stream dried up. God then told Elijah to go one hundred miles farther out to a place called Zarephath, "blast furnace," where he lived the next three years in the hand-to-mouth existence of a survivor in famine.

What do you think Elijah thought about in those hot, listless daylight hours waiting for the ravens to return? What must it be like to see the flow that means life reduced to a trickle and then to pools and then to damp sand? What must he have thought when God told him to move on from dryness into the blast furnace?

Are you living by an evaporating stream and facing even worse? The stream may be the declining health of you or a loved one. It may be the dwindling pool of love in a relationship that has gone dry from inattention. It may be revenues that won't equal expenses with reserves draining away. You may be seeking the miracle of relief and abundance but receiving no more than the grace of mere survival in the face of the inevitable. God may be telling you to move on to the smelting furnace of a Zarephath for further refinement to eliminate any vestigial self-reliance, independence, or pride. You may be struggling and reduced to begging from those who can scarcely feed themselves. In those moments of withering aridity, it is difficult not to cry out to God in the words of Jeremiah,

Why is my pain unceasing,
    my wound incurable,
    refusing to be healed?
Truly, you are to me like a deceitful brook,
    like waters that fail.[4]

The nineteenth-century pastor F. B. Meyer wrote a commentary on Elijah's experience. His words struck a deep chord in my soul:

> Most of us would have become anxious and worn with planning long before this. And probably, long before the brook was dry, we would have devised some plan, and asking God's blessing on it, would have started off elsewhere. He often extricates us because His mercy endures forever; but if we had only waited first to see the unfolding of His plans, we would never have found ourselves landed in such an inextricable labyrinth. Would that we were content to wait for God to unveil His plan, so that our life might be simply the working out of His thought, the exemplification of His ideal! . . .
>
> Our only need is to inquire if we are at that point in God's pattern where He would have us be. If we are, though it may seem impossible for us to be sustained, the thing impossible will be done. We will be sustained by a miracle, if no ordinary means will suffice. "Seek first the kingdom of God, and his righteousness, and all these things will be given you"(Mt. 6:33).[5]

What the seasonal streams of our existence teach us is to trust the provision of today. God, whose power cut the channel through the earth and fills it in season, will feed and water us where we stand, or, elsewhere at the place He sends us. David prayed thus:

But I trust in you, O LORD;
    I say, "You are my God."
My times are in your hand;
    deliver me from the hand of my enemies and persecutors.
Let your face shine upon your servant;
    save me in your steadfast love.[6]

Both the waiting and the journey, in their ways, will take us through the drought of the Cross, a place so dry that the Creator himself cried out from it in parched, human agony, " 'I thirst.' "[7] For those willing to stay or move at His word, however, there is a permanent home beside "the river of the water of life, bright as crystal, flowing from the throne of God and of the Lamb through the middle of the street of the city. On either side of the river is the tree of life with its twelve kinds of fruit, producing its fruit each month, and the leaves of the tree are for the healing of the nations. . . .

"The Spirit and the bride say, 'Come.'

"And let everyone who hears say, 'Come.'

"And let everyone who is thirsty come.

"Let anyone who wishes take the water of life as a gift."[8]

Thirsty child, waiting out the dry season for a drink of grace, I have a word of hope for you. "After many days the word of the Lord came to Elijah, in the third year of the drought, saying 'Go, present yourself to Ahab; I will send rain on the earth.' "[9] "Elijah was a human being like us, and he prayed fervently that it might not rain, and for three years and six months it did not rain on the earth. Then he prayed again, and the heaven gave rain and the earth yielded its harvest."[10]

_____ *Questions for Reflection* _____

1. Why might God place you next to an evaporating stream?
2. Why would God lead you from a dry place to a hotter, dryer place of existence?
3. What awaits you if you move with Christ through the parched agony of the Cross?

34

Learning From Jesus

It doesn't require perfection to learn from Jesus.

" 'Come to me, all you that are weary and are carrying heavy burdens, and I will give you rest. Take my yoke upon you, and learn from me; for I am gentle and humble in heart, and you will find rest for your souls. For my yoke is easy, and my burden is light.' "[1]

How long has it been since you considered the impact of those words as something more than a beautiful sentiment? Have you plumbed the depths of what Jesus is asking you to do?

The Creator of the universe and the Savior of the world is asking you to set aside what occupies your mind and heart and take on His burdens as your own. If that request doesn't drop you to your knees, what will?

Did you grow up with a view of a capricious, punitive God who is "out to get you" if you don't please Him with perfection? Then the invitation to take on His "easy" yoke and "light" burdens may sound like a trick.

Or you may be tempted to attempt to fix everything and everyone, including yourself, in the effort to be like Jesus. You may have been taught that Jesus is your example, and you are working on conforming to the template of His perfection.

But I have something surprising to tell you: attempting to be godlike is not a good thing. "The serpent said to the woman, 'You will not die; for God knows that when you eat of it your eyes will be opened, *and you will be like God,* knowing good and evil.' "[2] "You must understand this, that in the last days distressing times will come. For people will be lovers of themselves . . . holding to the outward form of godliness but denying its power."[3]

The late Lewis Smedes wrote about his childhood guilt created by the effort to match Jesus stride for stride.

> I felt that I had a duty to be perfect the way that God is perfect. Jesus himself said so: "You must be perfect the way God is perfect. You must, therefore, be perfect as your Father in heaven is perfect." The general impression this left me with was that I had to be like Jesus, not now and then, but all the time.
>
> > Be like Jesus, this my song,
> > In the home and in the throng,
> > Be like Jesus all day long,
> > I would be like Jesus.
>
> I was not sure whether I wanted to be like Jesus all day long. Nor did I have a clear notion of what it would take for a puny kid like me to be like an ancient Jewish rabbi on his way to being Savior of the world.
>
> I did understand that the only way for me to become like Jesus all day long was to be truly born again. So I was born again; it happened when I was twelve or thirteen years old. I do not recall that the experience gave me much joy. In fact, being born again added to my shame. I figured that my folks would expect a born-again boy to be like Jesus all day long, in the home and in the throng—and I could not see myself becoming that good so soon.[4]

Here is a further elaboration of the "Jesus as example" lived out as an adult:

> I had become an out-of-control work addict, what author and educator Parker Palmer calls a "functional atheist." Although I spoke of God as being powerful and in control, my actions told a different story, that God either didn't exist or was seriously ill. I lived in the illusion that unless I was making it happen, nothing was happening. Not only was my life shaped by an incorrect view of a too-small God, an equally incorrect view of a too-big me made matters worse. Once firmly planted, my mistaken views made arrogance second nature . . . and my life dangerously active.

I elevated my self-importance and diminished God's to the extent that even the act of coming to God was something I took credit for, speaking of "my" decision to follow God, as if Jesus was some innocent bystander with no part to play in the drama of my life. I had ignored Jesus' words, "No one can come to me unless drawn by the Father who sent me."[5]

The tree forbidden in to us in Eden bore the fruit of "the knowledge of good and evil."[6] Swallow hard and understand that living a good life by diligence, discipline, and effort in our own strength is as much a departure from God's plan for us as is indulging every lustful temptation of our flesh. It was about very religious people and "good" citizens that Jesus' pronounced the prophecy of Isaiah:

> " 'You will indeed listen, but never understand,
>   and you will indeed look, but never perceive.
> For this people's heart has grown dull,
>   and their ears are hard of hearing,
>   and they have shut their eyes;
>   so that they might not look with their eyes,
>   and listen with their ears,
> and understand with their heart and turn—
>   and I would heal them.' . . .
> Truly I tell you, many prophets and righteous people longed to see what you see, but did not see it, and to hear what you hear, but did not hear it."[7]

If we think we can live right by tracing out a pattern and coloring carefully within the lines, we have to consider the contingencies of when the crayons break or are used up; the Crayola manufacturers come out with a new color and eliminate an old one; our companions have the 128-color super box with a built-in sharpener while we have only the 8-color box; our fine-motor control fails us, and we color outside a tight corner in the lines and can't erase the result and ruin the picture; our stroke is too heavy in our enthusiasm and lays down a too-thick layer of wax; or a careless spill of milk curls our page, blurs the lines, and glues the book shut. Then there is the possibility that the teacher will like another child's choice of colors and neatness more and give him or her the gold star and us the silver star or the honorable mention, or will run out of stars before she examines our picture.

What a tragedy to be found head down, concentrating on not coloring outside the line so we can win the gold star, when outside the window Venus is rising in the western sky! This is exactly how spiritual blindness develops.

We can learn our Scripture, filling in blanks in workbooks and our doctrine sitting straight and neat in the pews. Does that please a God who empties His paint buckets in autumn forests, makes no two snowflakes alike, combines colors in a sunset that would get you evicted by a homeowners' association if you painted your house that way, enters the world through an unwed mother and leaves it as a criminal, and spends the time in between with sinners, not the righteous? What would please a God who would rather let kids climb into His lap and pull His beard, spend time with beggars on the roadside, and enjoy the conviviality of a group of hard-partying accountants than keep the schedule of His advance team? "Learn of me" invites Jesus. "I have an easy method and light requirements," but we demand to know, "Is the final exam going to be open book?" "Will it be comprehensive?" "How much am I going to have to study to get an A?" "Will I have to buy the book, or will there be handouts?" "How can I earn extra credit?"

God does not call us to be God.

"Hear, O my people, and I will speak,
    O, Israel, I will testify against you.
I am God, your God. . . .
    you thought that I was one just like yourself.
But now I rebuke you, and lay the charge before you.

"Mark this, then you who forget God,
    or I will tear you apart, and there will be no one to deliver."[8]

God looks down from heaven on humankind
    to see if there are any who are wise,
    who seek after God.

They have all fallen away, they are all alike perverse;
    there is no one who does good,
    no, not one.[9]

What does God do when He sees our imperfections?

As a father has compassion for his children,
> so the LORD has compassion for those who fear him.
For he knows how we were made;
> he remembers that we are dust.[10]

No, God calls us to be human, not superhuman.

Let the same mind be in you that was in Christ Jesus,
> who, though he was in the form of God,
>> did not regard equality with God
>> as something to be exploited,
> but emptied himself,
>> taking the form of a slave,
>> being born in human likeness.
> And being found in human form,
>> he humbled himself
>> and became obedient to the point of death—
>> even death on a cross.[11]

Humiliation to the point of a life of slavery and a death by crucifixion hardly seem like an easy yoke or light burden either. But we must remember that the Lord of the universe lived in our constraints and was executed as one of us so that we don't have to live that way anymore. The verse in Philippians continues,

> Therefore God also highly exalted him
>> and gave him the name
>> that is above every name,
> so that at the name of Jesus
>> every knee should bend,
>> in heaven and on earth and under the earth,
> and every tongue should confess
>> that Jesus Christ is Lord,
>> to the glory of God the Father.

> Therefore, my beloved . . . work out your own salvation with fear and trembling; for it is God who is at work in you, enabling you both to will and to work for his pleasure.[12]

God works in us, enabling us to please Him. God does for us what

186

we can't. Again, I say, God does not expect us to be God. "God," in the words of Brennan Manning, "expects more failure of us than we do."

Christ enters our very fingernail-chewing, inarticulate, high-carb, low-thinking humanity, and dwells there to transform us into a temple of His light and love.[13] " 'Because I live, you also will live,' " said Jesus.[14] Paul entered the debate between grace and performance and told the Galatians, "I have been crucified with Christ; and it is no longer I who live, but it is Christ who lives in me. And the life I now live in the flesh I live by faith in the Son of God, who loved me and gave himself for me."[15]

Christ's yoke is easy and his burden is light precisely because it is God's yoke and God's burden. "Jesus said to them, 'Very truly, I tell you, the Son can do nothing on his own, but only what he sees the Father doing; for whatever the Father does, the Son does likewise. The Father loves the Son and shows him all that he himself is doing; and he will show him greater works than these, so that you will be astonished. Indeed, just as the Father raises the dead and gives them life, so also the Son gives life to whomever he wishes.' "[16]

Just as Jesus lived in a close, responsive relationship with His Father, we are invited to live in a close, responsive relationship with him. He has no desire to jerk us around, pile baggage on us, yell at us, or force us to a mind-numbing conformity to get us to do what He wants us to do. Patricia and I have been married for thirty years. If I catch her eye or she catches mine across a crowded room, we can see the love in the other and know what the other is thinking. That is Christ's intention for our relationship with him.

> I will instruct you and teach you the way you should go;
> I will counsel you with my eye upon you.
> Do not be like a horse or a mule, without understanding,
> whose temper must be curbed with bit and bridle,
> else it will not stay with you.[17]

Jesus asks, " 'Are you tired? Worn out? Burned out on religion? Come to me. Get away with me and you'll recover your life. I'll show you how to take a real rest. Walk with me and work with me—watch how I do it. Learn the unforced rhythms of grace. I won't lay anything heavy or ill-fitting on you. Keep company with me and you'll learn to live freely and lightly.' "[18]

There's only one response worthy of that invitation. It's unconditional. David prayed it:

Examine me, God, from head to foot,
order your battery of tests.
Make sure I'm fit
inside and out.
So I never lose
sight of your love,
But keep in step with you,
never missing a beat.[19]

Questions for Reflection

1. What is the problem with seeking to be good in your own strength?
2. If your efforts don't earn the approval of God, what will?
3. What is Jesus' invitation to the exhausted and those carrying heavy burdens? What do you say to answer this invitation with prayer?

Experiencing God's Love Through Prayer

35

"I Am Not a Monster!"

An attorney's client facing a loss of reputation and career takes a first step of prayer on the pathway to Christ.

I stood on a stair landing outside a hearing room and watched a man cry. His career is distinguished by international prominence and service. His name is renowned for excellence in his profession and his scholarship. Yet only seconds before, as he broke under a concerted, vicious attack from colleagues, I had taken his arm and led him out of the room.

Now I, his advocate, stood beside him, as he fought for a composure that would not come. He hung his head over the railing, sobbing over and over, "I am not who they say I am. I am not a monster."

I longed to tell him what was on my heart, some lines from my favorite psalm:

How long will you assail a person,
    will you batter your victim, all of you,
        as you would a leaning wall, a tottering fence?
Their only plan is to bring down a person of prominence.
    They take pleasure in falsehood;
they bless with their mouths,
    but inwardly they curse.

For God alone my soul waits in silence,
    for my hope is from him.

He alone is my rock and my salvation,
　　my fortress; I shall not be shaken.
On God rests my deliverance and my honor;
　　my mighty rock, my refuge is in God.[1]

But I knew that my client did not believe in my God, and so I draped my arm around his shoulders and prayed silently for his healing and for justice to be done. "O God, if not for his unbelief, then for my belief—hear my prayer and be glorified through your justice."

I've encountered this dilemma before. What does a person in distress and grief do when he or she has no center, no God to call home, no Christ to still the troubled waters?

When I attended law school at a secular university, Patricia and I were the head residents of a large undergraduate coed dormitory. We were products of a sheltered Christian upbringing, and we were dismayed by the angst of our students. These were children of wealth and privilege. Yet the smallest of things—an argument with a roommate, a break-up with a girlfriend or boyfriend, or a bad test score—could emotionally stagger them, some to the point of suicidal thoughts. Much worse were the problems when the phone call would come from parents who had decided to divorce after their child had left home for college or when freshman women would return from the abortion clinic having been "stood-up" by the boyfriends who promised them anything on the night of the date, but were nowhere to be found on the day of the decision.

Whether experiencing small inconveniences or large tragedies, these students displayed a despair beyond anything Patricia and I had ever seen. After a while it dawned on us—these kids had no center, no internal compass, no knowledge of an ever-present Christ to come home to in their hearts. There were plenty of people around who rolled their eyes and sneered at our Christian education, but I realized in dealing with these problems that this is exactly where the "Christ" part of that education really counts.

As I stood beside my atheist, humanist friend twenty-two years later, I was looking at the same issue. When you have no center, externals are everything. What someone else thinks about you and how you stand with others becomes your life. When treachery or loss comes, you have nothing else to rely upon and no place to go for solace. The effect is like falling, flailing and thrashing, into a bottomless abyss. The night before his collapse, I had again reminded my friend of the hope to be found in my Jesus, but he responded, "It's nice that you can take such comfort in a myth."

When his sobs subsided, I told him, "The currency of your life has been devalued. I know what's happening here is beyond your enduring, but you must go back in there and endure the unendurable. I will go with you and get you through this to the end. We have a job to do here, and we aren't finished." Even as I spoke these words, the cry of my heart was, "O Father, be the glory and the lifter of this man that I love. He does not know how to hold on to you, but please hold on to him until he learns."

What is the state of your soul as you read this? Are you enduring the unendurable? Are you over your head in a foul mess of treachery or shame, falling down with no more hope that you will ever reach bottom or see the surface again?

Christ calls you home to the center, away from the troubled surface. He makes all the difference of sunrise and sunset in His very presence, wherever you are and however deep your circumstance. I have been blessed by this truth in the story of a Chinese pastor who spent eighteen years in prison for his faith. Somehow he emerged from that experience with his faith and health intact.

His job in the camp was extraordinarily difficult and repugnant. The camp authorities assigned him to empty the human-waste cesspool.

The pastor was well-educated, from a wealthy family—and he was a Christian leader. The atheist guards delighted in putting this refined man to work in the human waste cesspool where the other prisoners and guards hated to go. What the authorities did not know was how much the pastor enjoyed the job.

The cesspool was about ten feet wide by ten feet long, filled with human waste collected from the entire camp each day. When the pit was full, the human waste was allowed to "ripen." It was the pastor's job to dig out the waste to send to the fields as fertilizer. The pit was too deep to stand outside and empty it, so the pastor had to walk into the disease-ridden filth and scoop out the successive layers of human waste. The stench was overpowering, and he had to breathe it.

The guards and all the prisoners kept their distance because of the stench. This gave the pastor solitude, which he enjoyed very much. All the prisoners in the camp were under strict surveillance. No one was permitted to be alone. In the cesspool, however, the pastor could be alone and could pray to his Lord as loudly as he wanted. He could sing hymns and recite the Scriptures, including all the psalms he still remembered. There was no one close enough to stop him. He actually enjoyed this time of praise and worship each day.

One of his favorite hymns was "In the Garden." He hadn't understood the real meaning of this hymn before his arrest and confinement. Now, in the worst possible conditions, the hymn brought him fellowship and peace in his Lord's presence.

> I come to the garden alone
> While the dew is still on the roses;
> And the voice I hear falling on my ear,
> The Son of God discloses,
> And he walks with me, and he talks with me,
> And he tells me I am his own,
> And the joy we share as we tarry there
> None other has ever known.

The Lord stood with the pastor in those years. The pastor said, "He never left me or forsook me. And so I survived, and the cesspool became my private garden."[2]

A God who can turn the cesspool of our existence into the garden of our heart is the God we need at the center of our soul. Lawyer that I am, I rest my case for grace.

There is a postscript to the story of my client. A week after the long hearing concluded with his testimony, he sent me a note. I read it through eyes filling with tears:

Dear Kent:

I want to express my gratitude for your attention to me and my case. I know that you would do your professional best for any client, but I also know that I have benefited from your personal solicitude for me. . . . Your attention has meant a lot to me. I think the best way to say what I want to say is to tell you this anecdote. You are in a special position to appreciate it. You understand that I am a humanist, but this anecdote comes to you without any irony at all.

When I finally got to testify to the Committee, I was apprehensive about what the Committee thought about me and my case. My spirits were buoyed when at the end of the testimony the Chairperson said to me something to the effect that soon this nightmare would be behind me. Later in the day, relief replaced apprehension.

When my wife and son and I sat down to our evening meal, I spontaneously said a prayer. This is perhaps the only authentic prayer I have ever said. As I sat in my chair at the dining table, I put my arms on the table alongside the place setting. I involuntarily bowed my head. Silently I said, "Dear God, thank you for my family and my attorney."

My friend took a small, but essential, first step on the pathway to Christ. An honest "thank you" spoken to God is a password to the kingdom. An angel told the prophet Zechariah, " 'Whoever has despised the day of small things shall rejoice.' "[3] Whatever the faint stirring of life and love in your heart right now, do not despise it. It is the seed of new life breaking out of its hard shell on its journey of growth and fruitfulness in the garden of grace.

_____ *Questions for Reflection* _____

1. Can you think of a time when the actions of others seemed to have devalued the worth of your life?
2. Are you struggling in your thoughts and emotions over what someone else thinks about you?
3. What will it take for God's love and approval to be enough for you?

36

Finding Christ in Downtown Pittsburgh

An anxious husband and father, three thousand miles from home,
finds healing and comfort in the body of Christ on a cold, winter day.

I wandered the streets of Pittsburgh alone on President's Day morning, 2003. The biggest blizzard of twenty years blended streets, parks, and sidewalks into white meadows under cliffs of icy building facades. Because it was a holiday, the streets were not plowed.

Only a bit of traffic scuttled across the icy intersections. Offices were closed. I had come to the city the night before on the last flight before the storm shut down the airport.

My thoughts were colder than the air temperature. When I'd called back to California after arriving at the hotel at midnight, Patricia told me our son was dangerously ill. I made another call to arrange for emergency hospital admission. Since then I'd been out of contact with Patricia and Andrew.

I almost hadn't come on this trip to speak to a group of Christian school administrators. Patricia was struggling with a chronic illness. Work was piled up on my desk. Now our happy, active, tennis-playing son was sick to the point his own future was in doubt. I was tramping in snowbound solitude across an abandoned city three thousand miles from home. My heart was crushed with the weight of fear, uselessness, and love that could not be expressed in care.

The department stores were open for President's Day sales, and in two hours and three stores I saw only seven other people including sales staff. I don't know that I've ever felt more alone than I did on that chilled, empty morning.

195

The snow packed and crunched under my feet as I trudged back to the hotel before lunch. I came to a sandwich board sign on the sidewalk across from the steel and glass U.S. Steel Tower on Grant Street. It said, "The Holy Eucharist for Healing, 12:10." I looked around at an impressive, old, brownstone, Neo-Gothic church. It bore another sign, "First Lutheran Church."

I paused and thought of the two people I love most who so needed healing this day. I had never been in a Lutheran church in my life. My religious life has been spent in a denomination that claims roots in the Lutheran Reformation, and I've studied church history. I knew that we share beliefs in the sole authority of Scripture and salvation by grace alone.

But there was that term *eucharist*, a word of Greek origin meaning "gratitude," but not in vogue in my sectarian, plain-spoken, rational Protestant heritage. We use the word *communion* to describe the table of the Lord. I was raised to believe that the bread and wine are a symbol of Christ received by faith. I remembered from somewhere that Lutherans believe Christ is really present in the bread and elements. As for a healing service, my people believe God heals, but we are inclined to ask, "Isn't that why God made physicians and hospitals?" Healing prayer for us in practice is most often the ribbon on the package of traditional health care rather than an act of worship. These thoughts tumbled through my mind.

I needed to get back to the hotel, warm up, and prepare for my presentations. Yet a thought nagged me that a sign for a healing service on an empty street on a day when my family needed healing could not be a mere coincidence. I looked over the sign and the church portico again before starting on my way.

Another call to Patricia told me that Andrew was stabilized. He was being prodded and pricked for tests. She had spent the night beside him in the hospital room. I talked to him, and he sounded scared but brave.

By the time I got off the phone and groomed, it was noon. The conflict about attending the healing service was resolved in my mind in an instant. I pulled on my gloves and big black overcoat so foreign to my southern California sensibilities and gingerly picked my way back down the slick sidewalks to the First Lutheran Church.

Church bells began to intone the service as I approached the steps. The first person I encountered inside was a gray-haired, bearded, bespectacled pastor in a green surplice preparing the sacraments. Another sign said, "The healing service will be in the area of the baptistry today."

I slipped into a pew. The sanctuary was dark with beautiful stained glass windows, but to tell you the truth, the setting was a blur to me.

The effort of focusing on Christ through my daze of care and worry was all my tired, distressed mind could bear. I did make out that there were six men and women sitting around me looking a bit worn and frayed. *They must really want something to come down here through the unplowed streets,* I thought.

The pastor began the liturgy of healing. His homily was drawn from Mark 8:11, 12: "The Pharisees came and began to argue with him, asking him for a sign from heaven, to test him. And he sighed deeply in his spirit and said, 'Why does this generation ask for a sign? Truly I tell you, no sign will be given to this generation.' And he left them, and getting into the boat again, he went across to the other side."

"They were looking for a sign," the pastor said, "for the skies to open and fire to come down, or the earth to open up or something else to dazzle and prove that Jesus was God, and so do we, but we receive no sign of that kind. . . . Perhaps the sign is that in the midst of what we are going through we see Jesus."

Tears welled to my eyes, the spray from hope and distress sloshing around together in my soul. Four of the six ragamuffins in the pews went up to the rail and knelt for healing prayer. I was the last in the line. The pastor prayed, "Holy and blessed Trinity, sustain your servants with your presence; drive away sickness of body or spirit; and give them that victory of life and peace which will enable them to serve you now and evermore."

I begged for the grace of Christ to heal Patricia and Andrew, so far away. I would have to stand in this day by representation as husband and father.

The pastor prayed for each person in turn by name, first anointing them with oil on the forehead. When he reached me, he whispered, "What is your name?"

"Kent," I whispered back.

He laid his hands on my head as my mind sought connection with God and my loved ones.

The pastor waited a long time. His hands were gentle on my head. He prayed for me by name that I would know the healing of Christ for those suffering in the world and in my life.

I returned to my pew. The pastor pronounced a blessing: "May the almighty Lord, a strong tower to all who put their trust in him, to whom all things in heaven, on earth, and under the earth bow and whom they obey, be now and evermore your defense, and make you know and feel that the only name under heaven given for health and salvation is the name of our Lord Jesus Christ.

"The peace of the Lord be with you always," he said.

"And also with you." We greeted each other, "The peace of Christ be with you."

We prayed thanks and praise to the Lord.

I took the bread of communion, the pastor handing it to each one of us in turn.

Three thousand miles from home, in great anguish, snow barring any movement of return, I was powerless to help those I love most. But as we exchanged the peace of Christ with each other, I knew that I was not alone even in gray, slushy downtown Pittsburgh. Comforted with the knowledge that Christ knew and would not forget Patricia and Andrew, I received the postcommunion blessing. "The body and blood of our Lord Jesus Christ strengthen you and keep you in His grace. Amen. Go in peace; serve the Lord."

I returned quickly out into the cold street, but now warmed and relieved inside.

The next two days are a haze. I made phone calls home and to the hospital, gave my talks, hugged an old friend and shared spiritual blessings of God's abiding presence with her, conversed with other old friends, all the while confirmed in the grace of the Lord.

On the flight back I read the bulletin that I had received at the healing service. On the back was this message:

WELCOME! The Lord has entrusted his people at First Lutheran Church with the opportunity for ministry to downtown Pittsburgh. We count it a privilege to serve those who live and work here. In our ministry we strive to be faithful to the Word of Holy Scripture and the historic Confessions of the Lutheran tradition. . . . The Table before us is the Lord's. It is not for Lutherans only but for all who desire to receive Christ. All baptized Christians are welcome to receive their Lord in the bread and the wine of the Eucharist. Those who, for any reason, cannot receive the wine are free to receive the Sacrament under the form of bread alone. In doing so, a believer still receives the whole Christ.

Andrew was diagnosed and stabilized. Patricia's keen mother's eyes and intuition made a huge difference in catching the problem and obtaining medical attention early. The year that followed was one of increased health and stability for both mother and son.

The pastor's admonition was true. We received no dazzling miracle, no signs and wonders of lightning brilliance. But we have recognized Jesus in the midst of our little family, acquainted with our sorrows and afflicted for our sake, and bringing His gifts of love, peace, and hope into our conversations of prayer and His mercies that are renewed every morning. Christ lives with us. The first thing that I do in the morning is talk with Him, and the last thing that Andrew and I do each night is discuss the day's events with Him and go over our plans and concerns for tomorrow to obtain His blessing.

There are men and women of my acquaintance who ask, "Why follow Christ? Why be a Christian? Isn't it enough just to be a good person and do your best?"

These questions will often lead to another question, "If Christ is everything necessary for our salvation and life, why are there different denominations and so much division among His followers?"

Answering for myself, I have stumbled across many sharp and im-passable objects of injury, illness, and insult in this world. I cannot con-clude that things are as they were intended to be. In fear of death and observation of finite resources for our meager survival, we shove and el-bow and climb up the backs of one another like people taking the last elevator down from a burning building. My twenty years of formally educated, leading-citizen, hard-working, family man "best," even taken to its limit, leaves me short of eternity.

I accept that I have a Creator of good intentions and a Savior of grace who took pity on my plight and exchanged His own eternal life for my limited, broken one. Jesus Christ experienced the misery of all of us to the point of breaking and dying Himself in order to lead us to the power and glory of God the Father poured out for us in new life. This was ac-complished in His crucifixion and resurrection and is available to all who accept Christ as their Savior, trusting His gift of eternal life and living day by day in belief that His power at work in us is certain and true.

It all seems pretty abstract at first thought, but I realize freedom in the knowledge that I will live forever with Christ because He loved me enough to come and suffer for me to make it possible. His body, blood, and breath become my own. He frees me from the desperate need to indulge myself now because of my delusion that what I have now is all there is. Knowing I am loved allows me to give up my fight for identity and survival that hurts so many around me. Knowing I am loved gives me courage when others make their own violent grabs for life from me.

I know that my relationship with Christ is love because He offers himself to me with the full choice of acceptance or rejection that is the doorway to true love and does not force His will upon me as a robotic existence. Because the eternal consequence of my choice is both obvious to me and yet beyond my ability to empower, I believe in the God who came for me and stays with me in the form of Jesus Christ to make the choice a living reality. As a scuba instructor lifts a disabled student, sharing air until both break the surface to breathe free, His life becomes my life, His health becomes my health. That is the power, the grace, and the recognition of the communion service.

The fact that the body of Christ is divided by its adherents into specialties of the right or left feet, hands, eyes, or lungs is sad and silly.[1] But there can be no denying that there is only one Heart and one Head.[2] The light shines in our windows at different angles, illuminating different things at various times of the day. In our humanity and the faith heaven grants us for that moment, we may have our favorite times of the day.

> But the path of the righteous is like the light of dawn,
>   which shines brighter and brighter until full day.
> The way of the wicked is like deep darkness;
>   they do not know what they stumble over.[3]

In the full light of day, the gift is revealed as Jesus Christ Himself. Just as we concede to our human limitations when we divide up the Body of Christ into its component parts of our choosing, we sell His glory and love short when we seek the gifts and not the Giver. If we seek Christ only as our "physician," we are looking for an external phenomenon, much like the Pharisees who demanded a sign of proof. If we seek only a "healing," we are asking no more than for God to respond to our need in the limitation of our circumstance. But if we seek Christ, we receive a new and eternal life, and considerations of health are subsumed in the personality of our Healer who is our health. Like Paul, we appeal to Christ for the relief of our afflictions, but He replies, " 'My grace is sufficient for you, for power is made perfect in weakness.' "[4] It does not get better than this.

I entered the First Lutheran Church of Pittsburgh on a Monday noon when the best that humans could do through commerce and technology was paralyzed and made impotent by snow and ice. I was desperate in my absence and distance from those I loved and powerless to change their circumstances of pain and need. Yet, even in that frozen hell, a little fellowship gathered in the belief that Christ is present in liberating grace wherever even two or three of us gather in His name.[5] We believed that "God gave us eternal life, and this life is in his Son. Whoever has the Son has life; whoever does not have the Son of God does not have life."[6]

The mere fact that the church cleared the snow off its steps and faithfully placed its sign "Holy Eucharist for Healing, 12:10" proclaims the life that is in Christ. The gathering of the fellowship in spite of the storm and the inclusion of an attorney from California of troubled mind and spirit gives witness to the power of that life. The comfort and peace that I received from Christ in Communion with Him and His children in that place and the thankfulness with which I departed that Communion testify to the truth of His life.

I continue to live secure in the knowledge that was refreshed that day. The journey home is long and difficult and disillusioning. But along the way, God loves us and prepares a table for us in the presence of our enemies of doubt and fear. His faithfulness is the surest sign of a future and a hope. The apostle John described this liberating knowledge in his first letter to the churches:

> The God-begotten are also the God-protected. The Evil One can't lay a hand on them. We know that we are held firm by God; it's only the people of the world who continue in the grip of the Evil One. And we know that the Son of God came so we could recognize and understand the truth of God—what a gift!—and we are living in the Truth itself, in God's Son, Jesus Christ. This Jesus is both True God and Real Life. Dear Children, be on guard against all clever facsimiles.[7]

I keep moving in this knowledge that I am free to live and love because Christ gives me His love and His life to prove it. Patricia and Andrew live on in the same knowledge. Possessing Christ and being possessed by Christ is our true health for eternity.

Questions for Reflection

1. Think of a time when a loved one was in need of help and you were powerless to respond. What did this experience mean for your prayer life?
2. When have you experienced the Lord preparing a table for you in the presence of your enemies of doubt and fear?
3. What strength do you receive from enjoying the sacrament of Communion with your brothers and sisters in Christ?

37

Sparrow Economics

101

A work-day conversation in a busy office leads to the shining truth that Jesus Christ writes off no one.

I visited a client's office late on a hot Wednesday afternoon. I announced myself to the administrative assistant and sat down on a chair opposite her desk. She is a lovely woman, always immaculately dressed, gracious and helpful without fail, and shrewd in dealing with the demanding clientele of her employers to whom she is invaluable and their number-one public-relations asset. She loves Christ and has shown me a thing or two over the years about following Him.

The counter in front of her desk always has a brightly colored can collecting donations for the causes like children's health or breast cancer research that are her passion. I looked at the can and then glanced at the photographs and decorations around her desk. There was a round piece of white paper with blue circular printing around the rim, accented with musical notes. It said, "I Sing Because I'm Happy."

The song rolled up out of my heart.

> Why should I feel discouraged,
> Why should the shadows come,
> Why should my heart be lonely,
> And long for heaven and home,
> When Jesus is my portion?
> My constant friend is He:
> His eye is on the sparrow,

And I know He watches me;
His eye is on the sparrow,
And I know He watches me.
I sing because I'm happy,
I sing because I'm free,
For His eye is on the sparrow,
And I know He watches me.[1]

"I sing because I'm happy," I said out loud, quoting the lyric of the chorus. "I sing because I'm free, for His eye is on the sparrow, and I know He watches me."

She said the last line of the chorus with me. "That was my mother's favorite song."

"I love it too," I told her. "When I was a kid, our family watched the Billy Graham crusades on TV. Ethel Waters would always sing it, and my Dad loved to hear it. He would smile and say, 'Listen,' when she was announced, and we would sit still and hear her sing that song like she was telling a story."

"There you go." She smiled.

"You know there's a wonderful thing in the Gospels about the point of the song," I told her. "It's economics according to Jesus. Hold on," I said, "let me show you." I pulled my dog-eared NIV New Testament out of the inner pocket of my coat.

Then I realized I'd spoken too soon. I didn't know exactly where the texts appeared. "I think what I'm looking for is in Matthew and Luke. Just go on with what you're doing, and I'll let you know when I've found it."

"OK."

I thumbed through and found the texts.

"Here's what I wanted. Listen closely. Think about the math in what Jesus said about the price of sparrows."

"First, I'll read Matthew chapter ten, verses twenty-nine and thirty. ' "Are not two sparrows sold for a penny? Yet not one of them will fall to the ground apart from the will of your Father. And even the very hairs of your head are all numbered. So don't be afraid; you are worth more than many sparrows." '

"The market price of sparrows sold as pets in the marketplace was two sparrows for a penny.

"Now listen to Luke chapter twelve, verses six and seven. ' "Are not five sparrows sold for two pennies? Yet not one of them is forgotten by

God. Indeed, the very hairs of your head are all numbered. Don't be afraid; you are worth more than many sparrows." ' "

She looked at me quizzically. I explained my point.

"In Matthew's account, Jesus said sparrows were sold two for a penny. In Luke's account, the price was the same but with a volume discount. If one bought four sparrows for two pennies an extra sparrow was thrown into the deal. The extra sparrow wasn't even valued by its owner at a half-penny. Its price was written down, and it was thrown in as a 'loss leader' to seal the deal the same way Wal-Mart will throw in a third pair of socks if you buy two pair.

"Imagine the advertisement: 'Buy four sparrows and get one free.' A child pulls at the sleeve of her mom, 'We get a free sparrow if we buy two pair.'

" 'Quiet!' her mom would say. 'We'd have to buy a cage, and who is going to feed and clean up after them! Besides, that's the way they get rid of sick or hurt birds—by palming them off on us!'

"The value of every one of us is written down, or written off, sometime in our life. Someone we hope will love us may end up heavily discounting us and trading us off. It's a hard thing to be the fifth sparrow in a four-sparrow transaction."

She nodded at this thought. I suspect she knows the painful reality of what I was telling her.

"But Jesus said, 'That's not how God looks at it.' He says, 'God watches every sparrow, including ones that humans count as having no value. He sees their flights and their falls. Not one of them is written off or discounted in His sight. It is the same way with His children. He doesn't discount or count any one of us as worthless or trade-bait for a better deal. He loves each one of us. He numbers the hairs of our heads and writes our names in the palms of His hand because He delights in us and values each one of us the same. He saves us regardless of how worthless we see ourselves or we see each other.' "

As I spoke, I watched her face. She cupped her chin in her hand and sat still and silent while I could see the lights and shadows of thought flow through her beautiful dark eyes.

What is she thinking? I wondered. *Is she doing the calculation to check my math? Have I presumed too much in telling her this on a workday afternoon at her desk?*

"It is very interesting that you are telling me this," she finally said. "My mother used to tell us this when I was a little girl. She told us this in her own way without the benefit of much education. I didn't really get it then, but there was something there. She said how God thinks about the sparrows is how He thinks about us, and He sees every one of us the same way.

"Now, I see it from what you just told me. Thank you."

"It is great, isn't it?" I said.

I stood up then and went in to see the executive whom I had come to see. The conversation has stayed with me though.

It's not a big, dramatic story. It was just a five-minute exchange between two busy people on a Wednesday afternoon, but it carries the most important point of all.

I am writing about this because I think you need to hear exactly what God thinks about you and what Jesus Christ did for you in that thought. He loves you so much that He hoed the tough row of human existence Himself to identify with every ache and pain you suffer, with your lousy choices, mistakes, and shame. He loves you so much that He would rather have died than to live without you. Regardless of how anyone else has discounted you as worthless, He offers you eternal life with the same power that separated light from darkness at the creation of the world.[2]

The song has more verses.

"Let not your heart be troubled,"
His tender word I hear,
And resting on His goodness,
I lose my doubts and fears;
Tho' by the path He leadeth,
But one step I may see:
His eye is on the sparrow,
And I know He watches me;
His eye is on the sparrow,
And I know he watches me.

Whenever I am tempted,
Whenever clouds arise.
When song gives place to sighing,
When hope within me dies,
I draw the closer to Him,
From care He sets me free:
His eye is on the sparrow,
And I know He cares for me;

His eye is on the sparrow,
And I know He cares for me.
I sing because I'm happy,
I sing because I'm free,
For His eye is on the sparrow,
And I know He watches me.

Jesus touched lepers, spoke peace to the angry and violent, conversed with the morally disreputable, welcomed persons of different backgrounds and culture, invited the scruffy to dinner, forgave the shamed, and calmed the overbusy. He asked for nothing in return except acceptance of His love as the compelling power of their lives. The economics of the kingdom of God are the economics of grace—and in grace there are no write-offs for damaged goods. There is only Christ's unconditional offer to exchange your brokenness for His wholeness in the perfection of His love.

Even if no human can be found to come to your defense and extend you this grace—if your ex-spouse says, "I don't love you anymore," your parents announce, "You're a disgrace unworthy of our time and attention," your congregation deems you a moral leper and denies you fellowship, your boss tells you, "I can get lots of sparrows at a half-penny a piece and you have no value to me"—remember that your Father in heaven says, "Your fall has not escaped my notice. I know every detail of your fallen condition, and I love you still. Why, if you were the only sparrow out there, I would come for you! My grace is sufficient for you. Trust your broken wing to me for healing."

Is this too much to believe? Hardly! It's the first and last lesson of basic sparrow economics.

Questions for Reflection

1. When have you felt like a "write-off" sparrow?
2. What does it mean for your prayer life that Jesus became human to experience everything that you experience?
3. What lesson of "sparrow economics" can you take away from this story for your own life?

38

The Fullness of Peace

The moon illuminates prayer as a love story.

NOT for me is the love that knows no restraint but like the foaming wine that having burst its vessel in a moment would run to waste.

Send me the love that is cool and pure like your rain that blesses the thirsty earth and fills the homely earthen jars.

Send me the love that would soak down into the centre of being, and from there would spread like the unseen sap through the branching tree of life, giving birth to fruits and flowers.

Send me the love that keeps the heart still with the fulness of peace.[1]

This past work week began for me with an emergency call on Sunday afternoon regarding a medical-ethics issue in the care of a dying woman. The week steadily became more complicated and difficult from that point.

By Monday, I was well into a detailed reply to a long, hair-splitting, tedious, unrealistic response by a party to my client's offer of a contract. When I am frustrated, I have a tendency to unconsciously rub the top of my ears. By Monday evening, I had blisters on my right ear.

The rest of the week was filled with meetings. This aggravated my frustration because committee meetings are the pernicious anemia of organizational life. In corporate culture, the famous maxim of René Descartes, "I think, therefore I am," degenerates into "We meet, therefore our existence is confirmed." Over time, critical thought dissipates as to whether most standing meetings have any worthwhile point. Meetings creep onto the calendar and cling there tenaciously, where they suck the life out of the work day.

On Tuesday evening, an executive called me with an urgent request for overnight legal help in an intense battle with a competitor of my client. I vigorously resisted the request at first but ended up researching and writing an opinion letter until 2:30 A.M.

The late night made me a bit growlly for my Wednesday appointments, but I was enlivened by the sharp repartee and laughter of my closest colleagues as we planned a contracts seminar for corporate managers. There were more meetings about possible errors in a client's accounts and how to correct them.

The best part of the week came Thursday afternoon, when I got to speak to the fund-raising team of the medical center about their life and work as prayer in carrying out the healing ministry of Christ in that place. But my pile of contracts, correspondence, and document requests had grown so large by Thursday evening that I had to stop to review them, list them single-spaced on two full pages of a legal pad, and set priorities for follow-up. I also had to read and think about e-mail messages making complaints, asking advice, and scheduling yet more meetings.

Friday morning brought unexpected management challenges at the law firm, conference calls, a wearying presentation for two hours to over two hundred employees on sexual harassment awareness and prevention, followed by a meeting with the physician leaders of a hospital medical staff. During that meeting, I received five urgent pages of phone calls that I needed to return, and I ended the afternoon with a session with three executives to receive a status report on the battle of a client against a competitor to win the hearts and minds of the local community.

The twenty-five miles of crowded freeway required tense maneuvering on my way home. When I arrived in our driveway, I was talking on the cell phone with a friend and colleague about the events of the past week and what was ahead for the next. We shared laughter and mutual encouragement. I wandered around the backyard while I finished the conversation. Maggie, our cat, was glad to see me out there and came over for the obligatory scratching of her ears. She rubbed against my legs, stretched, and purred with pleasure.

The thick thatch of the St. Augustine grass under my feet was soft and soothing. The tangerine tree I planted twenty years ago caught my eye just as I said "Good-bye" and clicked off the cell phone conversation. The leaves were dark and gleaming in the windless summer evening, but the surprising thing was the large size of the rough green globes of fruit hanging all over the tree. The fruit is coming on early for some reason. Last season, the tree yielded little fruit, and we were disappointed. What I saw Friday evening was a stage of growth that usually doesn't occur until late September.

Seeing the tree coming on strong through the heat of August spoke to my heart with a message of life and love in an unexpected time and place. I stood there in the backyard as the setting sun gently spread a silken cloth of twilight on the living altar before me. I thought of the one-line poem by Tagore, "Be still, my heart, these great trees are prayers."[2] Our tangerine tree is not as great in size as the forest giants of India that Tagore was viewing, but its rich verdure is no less a prayer of intercession to the Creator God speaking grace for the replenishment of my depleted soul.

After sundown, Patricia and I took our nightly walk. Our direction starts out west and follows a circular route. On our turn east, we walked toward the startling bright yellow glow of the moon rising over the rooftops and pines of the neighborhood.

From the beginning of human history, time has been measured by the phases of the moon. The moon marks off the seasons.[3] The Old English root of our word *moon* means "to measure time." In ancient Native American cultures, the August moon was the "green corn moon," representing the time when the first green ears of corn formed on the stalks. The Cherokees called it the "fruit moon" because tree fruits and berries ripened in August in their homeland of the Smoky Mountains.

The appearance of the tangerines and the rising moon brought a renewing sense of God's presence to me. A question from Solomon's Song of Songs rose from my soul,

Who is this that appears like the dawn,
    fair as the moon, bright as the sun,
    majestic as the stars in procession?[4]

The moon speaks of the permanence of God over a world destined for impermanence. Ethan the Ezrahite wrote of the moon as a metaphor for God's enduring covenant to His people even if our fickleness and sin incur His correcting hand. "It shall be established forever like the moon, / an enduring witness in the skies."[5]

Why am I telling you all this? Certainly not because I think my schedule is special or unique from yours. Major malls feature stores selling lines of time management products, technology flourishes for faster communication (meaning we do more work with the saved time), and the price of real estate means workers commute farther in more dense congestion than ever before. Our eyes are glued to the artificial light of the computer monitor. We are missing the moon and its testimony.

I believe that you can identify with what I am saying. The tide of our endeavors is sweeping us all in its desperate urgency. Who can doubt that we live in the time of the end prophesied by Daniel when "many shall be running back and forth, and knowledge shall increase."[6] The "many" aren't some other people toward whom we can point in judgment. The many are us, and we are inexorably running out of time and resources. We are facing the growing darkness that results from increasing competition for the transient and finite things of our fading material world. This competition is the distracting reality of my daily life and yours.

Henry Wadsworth Longfellow wrote the truth about the moon's commentary on our existence here: "Nothing that is can pause or stay; / The moon will wax, the moon will wane."[7]

We need the story God tells us by the moon. "God made the two great lights—the greater light to rule the day and the lesser light to rule the night—and the stars. God set them in the dome of the sky to give light upon the earth, to rule over the day and over the night, and to separate the light from the darkness. And God saw that it was good."[8] We need the moon to tell us, through contemplation of its reflected light, of the "true light, which enlightens everyone,"[9] Jesus Christ, whose sovereign grace covers us and whose intention toward us is saving love. "What has come into being in him was life, and the life was the light of all people. The light shines in the darkness, and the darkness did not overcome it."[10]

At the end of another week of frenetic endeavor to pound the square peg of legal principle into the round hole of human compliance, I needed the graceful witness of the flourishing tangerine tree to point me toward the Savior who is coming to take me home. Jesus said of the time of the end when Christ would return for His loved and His own, " 'From the fig tree learn its lesson: as soon as its branch becomes tender and puts forth its leaves, you know that summer is near. So also, when you see these things taking place, you know that he is near, at the very gates.' "[11]

In the summer twilight, as I see the green tenderness of the tangerine and the faithfulness of the rising moon, I sense the closeness of Abba and Jesus Christ whom He sent to forgive our sins. He will come a second time, "not to deal with sin, but to save those who are eagerly waiting for him."[12]

How long has it been since you "eagerly waited" for the One who loves you best and most? What are you seeing in these summer days and nights, and what is it telling you?

There's a love story out there for you in the sun and the moon and the green foliage, found not just in themselves but also in their Source. "Long ago God spoke to our ancestors in many and various ways by the prophets, but in these last days he has spoken to us by a Son, whom he appointed heir of all things, through whom he also created the worlds. He is the reflection of God's glory and the exact imprint of God's very being, and he sustains all things by his powerful word."[13]

My parents taught me the following words as a love song when I was a little boy. I have sung them at twilight on three continents. I believe them to express the deepest longing of your heart and mine despite whatever else we have allowed in there. The green corn moon brought them back to my mind. Pray them through with me now.

> Day is dying in the west;
> Heaven is touching earth with rest;
> Wait and worship while the night
> Sets her evening lamps a-light
> Through all the sky.
>
> Holy, holy, holy, Lord God of hosts!
> Heaven and earth are full of Thee;
> Heaven and earth are praising Thee,
> O Lord most high!
>
> Lord of life, beneath the dome
> Of the Universe, Thy home,
> Gather us who seek Thy face
> To the fold of Thy embrace,
> For Thou art nigh.
>
> Holy, holy, holy, Lord God of hosts!
> Heaven and earth are full of Thee;

Heaven and earth are praising Thee,
O Lord most high!

While the deepening shadows fall,
Heart of love, enfolding all,
Thro' the glory and the grace
Of the stars that veil Thy face,
Our hearts ascend.

Holy, holy, holy, Lord God of hosts!
Heaven and earth are full of Thee;
Heaven and earth are praising Thee,
O Lord most high!

When forever from our sight
Pass the stars, the day, the night,
Lord of angels, on our eyes
Let eternal morning rise,
And shadows end.

Holy, holy, holy, Lord God of hosts!
Heaven and earth are full of Thee;
Heaven and earth are praising Thee,
O Lord most high.[14]

Questions for Reflection

1. What frustrations and tensions exist in your heart right now?
2. How do the moon and the sun remind you of the faithfulness of God?
3. What hymn brings you peace and comfort? Think through its words right now, or sing it out loud.

39

Hacking Our Way Through the Jungle From Prayer to Praise (Psalm 3, Part 1)

David's prayer when he fled Jerusalem during his son Absalom's rebellion gives us tools to break out of the turmoil and entanglements of relationships gone wrong.

The contract I am reviewing stinks. It places all the risks of the transaction and liability to third parties on my client and all the control of product and service delivery with the other party. The transactional benefits are illusory, but the responsible officer of my client insists that the salesman is a "good friend of mine" and the contract offers a great deal that will be lost unless the agreement is signed by tomorrow. I can't seem to convince him that tomorrow is by coincidence the end of the calendar quarter for which the salesman's performance bonus will be calculated, which is the reason for the "deadline." The salesman and his employer are in the business of selling. They won't stop selling if their artificial deadline isn't met by a buyer.

Then, there is lack of compliance with regulatory performance of a corporate client's contract with the government. I have advised that repayment and fines and penalties may result if the situation isn't "cleaned up" immediately, but with a smile the client's CEO tells me, "They'll have to catch us first, and then we'll worry about it." I will have to talk to the board of directors about this, pitting me directly against management.

A long-time client, a citrus grower, has been approached by a real estate developer who says, "I can develop your property for you into a housing tract and shopping center and make us both a lot of money. You put your land into a partnership with me. We'll use it to secure a loan. With my expertise in these kinds of deals, I'll use the loan proceeds to plan the development and build it out, and we will split the profits."

213

The grower is tired of low prices for fruit and high prices for water. He is dazzled by the thought of turning his land into productive assets so he can retire. I am trying to get through to him that the developer has no money in the deal and is going to leverage everything by putting my client's land at risk. The developer is telling my client, "Your attorney really doesn't have the experience to do the workout of a deal this large and sophisticated."

My desk is covered with the back-up for memos to be drafted and pink phone-message slips asking, "Where is that document I asked you to prepare?"

My son is discouraged over a misunderstanding with a teacher who I think is just plain arbitrary and insensitive. But I haven't been much different with my wife and my co-workers this week. My arthritic knee hurts, and there is surgery in my future.

I'm not telling you this to depress you. Welcome to what a business attorney brings into prayer with him. I've cited a few examples here. You probably dwell in a different context but with similar issues.

Many days, I seek to quiet my heart before God and offer up praise and thanks—but the issues, conflicts, disputes, fears, and criticisms boil up angry and inflamed in the midst of my prayer and carry my thoughts to to-do items, counterarguments, vengeance, and regrets.

Paul says to pray about everything,[1] and I wonder, *How can I pray with this much clutter and angst in my soul? How can I worship in the midst of turmoil?*

Some books about prayer recommend keeping a pad and pen next to you as you pray and writing down your concerns and what to do about them as they come to mind—and then returning to prayer. I find that to be obsession or brainstorming, not faithful prayer. The suggestion makes me feel more like saying, " 'Take these things out of here! Stop making my Father's house a marketplace!' "[2] rather than, "The LORD is in his holy temple; / let all the earth keep silence before him,"[3] which is the place and attitude of worship that I long for my own heart to become.

Surely David must have known such dilemmas when Absalom's rebellion forced him to flee Jerusalem. His own past sins, dysfunction and sins in his own family, the loss of his people's confidence in his rule, the embarrassing need to flee his own capital, betrayal by trusted advisers, and insults from old opponents would have occupied his thoughts and his prayers. I take counsel and heart from a prayer that David wrote down in those stressful times. It is Psalm 3.

> O LORD, how many are my foes!
>   Many are rising against me;
> many are saying to me,
>   "There is no help for you in God."[4]

You may be thinking, "I don't know where this is going, but I get along with people. My life is peaceful. I don't fight a battle every day." That may indeed be true. I am a lawyer and always work in combat, to some extent, so our experiences may differ. But if you think this way, I have to ask you, "How long have you been a hermit?"

The existentialist philosopher Sartre observed that "hell is people." I don't agree with Sartre on much, but you and I would have to concede that our greatest disappointments rise out of our relationships.

David was confronted with the attacks of real enemies and failed relationships that had him reeling. He had plenty to think about as well. Aren't the thoughts, doubts, weaknesses, and regrets that swirl through your prayers and quiet times "rising foes" that distract your focus and undermine your peace of mind?

> But you, O LORD, are a shield around me,
>   my glory, and the one who lifts up my head.
> I cry aloud to the LORD,
>   and he answers me from his holy hill.[5]

One of my favorite praise choruses draws its lyric from these verses. There are times when our prayers just drive us deeper into despair and upset. We want to be comforted in our hurt and vindicated in our causes, we seek agreement rather than resolution, and we aggravate the wounds and distress in our prayers. It is so important in those times to leave prayer that seeks our benefit and begin praising God for all of His glory and attributes. The armies of ancient Israel would go to battle led by choirs singing the praises of Yahweh. Such praise puts the source of our strength into focus and brings God to life in our circumstances.

Prayer puts us in the thick of battle, but praise announces the victory. At times our wounds are too deep and our burdens too heavy for us to pray. We may be disoriented, entangled in thoughts and feelings and laboring hard to break loose, or paralyzed not knowing what to do. Conventional Christian teaching is to pray harder at such times. After the burden is lifted and we are set free, then we can praise. But are we free in Christ or not? If we are, then we should praise our Savior for what He has accomplished even before the burden is lifted and the clouds have cleared.

Paul and Barnabas were unjustly arrested, beaten, and imprisoned in chains in the maximum security cell of the Philippian jail.[6] Philippi had a lot of springs and ground water. Its Roman underground jail was certain to be a dark, dank, gloomy place. Paul and Barnabas were in no place and no condition to want to sing praises. Praise, however, derives its very character from suffering and hopelessness. Praise is a sacrifice of our darkest thoughts and strongest feelings that rise in reaction to our circumstances and disappointments. Praise is a confession of faith that our God is greater than our circumstances. The Letter to the Hebrews states the point: "Jesus also suffered outside the city gate in order to sanctify the people by his blood. Let us then go to him outside the camp and bear the abuse he endured. . . . Through him, then, let us continually offer a sacrifice of praise to God, that is, the fruit of lips that confess his name."[7]

At midnight, as Paul and Silas were praying and praising God in song, an earthquake shook the prison off of its foundations, the cell doors were opened, and their chains were broken. Their fortunes turned, and their jailer and his entire household were saved in Christ out of the apostles' triumphant praise in the darkest hour.

The great Chinese Christian teacher and victim of persecution, Watchman Nee, explained this principle:

> Why is praise also triumph? Because when you pray, you are yet in the environment; but when you praise, you have risen above the environment. Whenever you are praying and pleading, you are involved in the thing that you ask for. The more you plead, the more you are bound by that thing, for it is before you all the time. But if you are brought by God beyond the prison, beyond the stocks, beyond the shame and suffering, then you are able to raise your voice and sing praise to the name of God.
>
> What prayer may fail to accomplish, praise can. This is a basic principle to be remembered. If you cannot pray, why not praise? The Lord has not only given us prayer but also praise that through it we may claim the victory. "But thanks be to God, who always leads in triumph in Christ."[8] Whenever your spirit is pressed beyond measure so that you can hardly breathe, let alone pray, why do you not try to praise God? Pray when you are able to pray; but praise when you cannot pray.[9]

The surpassing value of praise in bringing us out of our doldrums is underscored by the opening of Psalm 22.

My God, my God, why have you forsaken me?
> Why are you so far from
>> helping me, from the
>> words of my groaning?

O my God, I cry by day, but you do not answer;
> and by night, but find no rest.

Yet you are holy,
> enthroned on the praises of Israel.

In you our ancestors trusted;
> they trusted, and you delivered them.

To you they cried, and were saved;
> in you they trusted, and were
>> not put to shame.[10]

Another psalm pronounces the restorative power of praise:

Happy are those who live in your house,
> ever singing your praise.

Happy are those whose strength is in you,
> in whose heart are the highways to Zion.

As they go through the valley of Baca [weeping]
> they make it a place of springs;
> the early rain also covers it with pools.

They go from strength to strength;
> the God of gods will be seen in Zion.[11]

Praise is counterintuitive to human nature. We may be angry, shamed, and in pain, but praise refocuses us on our Helper and away from our plight. Salvation lies in the difference. A conscious submission to God's gracious will beyond our circumstances and a profound expressed gratitude for His love is required for the saving transformation of praise to occur.

____ *Questions for Reflection* ____

1. When has praying made your heart heavier rather than lighter?
2. How are praise and prayer connected?
3. Why does praising God help relieve your burdens?

40

Praying Yourself to Sleep
(Psalm 3, Part 2)

David found that the way to rest in the midst of threats and conflict
was to surrender his heart to God in prayer.

David was in retreat from the havoc caused by the rebellion of his son, Absalom. Yet he found calm and strength in spite of heartbreak and violence. He described this peace in the midst of ordeal in Psalm 3:

> I lie down and sleep;
>   I wake again, for the LORD sustains me.
> I am not afraid of ten thousands of people
>   who have set themselves against me all around.[1]

David was a fighter, often on the run during his early adulthood. He was on the run again late in life when he wrote these words. Lying down to sleep is both a luxury and a vulnerability for a combatant. Henri Nouwen wrote, "When the soldier sits down to eat he lays down his weapons because eating means peace and rest. When he stretches out his body to sleep he is more vulnerable than ever. Table and bed are the two places of intimacy where love can manifest itself in weakness."[2]

At times our agitated spirits refuse rest in the delusion that we can force the change of hearts and minds through our increased efforts. When my son, Andrew, was a toddler, the more he tired, the more he tried to do in a frenzy of action. We sometimes could do no more than watch him turn in circles in the living room until he collapsed in exhausted sleep.

Other times we will awaken in the night with grinding teeth, clenched fists, tears, and sinking hearts because of a powerful wrong that we have done or that has been done to us or because of our fear that we have not done enough. We may find the same toxicity seeping into our prayers.

Lying down and sleeping is putting down the weapons of our defensiveness and surrendering our cares to rest in the trust that tomorrow will be another day and the Lord will see us through no matter who or what we may encounter. Coming to quiet and calm in prayer requires the same surrender.

Spiritual advice from Archbishop Francois Fenelon to one who sought his counsel is instructive about this submission to God in our prayer.

> I have noticed a tendency in you to talk about problems rather than abandoning yourself to God and leaving them with Him. And you will be better off both physically and spiritually when you quietly place everything in God's hands.

> As the saying goes, "Let the water flow beneath the bridge." You can't change men from being men. People will always be weak, vain, unreliable, unfair, hypocritical and arrogant. The world will always be worldly. And you cannot change it. People will follow their own inclinations and habits. And since you cannot recast their personalities, the best course of action is to let them be what they are and bear with them. Do not allow yourself to be troubled and perplexed when you see people being unreasonable and unjust. Rest in peace in the bosom of God. He sees it all more clearly than you do, and yet He permits it. So be content to do whatever you feel you should, quietly and gently and don't worry about anything else.[3]

Not infrequently this submission to God takes enduring hand-to-hand combat between His spirit and our flesh to give up what we would rather thrash and subdue ourselves. Annie Lamott says, "Most things that I hand over to God have my claw marks on them."

> Rise up, O LORD!
>   Deliver me, O my God!
> For you strike all my enemies on the cheek;
>   you break the teeth of the wicked.[4]

We want out of the messes and conflict that we find ourselves in; we may not know how to get out, but we want out. "Rise up, O LORD! /

Deliver me, O my God!" is a complete prayer in and of itself. In His Sermon on the Mount, Jesus said, " 'When you are praying, do not heap up empty phrases as the Gentiles do; for they think that they will be heard because of their many words. Do not be like them, for your Father knows what you need before you ask him.' "[5]

"Forgive. . . .
". . . Do not worry. . . . Strive first for the kingdom of God and his righteousness, and all these things will be given to you as well. . . .
"Do not judge. . . . First take the log out of your own eye, and then you will see clearly to take the speck out of your neighbor's eye. . . .
"Ask, and it will be given you; search, and you will find; knock and the door will be opened for you."[6]

Nothing packs a punch with God like a short, honest prayer. He doesn't sponsor speech contests or talk shows.

Are you struggling with insults and fear of further wounds by enemies? God knows what you're feeling and thinking. " 'The insults of those who insult you have fallen on me,' " He says.[7] He can take care of the cheek slapping and defanging of those whose words and actions threaten to poison or devour us. More often than not, I find He accomplishes this by transforming my spirit from aggression and pride to a thankful acceptance that depends on His presence rather than my own planning and calculation. "Do not worry about anything, but in everything by prayer and supplication with thanksgiving let your requests be made known to God. And the peace of God, which surpasses all understanding, will guard your hearts and minds in Christ Jesus."[8]

Deliverance belongs to the LORD;
    may your blessing be on your people![9]

David wrestled through his own doubts and concerns, concluding that neither he nor anyone else could save the people he loved or himself from the devastation facing them. His own sovereignty and strength as a ruler, a father, and a man had obvious and finite limits. Even he, "a man after God's own heart," knew military, political, and relationship failures and moral lapses with shameful consequences. Neither his capabilities nor his devotion could deliver him. The authority and power for deliverance belongs to his

God, Yahweh, who once delivered his ancestors from captivity and repeatedly delivered them from the consequences of their own selfish choices because it is the very nature of God, manifest to us in Christ, to save.

We easily forget who saves us from our sins and redeems our fallen nature, but we live badly when we forget Him. Evil is the realm in which humanity attempts life without God. Our own knowledge of good and evil is no substitute for the power of God. Even our best efforts are evil without God. "No one is good but God alone," Jesus told the rich ruler who was seeking a formula of self-effort to secure eternal life. Jesus went on to explain that no matter what good the powerful man did, no matter how obedient he was to virtue and to Scripture, and regardless of how much wealth he possessed or controlled, he was always going to lack what it takes for salvation. " 'Then who can be saved?' " was the question of the shocked onlookers. Jesus told them, " 'What is impossible for mortals is possible for God.' "[10]

Frank Sinatra crooned, "I did it my way," and Frank Sinatra is dead. Our way is always going to be terminal. Deliverance belongs to God, who lavishly provides it to us in the life of His Son, Jesus Christ, not only for eternity, but for making it through what we are suffering here and now. " 'God so loved the world that he gave his only Son, so that everyone who believes in him may not perish but have eternal life.' "[11]

Wretched man that I am! Who can rescue me from this body of death? Thanks be to God through Christ Jesus our Lord! . . .

There is therefore now no condemnation for those who are in Christ Jesus. For the law of the Spirit of life in Christ Jesus has set you free from the law of sin and of death.[12]

We are aggrieved. Our wounds are real, our fears not unfounded, and our judgments are not formed without reason. But if we really could do something on our own to bring about lasting healing and peace and to live together in community without conflict, why has this not happened? Why are our happiness and security no more permanent than the next criticism or loss we receive? Why aren't there more happy and satisfied people on this earth? Why is the battle so desperate along the line between the "haves" and the "have nots"? Why do we not feel in control of everything and everyone who concerns us? Why do we keep trying the same things for the same reasons, expecting different results?

David concluded Psalm 3 with a request to God, "May your blessing be on your people." It was humbling for a king to recognize that his power to protect and help was transitory and weak. It is acutely painful for any parent to realize that the rebelliousness and actions of a child are causing so much destruction and dislocation in the lives of others and that even one's own household isn't safe. We are tempted to seethe and criticize and destroy in such moments, to eliminate whoever troubles us and confronts us with the awful facts of our own broken humanity and mistakes.

Paul Stevens's little story brings home the truth that instead of being upset by the inadequacies and failures of others and myself, I should regard them as a gift of discerning grace that should drive me to my knees in prayer.

> One of the most formative experiences in my wife's spiritual pilgrimage happened on a Pioneer Camp canoe trip as a teenager. Two of the girls were criticizing a third. But the counselor, a spiritually sensitive woman, said, "Have you considered that God has given us a spirit of discernment not to criticize but to pray?" Touché. Priests are people who progressively relinquish their tendency to assassinate the character of others verbally—either directly or indirectly in their absence—in order to touch God on their behalf through prayer. Priesthood, we have recognized, is both touching people and places for God, and touching God on behalf of people and places. Intercession is one of the deepest ministries of the Christian priest.[13]

We can read Psalm 3 through from beginning to end and watch David's mind change from outraged anxiety over the number and vileness of the attacks besetting him to a trust that God is the answer regardless of the specifics. The transformation continues into a restful vulnerability in that truth and a desire that God answer with a blessing rather than a curse. I have to go to the same well of prayer as David did almost every day. I know for a fact that this transformation of Spirit over flesh through prayer to the One who can really do something in me, if not around me, is possible because He loves me. He loves you, too, and that's why I am writing this to you.

Questions for Reflection

1. How can physical rest contribute to your prayer life?
2. Is quality or quantity more important in prayer? Why?
3. What is the power of prayer in dealing with insults and hurt feelings?

41

Owning an Ox Means a Messy Barn

A life well lived as our Creator intended involves risk and mess.

When I was in grade school, my Dad used to take me on Sundays to the houses he was building. He gave me a push broom and a dust pan and had me sweep out the house and clean up all the sawdust, blocks, chunks of sheet rock, bent nails, lead junction box plugs, and other debris that accumulates in a construction site. I hated the splinters from the 2" x 4" blocks. I hated the way the dust ground against the subflooring under the broom and the sawdust dribbled off the dust pan. Dad would pay me five dollars for doing this chore.

I rebelled one morning when I was in the sixth grade. "I don't want to do this. I hate it," I told Dad. He fixed me with his deep-set blue eyes and said, "Your grandfather hated doing this, I hated it, and now you hate it. But it has to be done—and you do it."

That was that. I swept when he told me to sweep and never complained about it again. My Dad never asked anyone to do anything unreasonable, but he never argued either. His punishment was swift, corporal, point-making, and fair.

I learned several things in my work with Dad that later graduated to helping him on the job in the summers. Reliable things that I take for granted, such as walls, a floor, and a roof, require hard and careful work. Making a mess is a necessary part of building. Cleaning up the mess is a necessary part of building. The most necessary work is often the toughest and most tedious, and there is no way around it.

It is strange but true: I think about sweeping out the houses when I have

223

to draft or revise corporate bylaws. I have to do that task frequently, and the novelty wore off a long time ago. I am a business lawyer, and drafting corporate bylaws is a basic part of my job. They are full of stiff, stuffy language, but when done well, they tell the boards and officers of my clients exactly what they need to do and when to do it to keep faithful to the corporate mission. Employees are sheltered and flourish, and customers are served under the structure of those bylaws. Drafting bylaws is tough and tedious but absolutely necessary to the survival and function of organizations and their institutions. That is that. I draft when they ask me to draft.

The sweeping lessons came to my mind this week when I was reading Proverbs 14. Verse 4 has this bit of wisdom from Solomon: "Where there are no oxen, the manger is clean, / but from the strength of an ox comes an abundant harvest" (NIV). This is an insightful observation about business, work, and life.

It is tempting to go to the job every morning and go through the motions and have as our highest goal a clean desk and a safe retirement. If you don't have plans for growth and improvement of your business or your job, you can keep your desk clean and pencils sharpened—and might make it all the way to collect the pension. Without the expectations of plowing, planting, and harvesting that come with an ox, you never have to refill a manger, muck out stables, and bring in fresh straw.

If, however, you seek to grow the business, improve your performance, and change the circumstances of your co-workers and customers, there are going to be some messes to clean up and some loose ends to tie off along the way. The oxen that help bring abundant crops will also bring manure that must be shoveled and feeding that must be done on time. It's hard work and it must be done, or there will be no enterprise.

My Dad built houses on speculation. He would buy a lot and build a custom home on it with a construction loan. Then he would sell it and pay off the loan. The profit over the loan repayment was what our family lived on. My sweeping was made necessary by Dad's work to provide for our family. If my Dad didn't have work, I wouldn't have to sweep—but our family would starve.

Right now, I am being challenged by a series of client business transactions that are different from and more intense and risk-laden than anything that particular client has attempted before. They are challenging and will involve more corporate bylaws and contracts that must be precise and will be tedious to produce. Old ways of doing things are going to have to give way to different management and information systems. There will be a lot of work and clean-up before it is over. If the client doesn't make the strategic moves, things will be simple and a lot easier to maintain, but the client will die of starvation due to a declining market share.

Why am I telling you this? Can an essay about work and risk possibly have anything to do with grace? Well, are you willing to accept that grace is something more than a pleasant saying on a refrigerator magnet or a needlepoint sampler? If so, you will find that without risk, mistakes, failure, and the resulting messes, shame, pain, and oppressive sense of futility, we would never know grace.

Humankind has taken God's creation the way a willful, reckless child insists on having his way with a toy, and we have broken it. First among the things we have broken are our own hearts and minds that He made for love but we have abused for selfishness and competition. Lacking the Creator's genius, we cannot repair what we have broken. There is a peculiar perverseness of the human spirit that tries to overcome this incompetence by willed insistence on perfection.

Many years ago I was called upon to mediate a dispute between a man and his wife. They were estranged and he, facing life-and-death uncertainties, desired reconciliation. He confessed to me his infidelity and his regret and asked me to do what I could to patch up things between them.

I met with the wife. She listened without expression as I relayed the husband's hope for healing. She then coolly described an affair of her own entered in anger over what she perceived as her husband's indifference to her. Both infidelities had occurred a long time before, but the anger remained—years of marital permafrost.

There was a gleaming exterior of a successful business, a beautiful home, children, and many friends. She was renowned for her dinner parties and the tasteful, precise decor of her home. The interior of the marriage, however, was icy and toxic with resentment and regret. Neither spouse would give the other a break. Their children labored under a cloud of disapproval for failing parental expectations.

I asked the wife, "What do all the beautiful furnishings, the 'apple-pie order,' the peaceful, pleasant social persona mean to you?"

"Oh," she said, "I have to have serenity."

"But what is the price of this serenity?" I asked.

"What do you mean?"

"I mean, could anyone really live with the burden of this perfection? Who could keep it up without breaking? It really is impossible to attain, you know, and all this cost to your family has been paid for the impossible."

She was visibly angry but silent. Steel determination and the sacrifice of imperfect relationships had not yielded the unblemished serenity she had desired.

I think if that woman had owned a barn, it would have been an art gallery. An ox would have been too messy even if the earth it plowed had improved the family's livelihood.

Jesus' warning about putting salvific reliance on neatness and order at the expense of substance was dire.

> "When the unclean spirit has gone out of a person, it wanders through waterless regions looking for a resting place, but it finds none. Then it says, 'I will return to my house from which I came.' When it comes, it finds it empty, swept, and put in order. Then it goes and brings along seven other spirits more evil than itself, and they enter and live there; and the last state of that person is worse than the first. So it will be also with this evil generation."[1]

Jesus' encounter with Martha before the resurrection of her brother Lazarus is instructive. Martha professed belief in Jesus as the Messiah, the Son of God, and therefore capable of raising her brother from the dead.[2] " 'Lord, if you had been here, my brother would not have died. But even now I know that God will give you whatever you ask of him.' "[3]

When Jesus asked that the stone be removed from the tomb, Martha's compulsion for neatness took over. " 'Lord,' " she remonstrated, " 'already there is a stench because he has been dead four days.' "[4] It can only be called a compulsion when one prefers death to a mess.

Fortunately, God's glory is sufficient to bring shining life out of any bad-smelling situation. "Jesus said to her, 'Did I not tell you that if you believed, you would see the glory of God?' "[5]

Jesus never instructed His followers to stand still and dwell in the *status quo*. Jesus defines the meaning of "change agent." In fact, the power of Christ in our souls is activated in repentance, that is, turning around and going another direction.

He told us to happily sell everything we have to obtain what is of greatest worth. Jesus told a story about a man who found a treasure in a pasture, hid it, sold everything he had, and went back and bought the whole farm to get the treasure. This story speaks of a shrewdness that borders on fraudulent. If the man went to the farm owner and said, "You have a treasure on your farm, and I want to buy it from you," there would obviously be no deal.

Property law has ever held that what you find in the way of treasure on the land of another belongs to the landowner, who wouldn't even have to pay a reward for the finder. So the man spotted a profit in the transaction that he was not obligated to disclose, legalese for, "he took the seller to the cleaners." To do so, he had to buy everything on that farm. Robert Capon wrote, "The man who discovered the treasure did not simply buy the cubic yard or so of clean dirt in which he cleverly buried it. He bought the whole property: sinkholes, dungheaps, poison ivy, and sticker bushes, plus all the rats, mice, flies and beetles that came with it."[6]

If in seeking the best, we are not willing to risk some bad, we are going to live out our lives as spiritual and emotional paralytics. I don't think there is anything so sad to Jesus Christ as well-defended, cautious hearts unwilling to risk change, growth, or even passion. You read it in His grief and anger over those who put prim, hard-bitten adherence to tradition ahead of healing the crippled and sightless and freeing those in bondage of body and spirit.[7] You hear His heartache when He said, " 'To what will I compare this generation? It is like children sitting in the marketplaces and calling to one another,

"We played the flute for you and you did not dance;
    we wailed, and you did not mourn." ' "[8]

His spirit cried out its anguish when He quoted Isaiah's prophecy that His ministry would be rejected by people smug and complacent in their ways and unwilling to accept the expansive, enlightening healing truth and grace of the Son of God.

" 'You will indeed listen, but never understand,
    and you will indeed look, but never perceive.
For this people's heart has grown dull,
    and their ears are hard of hearing,
      and they have shut their eyes;
      so that they might not look with their eyes,
    and listen with their ears,
and understand with their heart and turn—
    and I would heal them.' "[9]

Jesus described His kingdom as a mustard plant, a weed really, that became a tree,[10] as yeast that works into all the bread dough,[11] and as a wide-sweeping net.[12] Speaking of the propensity of religion to confuse its time-honored structures with life and meaning, He said right from the outset of His ministry, "Destroy this temple, and in three days I will raise it up." Our Jesus possesses the life that brought our Universe into being and that refuses to be boxed in. By emphasizing forgiveness as a release from the past and repentance as the route to the future and asking us to surrender to Him every claim we have to our own life, He brings us into eternity with Him.

Not owning an ox means a clean barn. Avoiding relationships and commitment means never risking rejection. Resisting growth means limiting tough decisions and not having to learn new things. Refusing change keeps us from the dangers of the unknown.

But you need to know some things before you decide to move on or stay where you are. First, those without fear are the stupid and the lost because "the fear of the LORD is the beginning of knowledge."[13] Next, Christ says to you, " 'My grace is sufficient for you, for power is made perfect in weakness.' "[14] Moreover, "I can do all things through Christ who strengthens me."[15] Then, "After you have suffered for a little while, the God of all grace, who has called you to his eternal glory in Christ, will himself restore, support, strengthen, and establish you."[16] Steady as you go, " 'My righteous one will live by faith. / My soul takes no pleasure in anyone who shrinks back.' "[17] Finally, for those who keep going and seek their home with God without turning back, "God is not ashamed to be called their God."[18]

> Therefore, since we are surrounded by so great a cloud of witnesses, let us also lay aside every weight and the sin that clings so closely, and let us run with perseverance the race that he has set before us, looking to Jesus the pioneer and perfecter of our faith, who for the sake of the joy that was set before him endured the cross, disregarding its shame, and has taken his seat at the right hand of the throne of God.
>
> Consider him who endured such hostility against himself from sinners, so that you may not grow weary or lose heart.[19]

Whatever is your barn, put an "ox" in it and look ahead to the future.

Questions for Reflection

1. What do the messes and loose ends of life mean for prayer?
2. Does prayer eliminate risk? Why or why not?
3. What was Jesus' point when He observed that the people neither danced nor mourned?

42

Can You Drink From the Cup?

Our cup is Christ's gift. Our thirst is Christ's opportunity.
Our grateful acceptance of the cup is the realization of eternal life.

A Central American orphanage was as poor as the children it served. The children were scarred and disfigured by neglect and malnutrition and the skin diseases that ravaged them even in this rough sanctuary. Their sunken little chests were racked by the respiratory infections they contracted from each other when sharing the same drinking cup.

The student missionary thought of the lovingly chosen, carefully washed dishes, drinking glasses, and cups back home in Colorado. She wrote home, and in a few weeks a package arrived addressed in her mom's neat script. Inside were enamel cups, one for each child. She hammered a row of nails into the wall, wrote each child's name on a piece of tape beneath the nails and hung the cups. The infections subsided; the night quieted with the absence of coughing.

A cup is a personal thing.

In many families it is traditional at the birth of a new child to give a silver cup engraved with the name and date of birth.

Men and women often have a favorite mug or cup at work or home. Woe be to the careless person who uses that cup without permission.

I prefer tin cups with blue-speckled enamel that are popular in the rural Western United States. Water seems colder drunk from a tin cup.

Nehemiah was the royal cupbearer to Cyrus, King of Persia, who rebuilt war-devastated Jerusalem in 445 B.C. He wrote the story in a book of Scripture that bears his name.

229

The cupbearer insured the safety of the king from poisoning during the inevitable palace intrigues. Nehemiah tasted the content of the king's cup first to see if it was lethal. The constant presence of a person who, if necessary, will die for you to save your life leads to a deep intimacy. The cupbearer had to be trustworthy, so he became the confidante and chief advisor to the king.

Life is often compared to a cup. There is a story about a teacher pouring tea for his student. The cup filled and overflowed, but the teacher kept pouring. The student exclaimed, "The cup is too full!" The teacher responded, "You are full of your opinions and speculations. Why don't you empty yourself of them so that I can teach you?"

To measure optimism or pessimism, we ask another person about his or her perspective: "Do you see the glass as half full or half empty?"

When our energy is drained and spent, we say, "My cup is empty."

Some cups are trophies of victories. Other cups, like the one Joseph hid in his brother Benjamin's saddlebag[1] or those we share in Communion, are doorways to forgiveness.

Jesus offered His disciples a cup at the Last Supper, and all of them drank from it. Jesus told them, " 'This is my blood of the covenant, which is poured out for many.' "[2] His life was being poured out in death so that they could have life. The result was a covenant, He said, a contractual guarantee.

It was not easy for Jesus to fulfill this contract. He'd taken on a human heart; made friends; and enjoyed parties, long tramps across the countryside, and sailing on the lake with His friends. He healed everyone who came to Him and was moved by spiritual growth in the lives of His followers. How much good could He accomplish if He lived and stayed?

We humans think that way, and Jesus was fully human. He knelt beside a boulder in a park and prayed out His concerns. Maybe His Father had something else in mind. He raised the possibility, " 'Abba, Father, for you all things are possible; remove this cup from me; yet, not what I want but what you want.' "[3]

As personal and intimate as a cup is, it is a childish and selfish thing to insist on holding on to your cup when someone else needs it more and there are other cups from which to choose. Jesus didn't clutch the cup of atonement in a white-knuckled grip. He held it loosely, ready to set it aside if His Father had other plans.

There is a difference between psychological denial and self-denial. When we insist on our goals to the exclusion of consideration of reality and changed circumstances, we are acting in delusion, not faith. Self-denial means that we give up our cup, accepting that our possession of it is subordinate to God's purpose for it. The person who holds his or her cup loosely, without attaching any conditions, says, "I would rather not go through this, yet, it's what You want, not what I want, that counts."

The brothers James and John solicited Jesus for impressive positions of authority in His kingdom. Jesus told them, " 'You do not know what you are asking. Are you able to drink the cup that I drink, or be baptized with the baptism that I am baptized with?' They replied, 'We are able.' Then Jesus said to them, 'The cup that I drink you will drink; and with the baptism with which I am baptized, you will be baptized; but to sit at my right hand or at my left is not mine to grant, but it is for those for whom it is prepared.' "[4]

The brothers were trying to control the circumstances of their life with God. They were quick to answer that they could deal with any obstacles on the way to their goals. Jesus told them, in essence, "You get to live your life, not control its outcome."

Most, if not all of us, fight against this truth. We struggle to keep a grip on our cup's handle without spilling anything in it. If anything were to change at all, we would wish it to be a better-looking cup with more delicious contents. Isn't that the way we think about our appearance, our relationships, our jobs, our homes, and our fortunes?

This was the challenge of Baruch, son of Neriah, a scribe who served as secretary to the prophet Jeremiah. He had what he thought was a great job working for a spiritual giant right at the center of the religious and public life of Judah. His boss, Jeremiah, had a penchant for speaking confrontational truth against the hypocrisy and weakness of the ruling class. When King Jehoiakim decided he had been told enough truth and sought to kill Jeremiah for telling it, Baruch felt sorry for himself and wished he were somewhere else doing something else. He said, " 'Woe is me! The LORD has added sorrow to my pain; I am weary with my groaning, and I find no rest.' "[5] Undoubtedly, we all have shared Baruch's feelings at least once or twice.

God gave Jeremiah a message for Baruch about the cup of his life. " 'Thus says the LORD: I am going to break down what I have built, and pluck up what I have planted—that is the whole land. And you, do you seek great things for yourself? Do not seek them; for I am going to bring disaster upon all flesh, says the LORD; but I will give you your life as a prize of war in every place to which you go.' "[6]

This is the same deal God offers us in a broken world. He gives us life and a choice whether to live it by trusting Him or trying it on our own. He does not give ideal circumstances to those who choose to trust His love, but He works in every detail of their lives for their good.[7]

Those who make the mistrustful choice to hang on to their cups for fear of risk and change or who insist on a cup of their exact specification can only be pitied because their hope is finite and dependent on their own strength.[8]

Jesus' final word about His own cup was acceptance. No one should force us to drink another cup or seek to spare us from drinking the cup God gives us. When the priests and temple police showed up to arrest Jesus in the garden, Peter whipped out his sword and slashed an ear off Malchus, the high priest's servant. "Jesus said to Peter, 'Put your sword back into its sheath. Am I not to drink the cup that the Father has given me?' "[9]

With His arrest, Jesus knew the Father had answered His prayer. He was not going to get a different cup. His blood was poured out for the salvation of us all. In that way, as Jesus told James and John, His cup would become our cup for those of us who believe.

There is only one response to the cup of life that God gives us and that is to drink it in thankfulness. Gratitude to God in the face of adverse circumstance is the sure mark of faith. This is what David was saying in his great prayer of Psalm 116.

> I walk before the LORD
> in the land of the living.
> I kept my faith, even when I said,
> "I am greatly afflicted";
> I said in my consternation,
> "Everyone is a liar."

> What shall I return to the LORD
> for all his bounty to me?
> I will lift up the cup of salvation
> and call on the name of the LORD,
> I will pay my vows to the LORD
> in the presence of all his people . . .
> I will offer to you a thanksgiving sacrifice
> and call on the name of the LORD.[10]

Every day of our life each one of us has a cup to drink, and we hear Jesus' question, "Can you drink the cup?"

If we are honest, we have to answer, "No, Lord, there is not a chance on our own."

He replies to us, " 'Write this, for these words are trustworthy and true.' . . . 'It is done! I am the Alpha and the Omega, the beginning and the end. To the thirsty I will give water as a gift from the spring of the water of life. Those who conquer will inherit these things, and I will be their God and they will be my children.' "[11]

Our cup is Christ's gift. Our thirst is Christ's opportunity. Our grateful acceptance of the cup is the realization of eternal life. This is Jesus' instruction and His promise: " 'Drink from it, all of you; for this is my blood of the covenant, which is poured out for many for the forgiveness of sins. I tell you, I will never again drink of this fruit of the vine until that day when I drink it new with you in my Father's kingdom.' "[12] This is the power and the hope of grace.

_____ *Questions for Reflection* _____

1. How is prayer like your favorite cup?
2. Do you pray as if "the cup" is half full or half empty?
3. When, like Jesus, have you asked your heavenly father to give you a different cup from which to drink?

43

Crossing the Lake

Christ takes us through our fears, not away from them.
A ship in harbour is safe, but that is not what ships are built for.
—William G. T. Shedd

Only the unknown frightens men.— Antoine de Saint-Exupery

In the evening after a long day, the Teacher said "Let's go across the lake to the other side." His companions were glad to hear this. They were men of the water, at ease under sail, competent with net and wind, strong at the oars. The crowds pressed close, and the teaching, while wonderful, was intense and disconcerting to the fishermen used to the wide-open sky and water. Living in tension on land was wearing to them, and they welcomed the chance to show off what they could do best.

A final wave to the crowd, and they took the Teacher just as He was, without baggage and tired to the bone. The boats of friends cast off with them, forming a little convoy into the last light. A bit of rowing out and then the sails snapped taut under the freshening sundown breeze from the Mediterranean to the west. A thousand nights of fishing had begun this way for them.

The men looked around for the smile of the Teacher. He was asleep on a mat in the stern. They were kind of disappointed. They wanted to share with Him their pride in their vessel and the joy of the run across the water.

Midpoint was reached, three miles out, in the deepest water. There was nothing to do but sit and watch the outline of the dark desert mountains against the night sky of late winter. It was a time to rest and think, heads down, coats pulled close against the moist chill.

Peter, who often noticed such things, felt the change first. A puff of warm desert wind in his face from the southeast. It was too early in the season for the *khamsin,* the name the desert people give to the east wind. He lifted his head and turned it slowly, waiting to feel it again, and there it was, unmistakable in its gritty menace.

Before he could even stir the others to action, the tempest compressed in the Trans-Jordan mountain passed and poured out on the lake. The strength of the blast from the east blew out the softer west wind. The boat shuddered to a halt and nosed down under the nearly vertical draft. They began taking on water. Peter untied the rope holding the boom in place. Struggling for his footing, he heaved the sail about, taking a crashing wave from the starboard as he did. The men sputtered up from their dozing, disoriented. Blowing spray and dust obscured the other boats and the shore.

The lake is only six miles wide and fifteen miles long. A strong wind increases to hurricane intensity when it funnels through the mountains, pushing the water down against the bottom. The water has no place else to go and towers up in steep waves that break on the western shore and then surge back, creating a sloshing swirl like bowl full of water shaken violently. At such times, an open fishing boat under sail is no place to be.

But that is exactly where they were—in an open boat on open water in an extreme gale. The boat bucked and wallowed, waves breaking fore and aft.

Peter clung to the boom and yelled for help. Others grabbed it too, but the conditions overpowered any possibility of steering. The sail was quickly blown to shreds anyway. The idea was to stop the boom from thrashing and knocking someone overboard. They had lived out their life on this lake, but now it was killing them. The roar reduced their shouts to incomprehensible shrieks.

They could feel the water in the boat rising to past their ankles. The weight was pulling them down in the troughs, bringing even more water over the sides. Stumbling about, they felt the Teacher, incredibly still asleep, laid out in the stern, waves breaking over him. It was maddening. Misery loves company. Desperation hates indifference. Who could sleep at a time like this? He is either the most confident being in the universe or a lunatic!

Hands grabbed the Teacher and shook Him awake. He sat up. "Teacher, we're dying here! Don't you care?" someone hollered. Other voices screamed variations of the question.

He rose to their panic. Later they would remember His silhouette standing straight up and steady, arms extended, palms against the wind. To their surprise, His voice was clear and distinct. "Stop blowing," He commanded the wind. Turning His palms down, He spoke to the churning waves, "Quiet! Calm down."

There was an instant and overpowering silence, no wind and not a ripple on the water. It was impossible, except they saw and heard it.

He spoke again with words that probed through the dark straight into their souls. "Why are you afraid? Do you still lack faith?" The words hung there in unanswered truth.

The day ended, and that evening began with the disciples certain of many things. They were devout men of strong principle and a hunger for God. They were sure they knew who Jesus was. They had taken Him on board "just as He was," and what He was to them was a teacher and storyteller, sometime miracle worker and bone-tired man. He was a celebrity, someone exciting to be around. It made them feel good to be useful to Him—to sail away with Him from the crowd on the shore that envied their closeness to Him.

They knew their home waters like the backs of their hands. They knew what it took to sail them and just where the fish would be feeding. They went out for a nice cruise that evening, certain they were in control.

Their certainties blew out with the sail. The storm almost killed them. They were powerless, adrift, one gust and wave from drowning. That's the most that they could know in their fear. And the Teacher had stopped it! He woke up, stood up, held out His hands, talked to the wind, talked to the water, and the storm was gone. There were no certainties in that—no "how" or "why," not even a "what." There was only a "Who" with a capital "W."

"Who, then, is this, that even the wind and waves obey Him?"

Phobos is the Greek word that Mark's Gospel uses for how the men felt in that moment when the lake perfectly mirrored the stars. It is the root word of *phobia*, an abnormal, intense, illogical fear. It was pathological terror devastating them to the core of their very being. It changed each one of them on that boat with Him that night forever. There was a tempest of demonic strength destroying them. Then Jesus stood up and overpowered it in an instant. They were more afraid of Jesus than the storm. "They feared exceedingly," the King James Version says in Mark 4:41. If you don't know what it means to fear Jesus more than the storm, you are still wading in shallow spiritual water.

It is the moment of conversion, you know, when you become more afraid of Jesus than the storm that threatens to destroy you. He tells you to cross the lake. He comes to you just as you are and climbs into your boat just as He is. You sail out with the other boats. You're proud to be in His company—Jesus and you sailing off together into the sunset, and He's picked your boat, not theirs! *It doesn't get any better than this—I'm taking Jesus for a ride,* you think. You even pride yourself that you've got everything under control so Jesus can sleep.

Then the wind changes and blows with a relentless keening that robs you of rational thought. The waves turn rough and hit you again and again and recoil and crash into you again from the other direction with no let up. Your carefully constructed little vessel begins to break up and take on water. *I'm sinking,* you think. *I'm dying!*

You forget that Jesus told you the destination and set the course and told you that you would go across together. How can He be your sailing buddy when He is asleep in the back of the boat?

Mustering up whatever you may remember from the lessons you learned by rote, you call out in desperation, even anger, "Teacher, don't You care that I'm dying?"

He'll calm the storm for your comfort, though it's not really necessary since He told you where you were going. It's your perception, not His reality, that has you scared. But He'll hold you and make the bad thing go away like a father holds His child who is screaming with night terrors, saying, "It's OK, Daddy's here."

But you're an adult, and the ease with which Jesus takes control scares you even more because you realize that you are truly powerless, and you are never again going to be able to wrap yourself in the security blanket of illusion. Even He leaves you with questions—"Why are you afraid? Have you still no faith?"

People are fond of slapping on cute little refrigerator magnets and hanging wall plaques proclaiming this verse: "The Lord is near. Do not worry about anything, but in everything by prayer and supplication with thanksgiving let your requests be made known to God. And the peace of God, which surpasses all understanding, will guard your hearts and your minds in Christ Jesus."[1]

Those of us battered by the wind and the waves struggle to find relief in that verse. Paul directs us to be thankful in spite of our misery and to keep asking God for help even when common sense tells us that we are beyond help. He even says that God's presence will give us a peace deeper than our ability to comprehend it. So even though we are overwhelmed by the storm, and everything looks hopeless, we are told, "Do not worry." It is hard not to respond, "Who are you kidding?"

It all comes down to Jesus. "Who then is this?" you ask, wrestling with your ego to accept the Prince of Peace when you don't know how He works that peace in the midst of the storm. If you could only know the details of how, when, where, and why, you could control the outcome. All you get, though, is a Who that you don't even understand!

You may think it's enough to have Jesus in your boat but are wondering why you are still wet, wind-blown, and cold, and your boat is sinking. "Don't You care?" you ask Jesus.

"Why are you afraid?" He asks back.

It is only later when the adrenaline subsides and your body stops quivering that you realize that Jesus does care because now the storm is gone, you are alive, and He made the difference. Paul says, The peace of God . . . that guards your hearts and minds is *in Christ Jesus!* It isn't what He is in, but Who you are in that makes that difference! And in case you are wondering, you *get in* Christ Jesus by *believing in* Christ Jesus as your Lord and Savior.

Where are you looking for the difference in your life? Put yourself in the story. Are you seeking your significance in the acceptance of the crowd waiting on the shore? In the number of boats that follow you out? In the fellowship of those sailing out with you? Do you require a clear sky and a calm sea before you venture out at Jesus' call? Are you putting your hope in a bigger boat or a water-tight hull of your own construction? Are you setting your course by the weather reports or by trusting your instincts to read the signs in the sky? Is Jesus disappointing you because your little boat seems to be sinking, and He doesn't seem to care? Do you fear the storm more than you believe Jesus' instruction to cross the lake?

Think about these questions—because this isn't a story about safe answers. It's a story about questions.

"Teacher, don't you care that we are perishing?"

"Why are you afraid? Have you still no faith?"

"Who is this that even the wind and the waves obey him?"

Honestly seek the answer to all three questions, and you will safely enter the harbor of the kingdom of God.

Questions for Reflection

1. How does Christ show His care for you?
2. How can you experience peace when you don't understand what's happening?
3. Is the solution to your fears a "what" or "Who"?

44

Winter in May

Hard times know no particular season.
That means any time is an opportunity for grace.

When they were drawing up the Russian-Finnish border, a
farmer had to decide if he wanted to be in Finland, but he did not
want to offend the Russian officials. They came to him and wanted
to know why he wanted to be in Finland. The farmer replied, "It
has always been my desire to live in Mother Russia, but at my age
I wouldn't be able to survive another Russian winter."[1]

David wrote these words:

Praise the LORD . . .
>   snow and frost,
>   stormy wind fulfilling his command.[2]

So, is winter to be avoided or to be praised? Why would this question
be raised in the middle of May?

Frost kills and snow buries in the equality of death. Stormy winds can
change everything in a gust, true enough.

I traveled to Washington, D.C., with business and educational leaders from my region to plead our case to legislators and bureaucrats for
support of various programs and projects. I was part of a small group that
met with a deputy cabinet secretary to obtain enhanced funding for
work-force development. We made our presentation in his office filled

with the photos and memorabilia acquired in proximity to the politically powerful.

The meeting went well, we told each other as we left the building and walked outside into the warm May sunshine. The Capitol dome stood above us in grandeur. A breeze stirred the flags. The green lawns and trees of the National Mall stretched before us.

We had some free time before our next appointment. A beloved friend in the group invited me to visit the National Gallery of Art with him. He has a reputation on three continents for his scholarship, vision, and flair. I am always stimulated by our conversations, and the thought of spending this moment with him in contemplation of great art excited me.

On the granite steps of the gallery, his cell phone rang. His spouse needed to return to California immediately to see a pain specialist. A slip of a scalpel some time before had damaged a nerve. Her waking life is seared with agony. Relief is sought whenever and wherever it might be found. Winter can occur in May, sending even the powerful to seek refuge against ravages of frostbite and wind.

To praise God for snow and frost and for the winds that bring them sounds like the crazed delusions of a luge sledder. What rational human soul can love a God who commands such events when He has the power to make every day springtime and pain free?

This week, a young man leaned over the table where I was signing copies of my book. "I heard you interviewed on the radio," he said. "I want to know how you deal with the things you talked about, like the loss of your sweetheart."

"It's hard," I said in the sudden intimacy of a shared story. "There are no easy answers, no quick fix."

"You're going to tell me it takes time, right?" he asked in a tone that told me he's heard this answer before like one more bumper sticker insisting on absolute truth in the transient flow of rush hour traffic.

How much can he know? I wondered as I looked at him. He was young, in his twenties I guessed, tall, spare, smiling, with a prematurely graying brush of hair.

"Yes, that's what I'm going to tell you because that's all I know. I didn't think I could breathe again when she died, but I did. The sun comes up in the morning and goes down at night. After a while you think, 'Well, what's one more day?' The days turn into weeks and months and years. What you thought would never happen, does. I've been married thirty years to a woman I love, and we have a wonderful son. Have you suffered a loss?" I asked him.

He hesitated, searching my eyes for a handhold of trust. "Not a death," he said, "a relationship."

"I'm sorry."

"It's not as bad as what happened to you—no chance for friendship, no chance to talk again. I might still be able to have that chance, though."

He obviously hadn't given up on her, but he was hurting enough to talk with a total stranger on a Sunday afternoon in a crowded bookstore. A cold wind was blowing through his May.

"It will get better," I told him. "I believe that life is a continuum, not a circle. Doors close behind us, but doors open before us all the way into eternity with new circumstances and new people. That's the one belief that makes us Christian, you know. Because of Jesus' coming to reconcile us with God, we will live with God forever. Heaven is a real place and God wants us there with Him, and that makes all the difference."

"Yes," he said in response.

I looked across the aisle to the gift section. I saw the Precious Moments® figurines inscribed with verses such as "Hope believes all things." I saw the potpourri sachets in little flower pots with inspirational sayings and the ubiquitous Thomas Kinkade prints with lighted cottages beside streams flowing through woods with no poison oak.

"God," I prayed, "help me make more sense to this man than platitudes on giftware."

"What's your name?" I asked.

"Ed."

"Ed, Paul says we suffer, we endure, we build character, and out of that we begin to hope, and that hope doesn't disappoint us because God's love is poured out into our hearts through the Holy Spirit that he gives us.[3] We get a process, not an answer. That process builds our hearts into something that God can fill with love. One step follows another the way spring follows winter. If this weren't true, I could never have written a book about grace because there was no way that I could make this up. God had to work this out in me for me. The same possibility is there for you."

"OK, I'll buy your book," he said.

I laughed.

The poet Shelley asked the truth in "Ode to a West Wind." "If Winter comes, can Spring be far behind?" The severity of that winter will determine the fertility of the spring that follows.

Our winter was soft and warm in the western United States. We are paying dearly for that with a reduced water supply and early forest fires. Rattlesnakes looking for a drink are found beside backyard pools and faucets. This usually happens in August and September, not May. Oh, we need winter all right. Winter clouds are what stand between us and the hell of unrelenting sunshine. Winter is what gives context to the words of grace whispered to each of us.

What happens if the frost comes early and kills the vines before harvest? What happens if the snow drifts far deeper than anything that we can handle? We wait, that's what. We wait while winter does its work reshaping, replenishing, and refreshing the dry and empty places. While we wait, we remember spring and Jesus Christ who said,

"I am on my way to the One who sent me. . . .

"In a day or so you're not going to see me, but then in another day or so you will see me." That stirred up a hornet's nest of questions among the disciples: "What's he talking about: 'In a day or so you're not going to see me, but then in another day or so you will see me?' And 'Because I'm on my way to the Father?' What is this 'day or so?' We don't know what he is talking about."

Jesus knew they were dying to ask him what he meant, so he said, "Are you trying to figure out among yourselves what I meant when I said, 'In a day or so you're not going to see me, but then in another day or so you will see me?' Then fix this firmly in your minds: You're going to be in deep mourning while the godless world throws a party. You'll be sad, very sad, but your sadness will develop into gladness.

"When a woman gives birth, she has a hard time, there's no getting around it. But when the baby is born, there is joy in the birth. This new life in the world wipes out memory of the pain. The sadness you have right now is similar to that pain, but the coming joy is also similar. When I see you again, you'll be full of joy, and it will be a joy no one can rob from you. You'll no longer be so full of questions.

"This is what I want you to do: Ask the Father for whatever is in keeping with the things I've revealed to you. Ask in my name, according to my will, and he'll most certainly give it to you. Your joy will be a river overflowing its banks!"[4]

Even as we contend with our winters, we trust that there will be other seasons. Richard Foster says, "Trust is confidence in the character of God. Firmly and deliberately you say, 'I do not understand what God is doing or even where God is, but I know that he is out to do me good.' This is trust. This is how to wait."[5]

I have lived through fifty-three winters, some of them harsher than others. It's been long enough to fill the aquifers of my soul with grace. These words are the spillage. There have been fifty-three springs, some of them drier than others. These all have taught me to trust the shared heartbreak of Ed and to cringe from the platitudes on Christian giftware.

When I was in college, I read and memorized these words from God to the prophet Isaiah:

> For as the heavens are higher than the earth,
>   so are my ways higher than your ways
>   and my thoughts than your thoughts.
>
> For as the rain and snow come down from heaven,
>   and do not return there until they have watered the earth,
> making it bring forth and sprout,
>   giving seed to the sower and bread to the eater,
> so shall my word be that goes out from my mouth;
>   it shall not return to me empty,
> but it will accomplish that which I purpose,
>   and succeed in the thing for which I sent it.
> For you shall go out with joy,
>   and be led back in peace;
> the mountains and the hills before you
>   shall burst into song,
>   and all the trees of the field shall clap their hands.
> Instead of the thorn shall come up the cypress;
>   instead of the brier shall come up the myrtle;
> and it shall be to the LORD for a memorial,
>   for an everlasting sign that shall not cut off.[6]

Let your winter in May do the work of God within you. It's called "grace."

Questions for Reflection

1. Why doesn't God make lives safe and perfect so that we don't need prayer?
2. How is the answer to your prayer sometimes a process and not a solution?
3. What has waiting for answers taught you about God?

45

Cleansing Fire, Healing Streams

Silence and solitude can burn away the underbrush and overgrowth of busyness and usefulness that drain us dry, permitting the springs of grace to flow again through our hearts.

The wet summer monsoons boil out of the central Pacific Ocean and gather strength in the Sonoran heat of the Gulf of California. They follow the spines of the Southwestern mountain ranges inland. By noon each late-summer day, the superheated air from the desert furnaces below ride up the mountainsides like smoke through chimneys, pushing up the subtropical moisture into towering columns of white cumulus cloud.

From my office window, fifty miles away, I watch the rising thunderheads inviting my head and my heart away from my phone calls and contracts. God was on the move in the mountains, and I ached to be with Him.

My faith tradition believes that nature is God's second book after the Scripture. I had not read that book for quite a while and suffered for the neglect.

I drove down the Angeles Crest Highway on an August day when the clouds shielded from the hot sun. To my surprise, streams ran down the sides of Mount Baden-Powell, Throop Peak, Mount Burnham, and Mount Islip. My explorations up the side canyons above the 6,000-foot level revealed the cause of the unexpected flows. The springs water the cedars, fir, and pines, allowing them to push their roots deep enough to hold firm on the steep mountainsides. Bunch grass, scrub willow, and buck brush also take the opportunity of the water to spread over the canyons. Eventually this brush sucks up the streams near their sources.

After many years without fires, during the past two summers, wild fires burned over the ridges and high ravines. The trees and brush closest to the water were consumed. The spring water is now released to tumble thousands of feet to the Mojave Desert floor.

God spoke to me through this view. I've worked harder the past three years than any other time in my life. Tall trees of genuine crises and the brush and grass of smaller demands have crowded in, drawing the life from the springs of my heart. The flows through my soul were drawn off and absorbed.

Finally, I developed the courage to take a summer Sabbath of three weeks, the longest vacation of my adult life. I left my pager with my office administrator and turned off my cell phone. I expected to spend long hours in spiritual reading and prayer during this time. Instead, I found my healing in the routines of home life with Patricia and Andrew. My cup needed to be refilled with the ordinary. I needed reconnection with real life. Toward the end of this respite, I gained the energy to journey into the mountains to listen to what God had to say.

When I sorted through the current state of my personal and public life, I learned that I have not been careful with my calling. The challenges and tasks that come my way need scrutiny before the Lord to determine those consistent with my calling and gifts and those best done by another. My tenacious refusal to surrender to grace in this area has choked the flow of my spirit and denied colleagues downstream the opportunities that are necessary for their growth and service. My life turned brittle and fragmented in the resulting dryness, leaving me vulnerable to both the fire and the flood of circumstance.

Does a mountain spring know the difference between the needs of cedar or scrub willow? It feeds them both. Similarly, I allowed demands to crowd out discernment and conscience.

These words of Thomas Merton both chastise and inspire me. "When we are not living up to our true vocation, thought deadens our life, or substitutes itself for life, or gives in to life so that our life drowns out our thinking and stifles the voice of conscience. When we find our vocation—thought and life are one."[1]

Solitude and silence are a fire that, if allowed to burn, will clear the underbrush and overgrowth of busyness and usefulness that overdraft our entire vocational capacity and demand even more. In the aftermath of that blaze, we can see that our worth is found in the grace that flows through us rather than the performance that is drawn from us. In the realization that we need mercy, we are disabused of the conceit that mercy is ours to give or withhold at will.

A stream flowing through a desert is a graphic depiction of mercy. It is the assurance of life beyond death and the cause for hope after devastation. It is a reminder that salvation depends on God's grace alone. Isaiah described this in beautiful words:

> The wilderness and the dry land shall be glad,
>   the desert shall rejoice and blossom;
> like the crocus it shall blossom abundantly,
>   and rejoice with joy and singing. . . .

> Strengthen the weak hands,
>   and make firm the weak knees.
> Say to those who are of a fearful heart,
>   "Be strong, do not fear!
> Here is your God . . .
>   He will come and save you."[2]

Questions for Reflection

1. How can the spiritual devastation of fire help you to release the water of grace in your life?
2. When have you experienced the spiritual equivalent of a spring in the desert?
3. What is the difference between God's grace and your performance in finding your worth?

46

Up the Mount
Tom Trail

A traveler's notes of a predawn prayer journey up a New England mountain.

I slip out of the inn into the fog-roofed darkness. A museum-quality stillness pervades the quintessential New England village of Woodstock, Vermont, in the predawn. The empty streets around the green await the buses of the fall-foliage tours and the Saabs and Subarus of the local folk.

The covered bridge and residential streets are familiar to me from walks during breaks in meetings the previous week. I easily maneuver the route to the town park. I hope the clunk of the rental-car door doesn't disturb anyone asleep in the beautiful old homes across the street. It occurs to me that a Californian would have a hard time explaining his presence here at five-thirty in the morning.

There's a walking stick in my right hand and in my left a bottle of water that I carried on the plane for three thousand miles. My plan is to hike up Mount Tom, the forested peak that borders Woodstock on the east. The brochure calls the route "a European-style walking path with many switchbacks and benches for the contemplation of nature." It is much too dark to reflect on nature at this moment. The only light comes from a couple of porch lights in adjacent yards. Barely making out the ground at my feet as I swish through leaves, I zigzag across the grass as I approach the forest, but I can't find the path. I drag the brass ferrule of the walking stick across the ground until it rasps on asphalt—and I'm off.

This is a hike I wanted to take from the time I first looked up Woodstock on the Internet when I knew that business would bring me here. I thought I had missed the chance, but when I was awake at four-thirty in the morning, with sleep not likely to return, I thought *It's now or never.* Patricia will note that I'm wearing my Levis and sneakers and took the water, and she'll figure out where I've gone.

Following Christ was like this. I didn't plan it. One afternoon I reached into a stack of books and picked the right one to read on a business trip. It stirred me awake. I prayed a halting, groping prayer that was answered by Christ's call, and my long spiritual torpor was a forgone possibility. It was only the start of the path, and I hadn't a clue where I was going, but the compulsion was "now or never."

The woods enclose me in blackness. I stop and squeeze my eyes shut for adjustment. On opening, I can make out only the tops of my white running shoes. My left knee is fragile with degenerative joint disease. I'm a continent away from home, and not another soul knows where I am in this moment. Maybe I should turn around and go back.

A disorienting moment follows the first footsteps after Jesus when you look up and realize that no one else is with you, and, no matter what you've been told, the path is different from the way it looked on the map and was described in the guidebook. You wonder if you missed something and whether you should turn around and go back. Prayer in that moment is eyes closed tight with the hope of seeing something when they open.

The dark enlivens the senses in a process of subtraction. Sound, sight, and breeze are absent. I sigh, and the musk of dust, pine, rock, and moss fills my nose and lungs. It is the universal smell of the forest, the same on the West Coast as the East. Each distinct smell is a reminder of places different, but familiar. Comforted by remembrance, I step forward, tapping my stick ahead of me like a blind man. Slowly, I move ahead over roots and stones. At an opening in the trees, I can pick out the silhouette of a bench in the ambient light, and I realize that I must be at the turn of a switchback. The town hall clock strikes six o'clock.

The first day after encountering Christ, I began to read the Gospels, starting with Matthew 1 and moving ahead. What I found there was familiar, but different. There was a time when I was graded on what I could remember of the Scriptures. The emphasis was on rote memory of strings of proof texts undergirding doctrinal constructs. Without the challenge of experience, the exercises often seemed absurd and useless. The texts lay at the back of my mind as dry and dead as the leaves and twigs I am now crunching underfoot. But in the springtime of Christ's love, the Scriptures opened to me like a poppy at daylight, and I began to see my way through them, enjoying the unexpected twists and turns.

A poem of Robert Frost, written about Vermont woods in the winter, lifts to mind with my heartbeats:

> The woods are lovely, dark and deep.
> But I have promises to keep,
> And miles to go before I sleep.[1]

The Congregational Church clock strikes six o'clock five minutes after the town hall clock. What is behind the discrepancy? A division of church and state? God versus mammon? Pride? An old feud? Which clock is right? "Avoid stupid controversies . . . dissensions, and quarrels about the law," Paul wrote Titus, "for they are unprofitable and worthless."[2]

My early efforts to talk with others about what I was learning in Scripture ran into some arguments about time. One friend was obsessed about an obscure bit of prophecy. "I don't think that's important," I told him in frustration. "And if we can't get beyond this, I'm done talking."

"It is important," he retorted, "because it's in the Bible."

"I don't think anything that obscure and hard to figure out could be important. Besides, every explanation of that idea I've ever heard required extrabiblical sources. God clues us in on what He wants us to know if we want to know it. I think something this complicated and trivial is just crazy-making."

"So what do you think is important?" he demanded.

"OK, here's what I think is important. We were created by God. He made us with the power to choose, and Adam and Eve chose to live by their own wits and effort and fell out of God's grace. We've been making the same mistake ever since. God loves us too much to give up on us. He started us back by calling people such as Abraham and Moses and formed a people for Himself with a set of instructions. They couldn't stay faithful to the instructions, so God's Son came to do it and gave His life on the cross to break the vicious cycle of effort and failure and lead us back to life. If we accept Christ as the way, the truth, and the life as it was meant to be, we are restored to grace as a new creation. Christ is going to return to finish the job physically that He has completed spiritually. Knowing this to be true, we are free to live the way God wants us to live. Those are the essentials of what I think is important. Everything else is crazy-making!"

Our fellowship was restored in agreement.

My pace is slower than normal because I'm watching my feet. Thoughts flit at random through my mind. I read, I've forgotten where, that the early Christians hiding in the Catacombs of Rome wore shoes with candleholders on their toes to guide their steps in the blackness. They would have had to walk slowly to avoid putting out the candles. "Your word is a lamp to my feet / and a light to my path."[3] I love the double perspective of this verse. It says I'm going somewhere, but I'm going there one step at a time. I can handle that but not more.

The trees begin to take form. Boulders hulk beside the trail. My knuckles graze them. Rock feels the same all over the world. It's elemental and dependable whether as a protection or an obstacle. Probably that's why it is a common metaphor for Jesus. He said of Himself,

> " 'The stone that the builders rejected
>   has become the cornerstone;
> this was the Lord's doing
>   and it is amazing in our eyes.'. . .
> "The one who falls on this stone will be broken to pieces; and it will crush anyone on whom it falls."[4]

The judgment of humanity in stark terms—fall over God and break, or God falls on you and crushes you. There is no hope for the complacent and the self-protective.

The benches keep me honest at the turns. Some of them are milled furniture; others are split logs cradled on stumps. I recall the switchbacks recorded on the map and try to count them to keep track of how far I've come. The guidebook was a help in orienting me. There's nothing, however, like walking the trail for yourself.

My parents took me to church every week. They sacrificed to send me to church school right through college. I learned the hymns and memorized the verses. I studied church history and doctrine. I attended chapel as required and mostly kept the rules. Twelve years ago after my mother read the story of my conversion at thirty-seven years of age, she looked at me grimly and asked, "Surely, we must have done something right?"

"Mom," I said, "do you think that my coming to God on my own reflects badly on you? I am thankful for the worships and the church school and the Bible studies and your and Dad's examples. Those are all stepping stones. But I had to experience God for myself. You couldn't do that for me. This isn't about you."

There are persons, some church leaders and parents, who expect the Christian colleges and universities I represent to graduate mature, conforming Christians and church members each time and every time. They become angry when it doesn't happen, and they add rules and change personnel to try to make it work. The cycle merely repeats itself in fear, pain, and loathing. The things of God, the angel told Zechariah, are accomplished " 'Not by might, not by power, but by my spirit, says the LORD of hosts.' "[5]

As, a wise old attorney-mentor once told me, "The thing about people is that they just won't mind. You have to persuade them." The most that can be expected of Christian education is that it supplies building blocks for faith, but the construction of faith cannot be forced. An insightful nineteenth-century author wrote, "Minds are constituted differently; while force may secure outward submission, the result with many children is a more determined rebellion of the heart. . . . It is not God's purpose that any mind should be thus dominated. Those who weaken or destroy individuality assume a responsibility that can result only in evil. . . . when the control ceases, the character will be found to lack strength and steadfastness."[6] The apostle John likewise noted that it was impossible to manufacture believers. "He [Jesus] came to what was his own, and his own people did not accept him. But to all who received him, who believed in his name, he gave power to become children of God, who were born, not of blood or of the will of the flesh or of the will of man, but of God."[7]

We read the maps and the guidebook, and, if we have a lick of sense, the information may give us landmarks to follow, but each of us has to walk the path for ourselves. To describe the path to someone without allowing him or her to walk it is crippling. It is an evil, even monstrous, thing to do to someone.

Persons of my heritage have climbed this slope since 1761, when the end of the French and Indian War made it safe to move into the area. I wonder who may have sat on the benches I find on the knoll overlooking the town. It looks like trail's end, but it's not. A wooden sign says "Mount Tom—200 yards." I look up in the growing light to see steps carved out of the rocky bluffs above. A cable and stanchions run beside the steep path for support and protection. Just as I haul myself to the top, the town hall clock strikes seven o'clock, the moment of dawn. Five minutes later, the church bell says its seven, but it's not true; dawn has already come.

Up top is a broad carriage path from the other side of the mountain. It was built by Frederick Billings, a lawyer who made a great fortune in mining and railroads in San Francisco during the gold rush before retiring as a gentleman farmer to his native Woodstock. The carriage paths allowed his guests the experience of the forest and vistas in comfort, not unlike the tour buses in the valleys below. The path continues through the kind of "yellow wood" that Robert Frost wrote about in another poem about the Vermont autumn. The mountain rolls on and on, and the carriage path winds around cleared pastures with green grass of an even height that would pass for lawn in California.

I startle two deer that crash off into the woods, white tails flashing. Then I walk out onto an immense pasture sloping north to south to a large pond called "The Pogue" on the map. Encircling the pasture are maples and birch in yellow, orange, pink, and scarlet so intense against an evergreen background that the effect is combustible even under the glowering, gray October sky. I walk to the center of the field and turn in circles, trying to absorb the glory. The viewfinder of my camera is inadequate to the task wherever I stand. So is my heart. The thing about glory is that to be real, it has to overwhelm. This is why you can go to all the seminars and lectures on worship that you can stomach, but worship will ever and always be a spontaneous response to transcendent, surpassing beauty. David stood in woods like this and exclaimed "Ascribe to the LORD the glory of his name; / worship the LORD in holy splendor."[8]

Regardless of the fumbling in the dark and the steepness of the trail and the rising, cold, west wind that is icing over my perspiration, the journey is worth it. I will never forget this morning. But I must go back. There is a check-out time and a plane to catch. By tonight I'll be back in California.

On the way down, I exchange greetings with a hiker whose accent and reserve identifies him as a "local." I'm envious. I flick a tick off my arm. Squirrels chatter. There is a thrashing in the leaves above followed by a sudden silence. I look up and see and hear a bronze-and-gray hawk pump its wings to power up and out of the trees with a squirrel in its talons. It is terrible and it is great. It is a benediction.

What would I have missed if I hadn't left my warm bed, searched for the path in the dark, and walked it one step at a time? Frost wrote,

> Two roads diverged into a wood,—and I,
> I took the one less traveled by,
> And that has made all the difference.[9]

Frost was right.

Questions for Reflection

1. What is required for Scripture to come alive for you?
2. How has family, school, and church influenced your walk with God?
3. What have you learned about God independent of family, school, and church?

47

Giving Up Our Nothing

Risking everything, even our emptiness, is the way of the Cross.

One day Jesus, visiting the temple with His disciples, made a keen observation recorded by Mark and Luke: "He looked up and saw rich people putting their gifts into the treasury; he also saw a poor widow put in two small copper coins. He said, 'Truly I tell you, this poor widow has put in more than all of them; for all of them have contributed out of their abundance, but she out of her poverty has put in all she had to live on.' "[1]

I think about this story when I picture the three little boys who were excited on a warm June Sunday. Their daddy was graduating from college.

The family had crammed into the un-air-conditioned, four-room, married student house for four years. They didn't mind. They were quiet when Daddy needed to study. They conquered their fears when Mom was absent at night, working as a nurse to put bread on the table. They roamed the lawns and sidewalks of the campus, learning secret places. They dreamed of the day when their family would begin a new life in a new home after Daddy earned his degree.

Now they were dressed in their best, hair combed and shoes shined, sitting in a smiling row in the campus church. Their eyes opened wide to take in the pomp and pageantry of their daddy's commencement. They clapped their hands hard and loud when his name was called and he crossed the platform to get his diploma.

The graduates marched out, and the boys risked a "shush" from Mom to wave and call out for his attention. He didn't look, though. He marched soberly past, and they watched his back down the aisle. They couldn't wait to see him outside. There was a special treat of cake and ice cream waiting at home for a surprise celebration.

When the boys and their mother got outside, they couldn't find him. They looked everywhere through families embracing and posing for pictures. After a while the others left. Mom and boys went home, and there was no daddy there. Only a note that Mom read and cried. Daddy had marched from his graduation into a new life with another woman. They did not hear from him again for more than ten years.

One of those boys told me the story many years later as we were driving down the freeway. Tears rolled from my eyes as I heard of my friend's pain.

The remarkable thing is that he grew up to be a reliable and good man, a loving husband and a great father to two sons and a daughter of his own. The wastelands of his youth have become flourishing gardens because he chose to love where there was no love.

The reactions of the 9/11 victim's families and friends are a similar marvel. The owner of the Cantor Fitzgerald bond brokerage firm, a ruthless businessman, vowed to spend the rest of his life taking care of the families of the seven hundred employees lost that day. Lisa Beamer, a young mother and youth leader with two young children and another on the way, lost her husband in the heroic fight to end the terrorist threat on United Flight 93. She established a foundation to support the children who lost their parents on the flight.

There are single parents who do a wonderful job of child rearing. We have all seen people rise up from unspeakable pain and loss to rebuild lives. We also know people who succumb to despair and bitterness, the acid of their misery killing off every living thing around them. What makes the difference?

I heard a memorable sermon on this topic by Jesse Jackson. "Jesus," he said, "could have gone through life on earth a self-pitying victim. My momma wasn't married to my daddy when she got pregnant. I was born in a barn 'cause we were so poor. My parents forgot me in Jerusalem for three days when I was only twelve. My hometown folks threw me out. My friends were a bunch of beach bums. The church leaders hated me. I didn't have a house or a bed to call my own. But Jesus didn't say these things. He chose to trust and move ahead. He said 'the one who sent me is with me, he has not left me alone.'[2] He helped other people with their problems instead of whining about his own."

One of the most insightful books that I've ever read is *Poverty of the Spirit* by the German theologian Johannes Metz. He writes,

> Christ did not "identify" with misery or "choose" it; it was his lot. That is the only way we really taste misery, for it has its own inscrutable laws. His life tells us that such neediness can become a blessed sacrament of "poverty of the spirit." With nothing of one's own to provide security, the wretched person has only hope—the virtue so quickly misunderstood by the secure and the rich. The latter confuse it with shallow optimism and a childish trust in life, whereas hope emerges in the shattering experience of living, "despite all hope" (Rom 4:18). We really hope when we no longer have anything of our own. Any possession or personal strength tempts us to a vain self-reliance, just as material wealth easily becomes a temptation to "spiritual opulence."[3]

Thus a tired, hungry, empty-handed Jesus could tell His disciples, " 'I have food to eat that you do not know about.' "[4] And he could say that the impoverished widow gave the greatest gift because she gave up to God the very thing that she depended on for survival.[5]

My friend reached down into the pocket of his heart and gave love to his family out of the emotional poverty of his childhood. This is grace you know—to risk your emptiness for another. The Creator of the universe relinquished His seat beside the Father to became a diapered, dependent infant, leaving His divine powers at home to live on the road. On a day of rejection, Jesus said, " 'For this reason the Father loves me, because I lay down my life in order to take it up again.' "[6]

Philip Yancey, in an essay on the life and work of the Harvard psychiatrist Robert Coles, included this haunting description of Jesus' gift of emptiness.

> Coles reflected on the peculiar circumstances of life that God had chosen in coming to earth: as a carpenter who associated with peasants and fishermen, his mother used to remind him, not as a doctor or lawyer or college professor. God did, in the words of Annie's father, the sharecropper, "come and see for Himself."
>
> "We have the mind of Jesus Christ in our heads," a migrant farm worker said in an interview, and at the time Coles, thinking like a doctor, wondered if the man was drunk or crazy or delirious or slow of thought. Only later, when Coles took time to reflect on

the mind of Jesus Christ as it was actually lived out—in exile and wandering, in pain, in scorn, isolation, loneliness, the "mind" of kenosis, or emptying—could he see the profound truth in what the man had said. "He didn't have to come here, you know," one little girl said of Jesus.[7]

Jesus calls us out of our self-reliance to put down our carefully honed survival skills, to drop our chameleon camouflage, to move beyond the walls of our sensitive distrust. Instinctively, we whisper, "No one is going to take care of me, so I will take care of myself." Our survival is the thought that we cling to in season and out, and it is our most difficult possession to put down. We can polish the "all I've got is me" idea into virtuous artifice of simplicity and humility. A striking story illustrates the problem:

A certain Christian thought it was of vital importance to be poor and austere. It had never dawned on him that the vitally important thing was to drop his ego; that the ego fattens on holiness just as much as on worldliness, on poverty as on riches, on austerity as on luxury. There is nothing the ego will not seize upon to inflate itself.

"Disciple: 'I have come to you with nothing in my hands.'
"Master: 'Then drop it at once!'
"Disciple: 'But how can I drop it? It is nothing.'
"Master: 'Then carry it around with you! You can make a possession of your nothing. And carry your renunciation around with you like a trophy. Don't drop your possessions. Drop your ego.' "[8]

If nothing is all that you have, then there is no greater gift that you can give to your Maker. Jesus Christ is relentless. He commands the surrender of our most intimate human relationships, "and even life itself" as a condition of discipleship.[9] He requires us to put down our baggage and carry the cross with both hands. " 'Whoever does not carry the cross and follow me cannot be my disciple. . . . So therefore, none of you can become my disciple if you do not give up all your possessions.' "[10] The mathematics of the kingdom begin with subtraction.

Does this frighten you? If so, that's understandable. It frightens me too. Here's another question. Do you want to lock and deadbolt your life as a survivor, or do you want to clean out the cupboards and empty the drawers and risk it all on the "riches of his grace that he lavishe[s] on us"?[11] This is the issue of Christianity. It may even be the question of the judgment. We can attempt to hoard our provisions against the day we have to pay up, or we can admit we don't have enough and are never going to have enough, and give it up and ask God to take care of us. That's what the widow did in throwing in her two coins at the temple that day. That's what my friend did in risking his broken heart in the love of his wife and children. That's what Jesus did in letting go of equality with God and becoming human to the point of dying as one of us for us.[12]

We are saved by grace and not by anything we do and not by anything we have.[13] This is not some abstract theological principle. This is life we are talking about. In the week ahead, take some quiet time to think about what and whom you can't live without. If it is anyone or anything other than Jesus Christ, then open your hands and give them or it up to God. The big gifts don't really come from those who have a lot of stuff. The gift that counts is the gift of whatever we think we have to live on, even if it is little or nothing. Remember, God didn't withhold His own Son for us. If a gift of infinite enormity was necessary for our salvation, how do we really think our grasping and hoarding can help us?

Questions for Reflection

1. How has a loss prepared you to receive grace?
2. What did Jesus Christ give up for you?
3. What are you willing to give up for Jesus Christ?

48

Answers in Surprise Packages

The answers to our prayers may require us to set aside our prejudices.

On the first day of Unleavened Bread, when the Passover lamb is sacrificed, his disciples said to him, "Where do you want us to go and make the preparations for you to eat the Passover?" So he sent two of his disciples, saying to them, "Go into the city, and a man carrying a jar of water will meet you; follow him, and wherever he enters, say to the owner of the house, 'The Teacher asks, Where is my guestroom where I may eat the Passover with my disciples?' He will show you a large room upstairs, furnished and ready. Make preparations for us there." So the disciples set out and went to the city, and found everything as he had told them; and they prepared the Passover meal.[1]

Tensions were high. This was the big religious and social event of the year. So much depended on the preparations and setting of the meal. A lot of families experience this kind of pressure at Thanksgiving and Christmas dinners. Traditions demand perfection, and the effort to meet the expectation strains human relationships.

It was late to be making arrangements for a large sit-down meal in a city where none of them lived. They asked Jesus where He wanted them to start, and His answer was surprising. He told them to go look for a man carrying a water jar and take it from there.

Men didn't generally carry the water jars in first-century Palestine. Fetching the water was women's work. Jesus' clue was about as subtle as a man walking in to an Oakland Raider's football game carrying a Gucci handbag.

Finding someone that nonconforming would be easy. The challenge was the instruction to follow him.

In my experience, people are rigid about their traditional meals. There are "rules" about who will come to dinner, in whose home the meal will be served, what ingredients will be used, where those ingredients will be purchased, who will be welcome in the kitchen, and who needs to stay out. Attendees of each gender generally assume certain roles. In that culture, the men made the meal, so no big deal there. I can, however, imagine Peter saying, "Let me get this straight, Lord! You want us to follow a GUY carrying a water jar? What if someone sees us!"

The expectations for spiritual leadership can be just as rigid. I remember one woman in a pastoral search committee announcing, "We need a man as big, strong, and forceful in speaking as the apostle Paul." I laughed out loud, which made her angry. Paul's contemporary critics said, " 'His bodily presence is weak, and his speech contemptible.' "[2] Paul himself, in defense, referred to himself as "a fool" and not as tough or authoritative as his critics demanded.[3]

There was an early time in my denomination when one couldn't be ordained a pastor unless one was a male with a beard. There was a later time when a pastor was deemed suspicious or even unfit if he had a beard. Now fights rage and congregations split over whether women can be ordained or speak in church. I once was ordered not to sing special music in a church because my duet partner was going to accompany us on the guitar, which the pastor deemed "a vulgar and common instrument." It's always amused me that the same pastor often performed for the congregation on his cherished instrument—a handsaw played with a fiddle bow. Go figure!

Some persons say that a person with tattoos and pierced body parts could never preach the gospel. I have been blessed and edified by the Word of God proclaimed by young men and women of that appearance even though such decorations would not be of my choosing. Paul was careful to point out that it is the shining treasure of the knowledge of the glory of God's love contained in the earthen vessel of the human witness that counts. It's our loss if we reject the treasure because we'd like it delivered in a more tasteful package.

Peter, in prayer, was led by God to do things that every bit of religious training and conviction that he possessed told him were "profane and unclean."[4] Peter's submission to that instruction opened the gospel to the entire non-Jewish world. When Peter first entered the home of the Roman centurion Cornelius, he told the assembled guests, " 'You yourselves know that it is unlawful for a Jew to associate with or to visit a Gentile; but God has shown me that I should not call anyone profane or unclean.' "[5] Later, in response to critics of this visit, Peter said, " 'As I began to speak, the Holy Spirit fell upon them just as it had upon us at the beginning. . . . If then God gave them the same gift that he gave us when we believed in the Lord Jesus Christ, who was I that I could hinder God?' "[6]

Am I making too much out of a simple set of directions to find a dining room? I don't think so when we consider the power of culture, the importance of that meal, and the fact that none of the twelve disciples were themselves fit candidates for the seminary. Jesus said a burly, temperamental fisherman exhibited the kind of revelation and faith upon which the church would be based, even though within minutes Jesus reproached him for being a tool of Satan.[7] More than that, it is human nature to be much more concerned about who's carrying the jar than what's in it. It isn't that far a stretch to say I wouldn't drink water carried by a man if, for the same motivation, you can say, "I can't stand to listen to a woman speaking in church."

The real issue, of course, is who is giving the instructions. Jesus told them to look for the man doing the unusual thing and follow him to the home where the owner would make the room available. "They found everything as he had told them." The meal was prepared and shared. Jesus washed feet in another surprising turnabout, and the secret of spiritual servanthood was revealed. The gospel was revealed and advanced that evening. It would have been an eternal tragedy if some had missed out because they could not accept the instructions that brought them together.

Each one of us must examine our hearts for prejudices that would stop us from obeying Jesus. If I find something or someone that sticks in my craw and causes me to say, "Don't ask me to accept this person, Lord," I know that I am still an idolater putting my images and expectations ahead of Jesus' will. There is nothing else to do in that moment except bow my head in submission and pray with Peter, "If God has given this man or this woman the same gift that I received when I believed in the Lord Jesus Christ, who am I to hinder God. Change my heart, God, and make me more like you."

Questions for Reflection

1. How have your cultural traditions and social environments influenced your expectations about answered prayer?
2. Think of an incident when God's leading seemed opposed to your religious traditions. How was that conflict resolved?
3. When has Jesus led you out of your bias and judgment to accept a person?

49

Do Whatever He Tells You to Do

The miracle of the wedding feast at Cana reveals a Savior who is concerned and willing to help us with every one of our embarrassments and disappointments.

I don't know about you, but it tickles me that Jesus' first miracle was to save a wedding reception from social failure by turning dishwater into fine wine. This is how the apostle John who witnessed the event described it:

> On the third day there was a wedding in Cana of Galilee, and the mother of Jesus was there. Jesus and his disciples had also been invited to the wedding. When the wine gave out, the mother of Jesus said to him, "They have no wine." And Jesus said to her, "Woman, what concern is that to you and to me? My hour has not yet come." His mother said to the servants, "Do whatever he tells you." Now standing there were six stone water jars for the Jewish rites of purification, each holding twenty or thirty gallons. Jesus said to them, "Fill the jars with water." And they filled them up to the brim. He said to them, "Now draw some out, and take it to the chief steward." So they took it. When the steward tasted the water that had become wine, and did not know where it came from (though the servants who had drawn the water knew), the steward called the bridegroom and said to him, "Everyone serves the good wine first, and then the inferior wine after the guests have become drunk. But you have kept the good wine until now." Jesus did this, the first of his signs, in Cana of Galilee, and revealed his glory, and his disciples believed in him.[1]

There are great lessons to be learned from this story about the power of Jesus to transform the ordinary into the wonderful.

> The gifts of Jesus are ever fresh and new. The feast that He provides for the soul never fails to give satisfaction and joy. Each new gift increases the capacity of the receiver to appreciate and enjoy the blessings of the Lord. He gives grace for grace. There can be no failure of supply. If you abide in Him, the fact that you receive a rich gift today insures the reception of a richer gift tomorrow.[2]

The Scripture says we should pray about everything.[3] There are always those self-appointed receptionists for God who claim this verse doesn't mean what it says and God can't be bothered except with the really "big stuff." Coincidentally, these people love arguments over "big stuff," such as whether Jesus changed the water into champagne or Welch's grape juice. (No, I'm not advocating alcohol, nor do I wish to enter that debate.) Running out of refreshments at a wedding reception sounds like a human failure to plan—hardly a concern to the Creator of the universe.

Of course, whether or not this was a big deal depends on whose doorstep the blame for the faux pas is laid. The wedding festivals in those days lasted several days. The bridegroom, who would have footed the bill, would have been highly embarrassed about the wine running out as would the chief steward, who functioned as the wedding coordinator. It was this embarrassment that Jesus relieved with His miracle. It is fair to conclude that our mistakes and social shortcomings are some of the "everything" that Paul said that we can pray about.

Mary, observing the predicament, told Jesus, "They have no wine." His answer to His mother was a bit harsh. "Woman," He called her. "Woman, what concern is that to you and me? My hour is not yet come."

Let's see—you are God incarnate, your conception was announced to your mother by an angel, you were conceived by the Holy Spirit, angels sang to shepherds at your birth, three brilliant scholars of prophecy and astronomy followed a star to your birthplace, you held your own at age twelve with the religious leadership of your nation, at your baptism a light shone on you and a dove flew to your shoulder and God spoke from the heavens, and you recently completed a forty-day fast in the wilderness facing down Satan's worst temptations by faith alone. Now your mother wants you to use your astonishing gifts as a party favor. I think the reaction is understandable. In fact, isn't that just like a mom? It's one of those passages that in its authentic humanity helps prove the Scripture to me.

If one struggles to get past the abrupt difficulty of Jesus' response, there is something to be gained from Mary's trust in Him to do what was best, even if His answer contained neither comfort nor clarity. All of us face that test of faith and often. Do we trust Jesus or our feelings?

"Do whatever he tells you to do," Mary told the servants. Now, there's a daunting thought. Sell the house and the car, close the office, move into the slums and help the poor. Go care for AIDS victims in Africa. Bathe, dress, and feed the developmentally disabled or invalid elderly. Forgive the unforgivable. Love your enemies. Be kind to those who spitefully use you. Don't marry that person who looks so good. What if he tells you to do a wild and crazy thing? You take this kind of advice, and it can blow up your whole life.

Whew! He only asked them to get the jars and fill them with water, not that it wasn't a task. Each jar was stone and held about twenty-five gallons. Imagine taking out your twenty-five-gallon trash can if it were hollowed out of rock! The jars were meant to hold water for washing hands and cooking utensils in a ritual of purification from the contamination of everyday life. The jars were hard, heavy, intended for cleansing, but empty, like the law of Moses engraved on tablets of stone explaining how to avoid getting dirty but proving ineffective in itself to cleanse from the grime of everyday life in a dirty world. Someone new was on the scene to change the water of cleansing into the wine of celebration and to fulfill the law with living, breathing grace.

How much grace? Around a hundred fifty gallons of wine, enough for nine hundred bottles or so. Ask the Creator and Savior of the world to cater a wedding reception, and what do you think you're going to get? He's used to ocean-size bowls. It's hard to downsize from that scale. And it was the "good stuff," the best they'd ever tasted. The chief steward, experienced in these matters, marveled at the taste and complimented the bridegroom on his class. "Most guys in your position would serve the best tasting drink at the start and serve cheaper brands the third day when no one cares. But you've saved the best for last."

A French horn instructor once told me, "However you play, whatever mistakes you make, always hit the last note and leave them with that." I think that it's the same idea. It's not the roughness of the beginning of the journey, but it's transformation along the way and the grace of the ending. "Better is the end of a thing than its beginning," wrote Solomon.[4]

Continuing that thought, the words "On the third day," which begin John's account, likely refer to the passage of time since Jesus had called His disciples. The "third day," however, is an important Scriptural allusion to the resurrection. Turning the water into wine has traditionally been believed to show Jesus' power over creation and thereby to produce new life. For this reason, it is significant that the miracle occurred at a wedding because, since Eden, marriage has been the God-ordained method of creating and nurturing new life. John the Baptist spoke of Jesus as Bridegroom.[5] Jesus often used weddings and wedding banquets as illustrations of grace.[6]

Some Eastern Orthodox commentators rank this miracle of life and love and joy as Jesus' first in importance as well as chronology. We can know this: Cana revealed a Savior of grace and kindness who cares about our embarrassments and disappointments no matter how trivial. He is a God who seeks intimacy with imperfect humanity. After all, the power of intimate love lies in the Lover's embrace of us in our mundane moments and over our blemishes and inadequacy. We are transformed by the Lover's unrestrained love and grace lavished on us. Thus the miracle of Cana revealed Christ's glory in a generous action of shining joy. John reported that as a result "his disciples believed in him."

John was an angry young man who found himself transformed into "the one whom Jesus loved."[7] He wrote at the beginning of his gospel, "From his fullness we have all received, grace upon grace. The law indeed was given through Moses; grace and truth came through Jesus Christ. No one has ever seen God. It is God the only Son, who is close to the Father's heart, who has made him known."[8] Author Richard Rohr says, "If Jesus is the revelation of the heart of God, it's very good news about the nature of God."[9] Think on these words of Jesus: "It is your Father's good pleasure to give you the kingdom." "I came that they might have life, and have it abundantly."[10] However heavy or empty your jar of stone is at this moment, consider that Jesus Christ wants you to have and enjoy life simply and wonderfully because He loves you. Do whatever He tells you to do, and He can transform the contents of that jar into something amazing. It's called "grace," and I bring you word of it.

Questions for Reflection

1. What is your reaction to the thought that Christ is concerned about your social embarrassments?
2. How does prayer address the conflicts between your trust for Christ and your fears?
3. When have you experienced the transformation of something ordinary into something extraordinary through prayer?

50

Praying in Tongues

Music swells with prayer from the deepest places of the heart.

> By day the LORD commands his steadfast love,
>   and at night his song is with me,
>   a prayer to the God of my life.[1]

Playing the piano in the dark late at night is on my short list of favorite things to do. I can't see the keys, but I can feel them and hear them, and there is only the music. The darkness allows me to express to God the deepest thoughts of my heart through the melody and chords.

A few years ago, a Pentecostal pastor took an interest in me and tried hard without success to get me to speak in tongues. I was not opposed on principle to the experience; I'm open to anything that God wants to do in my life, but it doesn't really matter to me whether I speak in tongues or not. The man invited me to the place he was staying, laid his hands on my head, and prayed and prayed. Finally, he gave up and told a colleague in amazement, "I have never seen anyone before who exhibits so much of the fruit of the Spirit who doesn't have the Holy Spirit."

This made me chuckle because you'd think the fruit of the Spirit has to come from the Spirit.[2] But the man continued to pray for me that I would receive the Holy Spirit.

I told Patricia about the encounter and she said, "But you do speak in tongues."

"What do you mean?"

"That's what playing the piano is for you."

It's true that I feel close to God when I'm playing in the darkness and the joy of God's presence wells up from my heart and rolls out in waves through my fingers. It is a resonance of the steadfast love that holds me in the embrace of my Abba and is truly a prayer to the God of my life. This experience is not confined to the night hours, nor does it require me to sit at the keyboard. There are times, especially on the weekends, when I will sit and play for an hour or so with Patricia sitting on the couch reading and singing softly. The Spirit of the living God stirs my soul in those moments with gratitude, and it is not unusual for me to finish unable to speak because of my tears of thankfulness at the faithfulness of Jesus Christ. A song I learned in childhood from my parents sums up this experience:

> In shady, green pastures, so rich and so sweet,
> God leads His dear children along;
> Where the water's cool flow bathes the weary one's feet,
> God leads His dear children along.
>
> Some through the waters, some through the flood,
> Some through the fire but all through the blood;
> Some through great sorrow, but God gives a song,
> In the night season and all the day long.
>
> Sometimes on the mount where the sun shines so bright,
> God leads His dear children along;
> Sometimes in the valley, in the darkest of night,
> God leads his dear children along.
>
> Some through the waters, some through the flood,
> Some through the fire but all through the blood;
> Some through great sorrow, but God gives a song,
> In the night season and all the day long.[3]

My family sang our faith. Around the piano in the evenings, on the road, day or night, we praised our God and called upon the memory of His loving compassion that the hymns and choruses evoked for us wherever we were, whatever we were traveling toward or coming from. The songs were recorded in my heart and are often replayed in my thoughts day and night.

It is a rare morning that I do not wake with a song running through my mind. This morning it was a hymn that brought back to my mind an experience two years ago when I went to speak in Boulder, Colorado. I stayed in the home of the woman who had extended the invitation to speak and her physician husband. His aged mother lived with them, frail and weak, unable to walk. She spent her waking hours on the couch in the family room, dozing and watching Christian TV, brought to her by satellite.

Late on Friday afternoon before we left for the first meeting, I sat down at their grand piano and played. I asked the old woman if there was a favorite hymn she would like to hear. Without hesitation she said, "Oh yes, 'All the Way My Savior Leads Me.' " I began to play. Her sweet, quivery voice followed me with the words of the wonderful blind song-writer, Fannie J. Crosby—words that clearly had illuminated the woman's journey through life to these final years, and she knew all of them as one who'd lived them out.

> All the way my Savior leads me; what have I to fear beside?
> Can I doubt His tender mercy, who through life has been my guide?
> Heavenly peace, divinest comfort, here by faith in Him to dwell;
> For I know what-e'er befall me, Jesus doeth all things well;
> For I know what-e'er befall me, Jesus doeth all things well.
>
> All the way my Savior leads me; cheers each winding path I tread;
> Gives me grace for every trial, feeds me with the living bread;
> Though my weary steps may falter, and my soul athirst may be,
> Gushing from the Rock before me, lo, a spring of joy I see;
> Gushing from the Rock before me, lo, a spring of joy I see.
>
> All the way my Savior leads me; O the fullness of His love;
> Perfect rest to me is promised in my Father's house above;
> When I wake to life immortal, wing my flight to realms of day,
> This my song through endless ages, Jesus led me all the way;
> This my song through endless ages, Jesus led me all the way.[4]

It's my fondest desire that the thoughts this song expresses be the truth of my life in its final moments. For now, I hear this song and other songs of faith in a gracious God as I traverse the exposed reaches of the days and endure the long night passages.

I have read many books and articles laboring over what it means to "rejoice always and pray without ceasing" as Scripture instructs us to do.[5] The attitude of praise and prayer that instruction calls for cannot be constructed by formula and effort. The apostle Peter wrote that rejoicing "with an indescribable and glorious joy" was the natural response to receiving "the salvation of your souls."[6] If you want to pray without ceasing, ask God to put His song in your heart and listen to it in silence until it becomes part of you. You will know solitude after that, but not loneliness.

I've known two people who said that they "hated music" and couldn't care less if they never heard it. I think there must be some deep, mad sadness in them. To hate music is to live life without the best lubrication for its frictions. When I lie tossing and doubtful in my bed at two in the morning, hearing the familiar words and music of faithfulness in the memory of my heart is a continuing reminder that the God who loves me steadfastly by day is still with me by night, lifting me over the rocks and shoals of trouble on the flood-tides of His grace. The song rising in my soul is an invitation to tell Christ, with no reservation, what is bothering me and then to yield to His loving arms like a brokenhearted child confessing to his understanding dad or mom.

Anne Lamott describes this divine power of hymns to move Mattie, the confused and longing heroine of her novel *Blue Shoe*. "The choir sang her favorite songs, 'Just As I Am' and 'Softly and Tenderly.' Mattie heard the desperation and generosity beneath the notes. She listened with her eyes closed to the sermon, which was about letting God into your worst drawers and closets, and how healing could not happen if you let God into a living room that had been cleaned for the occasion. If you wanted the healing, you had to show God the mess."[7]

I wandered from God in the early years of my adulthood. I was busy figuring things out for myself and was trying to prove that I didn't need anyone or anything. What kept me connected through all that time were the hymns that I'd learned growing up. My devotions during that period consisted of nothing more than playing those hymns on the piano late at night with the lights turned off. "Echoes of mercy, whispers of love," was how Fannie Crosby described such connections in my favorite hymn, "Blessed Assurance." Hearing those echoes and whispers in the darkness was enough to keep the flame of God's love flickering until the daybreak of His grace became my reality.

My experience is not unique. We will all need songs in the night until we see God face to face. "There will be no more night; they need no light of lamp or sun, for the Lord God will be their light, and they will reign forever and ever."[8] If you are listening for a particular melody or words, stop! Lie still in the darkness, surrender everything, even your hope, to Him and wait. God, himself, wants to be your song.

> O Thou in whose presence my soul takes delight,
> On whom in affliction I call,
> My comfort by day and my song in the night,
> My hope, my salvation, my all![9]

Questions for Reflection

1. When do you feel closest to God in prayer? Why?
2. How does music influence your prayer life?
3. What "songs in the night" encourage your faith and hope?

51

Under the Cross
One Morning . . .

God changes hearts through a prayer at the foot of the cross.

I experienced an encounter literally at the foot of the cross that brought home to me the power of prayer to reconcile and meld men and women of diverse backgrounds and thinking into the body of Christ.

It was a place I did not want to be at the time. My plan had been to spend the day with my son on a relaxed train jaunt into LA and back. The previous week had been tense and draining.

The phone rang in the early morning while I was reading. It was my friend Richard, inviting us to go join a small group on a hike up Mount Rubidoux, a big rocky hill between the city of Riverside and the Santa Ana River.

A big white cross made out of iron pipe is anchored into the highest point of Mount Rubidoux. The first Easter sunrise service was held there in 1909, and its tradition continues each spring.

I told Richard that I'd check with my family and call him right back. I was weary and grumpy and looking forward to time with my son, but as soon as Andrew heard that his friends were going, he wanted to hike. "Don't you want to ride the train?" I pleaded. I didn't think I could face anyone else.

"No, I want to go up to Mount Rubidoux," he said.

So I called Richard back and made arrangements for transportation. "Bring something along to read to us under the cross," he said.

"OK, I'll see what I can scrounge up."

A *Christianity Today* magazine had come with an excerpt from Philip Yancey's book *What's So Amazing About Grace.* I grabbed the copy and dropped it into my day pack.

Richard and Debbie and their two daughters Kelli and Katie arrived to pick us up in their van. Driving behind was Jill and two of her daughters, Tori and Hillary. The kids worked it out so they could ride together, and we were off.

We piled out at the gate and began to walk up the road. It was a mild fall day dappled with big white cumulus clouds. Pretty soon we were spread all over the hillside. The kids clambered straight up. Richard and I took a short-cut. Debbie and Jill took the road.

We were damp and breathless when we reached the top. The kids hopped up and down the stone terraces of the sunrise service amphitheater. Debbie warned them to stay in sight of the grown-ups at all times. Then we adults made our way to the base of the cross.

I sat on the cement pedestal with my back leaning against the cross. Jill, Debbie, and Richard found seats to their liking on the surrounding outcroppings.

It was peaceful. I pulled out my harmonica and played some tunes while looking over the landscape. The view was 360 degrees with the mountains and the valley of the river on one side and downtown Riverside on the other. "Do you want me to read?" I asked.

"Sure," Richard said.

The Yancey excerpt was a series of vignettes on the theme of grace. A penniless vagrant wins the lottery. A jilted bride throws her lavish wedding banquet for street people. An overextended entrepreneur finds his million dollar debt forgiven. In one of the most beautiful pieces of spiritual writing that I've read, a wayward teen-age girl from Traverse City, Michigan, makes her way home from the dregs of Detroit not knowing what she'd find when she arrived in the middle of the night. Her love-sick father and mother were waiting with a big welcome-home party. She begins to blurt out her apology when her Dad interrupts her. "Hush, child. We've got no time for that. No time for apologies. You'll be late for the party. A banquet's waiting for you at home."[1]

I could get through the teenager's story only by blinking back tears.

At some point, Debbie interrupted. She called out for Katie, who had drifted out of sight.

As we all stood and looked for the missing six-year-old, a man appeared out of the rocks. He was wearing jeans and a wool plaid shirt buttoned to the neck despite the warmth of the day. He was wearing a bright blue baseball cap with a large shiny, silver, plastic cross pinned to it. Another cross hung from his neck. He clutched a white plastic garbage bag as he walked up to us.

"Are you the one calling out to the little girl down below?" he asked Debbie.

"Yes."

"She's all right."

"She is?"

"She looks fine to me," he concluded, just as Katie's yellow curls bobbed back into view below us.

We thanked him, and he walked on past as I resumed reading. Yancey follows the parables with a personal commentary on grace and Jesus' desire for the lost even over His affinity for the righteous.

Suddenly a voice broke through, loud and harsh. "Are you people talking over how to bring this country back to God and kick the devil out on his rear!"

Shocked, I stopped reading, and we all looked up to see our baseball-capped friend standing beside us, his plastic crosses glittering in the late-morning sun.

"You know it's time for true Christians to stand up and be counted and take back this country for God, the way the Pilgrims intended. Is that what you're talking about?" he demanded.

I could see that he was angry and hear that he was rude too.

"We're talking about grace," I said quietly.

"Grace is good," he boomed out, "but we need true Christians to step out of the box and put prayer back in the schools and take this nation back for God. We've got to get Satan off our backs and fight the powers of evil!"

"God doesn't need our help to do that," Richard said. I could tell from many conversations that he was throwing out the bait.

The man was surprised. "Of course, He needs our help. God has been kicked out of government. He's been kicked out of the schools. There's filth all around us, and we can't just stand by."

He plunged ahead. "My wife cheated on me. I caught her in bed with another man. She divorced me and got the kids, and I was ordered to pay child support and couldn't say a thing about it."

He was ranting now. "She ran off and took the kids to Oregon, and I don't know where she is. I've got to reimburse the state for forty thousand dollars in welfare payments she received, and I don't know where she is or my kids either. Is that fair? Do you think that's fair? That's why I'm out here picking up cans—to pay off her welfare."

"I'm sorry," I said.

He gulped a breath and kept going. "We've got to get people back in church and get the churches working to turn this thing around. When a man's wife can cheat on him and then he loses his kids, that's wrong!"

Richard challenged him again. "I don't think church means anything in itself."

The man replied, "You're right! I don't think ninety percent of the churches are any good. My church don't stand for anything any more. 'Once saved, always saved.' " He laughed. "That means Satan is saved 'cause he was saved once."

I could tell that this was an old argument of his.

Our group was silent. Glancing around, I could see Jill and Debbie were tense. The man was really angry.

He said, "A lot of my friends think they can do anything they want 'cause they're saved. I can't believe the things that they do. They spend all their time looking at pornography on the Internet. They don't have time for their families. They have no time to do anything with me.

"I've asked a couple of times to help out at churches—to replace their roofs that are blowing off. They say, 'no.' They want a contractor even though they don't have any money to pay one, because they are afraid of liability. So they won't let me help."

I was thinking hard. *What can I say to this man?* I had spent much of the previous week arguing issues of religious liberty. Argument wasn't called for with him. I didn't want to say anything to set him off more or make me sound like I was trying to be superior.

What do I say, Lord? What do any of us say? We are reading about grace, and you sent us this man, angry and legalistic. We are literally sitting at the foot of the cross. What do You want said, Lord, or are You saying it already?

The man said, "I'll get out of your hair," but he made no move.

You can pray, the Holy Spirit whispered to me.

"You've got to help take this country back," the man started in again.

The Spirit moved in me again. *Pray, but wait until he really is ready to go,* I heard in my heart.

"Do you know that God loves you?" I asked him.

He looked up at me sitting above him and smiled. "Yes, I do. God loves me, and I know he wants to use me."

"Yes, he does," I agreed.

The man wasn't done yet. "God needs people. He can't leave it in the hands of college-educated computer-users who just screw up everything."

I didn't show it, but I smiled inside.

"God needs ordinary people to get up and fight the forces of evil all around us," the man pronounced.

"Well, I'll get out of your hair," he said again. He started to walk down the path.

"Wait a second," I called out. "May we pray for you and your family?"

He stopped still, then turned and squinted up and said, "Well . . . yeah . . . sure."

"Good," I said and opened up to God as he took off his cap.

"Father in heaven, we come in the name of Jesus and His love and grace to pray for this man, this brother, and his ex-wife and children. Father, we pray that your arms of love will hold him and your grace will pour over him, that you will protect him and reconcile him to his family. We lift his children up to you right now and pray that your love will re-store them. Lord, this brother has spoken of injustice in a legal system that is unfeeling and does not recognize the hurts and wounds of flesh and blood or meet the needs of a broken heart. We are on this mountain surrounded by the glories you have created—the mountains, the clouds, the sun—and we know that we are surrounded by your love."

I heard the man choke back a sob and gasp for air.

"Lord, be a shield about this man and his loved ones, be his glory and the lifter of his head. May the blood of Jesus cover his ex-wife and the children and him. May it wash them all in its grace. May Your love be his blessing as he leaves this place. We pray this in Jesus' name. Amen."

Even as I finished the prayer, I knew what this day was about—this moment—this man—were all in the plan of the Lord who had to over-come my resistance and selfishness to get me there to pray this prayer.

The man prayed himself. His voice was soft now. "Lord, bless these precious people. Amen."

"Be blessed," I said.

"I am blessed," he replied. "I'm already better, finding you precious people here."

He put his cap back on and adjusted it. He reached down and picked up his bag of cans and disappeared into the rocks.

God had spoken to all of us.

Questions for Reflection

1. How can God speak to you through a difficult encounter with a stranger?
2. What does Christ's sacrifice on the cross mean for your differ-ences with others? Read and reflect on Ephesians 2:11–22.
3. How could praying together bring peace between you and those who are challenging you?

52

From Where Will My Help Come?

Sometimes our devotional life can get in the way of intimacy with God.

To have found God and still to pursue Him is the soul's paradox of love, scorned indeed by the too-easily-satisfied religionist, but justified in happy experience by children of the burning heart.—A. W. Tozer

The Indian summer day got away from me as I meandered through sun-dappled Vermont woods. The trail required attention for its up and down course over rocky terrain interspersed with bogs.

About five o'clock, I realized that I might be in some trouble. The height of the ridge to the west would bring the sun down early in the forest. I was three thousand miles from home, in terrain that I hadn't seen before, with no flashlight, no food, no cell phone service, and no one else knowing my exact whereabouts. There wasn't a rule of safe hiking that I hadn't broken. It was a sure bet that I would not make my destination before night came on.

Now I knew what the guidebook meant when it said, "You will realize that you didn't set aside enough time for this hike." The moss-slick boulders and ledges, crevices, and mud holes made maintaining a steady pace difficult. The canopy of pines, oaks, and maples cast deceptive shadows.

But I had come too far to retrace my steps before darkness fell. At least I had a distinct landmark of a granite palisade behind me to the east and a lake off to my left that I was circling. I picked a point on the opposite shore that I wanted to reach by six o'clock and kept moving.

I'd entered these woods intending to pray and read, but there was no time for that. I prayed as I walked in rhythm with my breathing.

I'd passed a couple a while back who had canoed in to their campsite. My hope was to stay near the lake where my voice would carry across the water to them if I became lost or hurt after dark.

The sun set behind me as I rounded the west end of the lake and started east. A garter snake raced across the path, the blaze of its three yellow stripes the only thing to distinguish it against the shadowed green moss and duff of the forest floor.

Pressing on to use the remaining light, I found it harder to see the blue blazes on the trees. I was looking down most of the time to guard against a misstep. Then, in no more than a moment, I was lost. I raised my eyes and saw no trail to speak of and I had obviously wandered deeper into the woods and away from the lake.

Bushwhacking through the underbrush, I began to wonder what poison ivy looks like.

Poison oak grows in great matted thickets of shiny-leafed misery out in California where I am from. I know the slogan, "Leaves of three are bad for thee," but I hadn't a clue as to what was brushing against my legs and arms in the twilight.

Then from out of the darkness ahead of me blasted the incongruous sound of honky-tonk country music. This was Vermont! I might expect chamber music or even folk-rock maybe—but, country?

The music had to come from a vehicle because of the power of the sound. I headed toward the music and came into a clearing where about twenty young men, women, and children were laughing and talking, congregating for something—maybe line dancing.

They were surprised to see me with my walking pole and khaki bush hat, and one of them asked me, "Are you in charge?"

I didn't know how to answer that question, so I asked, "Do you know where the trail is?"

"We haven't seen it," was the reply as if to say, "Who needs a trail when you've got a Winnebago?"

The woods turned to swamp beyond the clearing because, from the looks of the downed trees, beavers had dammed an outlet of the lake. I started uphill to find dry ground but found more big rocks in the thick woods.

Step by step, I stumbled up to a dirt road in the last light. I could make out the silhouette of the granite cliff and knew I was close to the end of the trail. A turn on another road, and I was back to the trailhead and the car.

My drive back through Montpelier was beautiful. God spreads out darkness over the rises and folds of the Green Mountains like a jeweler spreads black velvet in a display case to show off diamonds—only God shows off His stars.

> Lift up your eyes on high and see:
>> Who created these?
> He who brings out their host and numbers them,
>> calling them all by name;
> because he is great in his strength,
>> mighty in power,
>> not one is missing.[1]

I made my way back to the lodge at the foot of Mount Mansfield, where I had come for meetings. My hope was to spend some quality time in study and reflection through some days of business and then vacation. But that was not to be.

Within an hour of the end of the meeting three days later, I hiked straight up a mountain. It again took longer than I thought it would, and I had to pick my way out of the woods in the dark. There was no time to read the Bible or the book that I lugged up and down the trail in my pack.

I moved down to an inn on an island in Lake Champlain with the same results. The green woods with their first tinges of yellow, orange, and red, fields of purple asters and blue daisies, the steady west wind and lap of the waves all drew me in to wander and wonder at their beauty.

The basic habit of my life is reading. It is the most disciplined thing that I do. Here I was with the time and the perfect place to read, and I was watching waves roll, rivers run, and leaves fall. But I was enjoying myself, and things were peaceful and easy between God and me. The words to a beloved hymn kept rising from out of my heart to my mind.

> O worship the Lord in the beauty of holiness
> Bow down before Him, His glory proclaim;
> With gold of obedience and incense of lowliness
> Kneel and adore Him; the Lord is His name.[2]

My prayers were mellow and full of thanks to God and loving concern for my dear ones so far away.

The message began to sink in to me that my devotional life had become an obstacle to my relationship with Christ. Head in a book, I would never have seen the flood of yellow leaves through the great gorge of Smuggler's Notch or the sunrise over the Green Mountains from the pier on Lake Champlain or had watched gulls cruise for the sheer fun of the updrafts over the bluffs and straits.

A passage of Scripture has haunted me over the years. God told the prophet Zechariah, "Say to all the people of the land and the priests: When you fasted and lamented in the fifth month and in the seventh, for these seventy years, was it for me that you fasted?"[3]

A fast isn't only about abstaining from food and drink. It is a giving up of anything of which one is otherwise privileged to partake. The purpose is devotion to God.

A fast isn't an excuse to diet, watch less TV, or recycle more. It is an emptying of one's soul to be filled by the Holy Spirit.

Our very efforts to seek God and do His will can get in the way of enjoying intimacy with Him. It's like a mother slaving over a holiday meal for her family, refusing to leave her kitchen tasks to sit down and have a conversation with her husband and children. "I'm expressing my love for you" is the frequent excuse given by such women and by men like me who work constant long hours on the premise that we're providing for our families. What do such efforts really mean without communication, without presence, without the knowing intimacy that takes spending the good, the bad, and the mostly ordinary times together?

Jesus put it straight to Martha: Relationships come first. Jesus was ruthless about His followers' self-deception, substituting their own hard effort and good works for intimacy with Him. " 'Not everyone who says to me, "Lord, Lord," will enter the kingdom of heaven, but only the one who does the will of my Father in heaven. On that day many will say to me, "Lord, Lord, did we not prophesy in your name, and cast out demons in your name, and do many deeds of power in your name?" Then I will declare to them, "I never knew you; go away from me, you evildoers." ' "[4]

I take books with me whenever I travel. They are heavy and create packing problems, but I learn from them and am supported by them and speak to others from what I read. I hate the very possibility but have to wonder whether my books become a crutch, or worse, an idol? Kierkegaard compared a scholar consulting his commentaries with a small boy stuffing his pants with a pillow to cushion the spanking that he was about to receive.

The books filter thoughts and ideas about God for me, but no book makes the demands on me that simply reading the Word and silent listening do. Isaac of Nineveh, an early Christian patriarch, wrote, "Every man who delights in a multitude of words, even though he says admirable things, is empty within. If you love truth, be a lover of silence."

My sense is that Christ is teaching me fundamental things these days—surrender, dependence, patience, and acceptance—things as simple and harmonized as the colors of the Vermont Indian summer.

I equally disdain the oversimplifying and the overintellectualizing of the gospel, but I may have lost something in my search for the novel and the new.

Too often, when I glimpse a spiritual insight, I think about how it will read as a Word of Grace message or sound as a sermon or even a prayer prayed for and with a friend. There is more than a hint of arrogance in that reaction. The real question is, What is the Holy Spirit speaking to me?

I fill many roles and attempt to excel at all of them. I cannot possibly do so, yet, I try harder because . . . because I doubt that I will be loved and accepted if I don't achieve. I know that I am not alone in this.

Reading the following description of workaholism convicted me:

> Workaholics want to find their identity and fulfillment in only one of their three, full-time jobs (communion, community-building, and cocreativity), whether it is mothering, administering, counseling, selling, or preaching. We were meant to experience a balanced life of living wholly and completely for God. But workaholics invest all of their energies in one part of the human vocation, usually the "cocreativity" part in society. The reasons are well-documented. Usually raised in non-affirming environments, workaholics are attempting unconsciously to prove worthy of the approval of their parents and others. Workaholics are consumed by this inner drivenness and cannot play without feeling guilty. They have to work at play and cannot play at work. Work is too serious a matter. It often becomes misdirected worship as they use work to fill the God-shaped vacuum in their souls. A definition of idolatry is simply making something one's ultimate concern, other than the One who is ultimate. Even on vacations (if they take them at all) workaholics plan the next piece of work. Amos may be describing them when he rails against the people who spend their Sabbaths figuring out how to make more money as soon as it is over (Amos 8:5). The whole of life is oriented around what becomes one continuous workweek. But the outside effect of the workaholic is the same as the idler: they are a burden to all around them.[5]

When ancient Israel became entangled in the degrading pursuit of conditional acceptance and love from her neighbors to the point that God was forgotten in the life of the nation, God told the prophet Hosea,

I will now allure her,
> and bring her into the wilderness,
> and speak tenderly to her.[6]

"Come to me, all of you who are overburdened and laboring, and I will give you rest," said Jesus. "Learn from me for my tether to you is not taut to jerk you around and my requirements for you are light—You believe and I'll do the rowing while you rest."[7] From the context, it appears he said those words on a Sabbath walk through the fields that was disrupted by a specious argument over His grace versus the Pharisaical demand for exacting religious performance. " 'But if you had known what this means, "I desire mercy and not sacrifice," you would not have condemned the guiltless,' " Jesus told His critics.[8]

I read a card in Vermont that quoted Alex Ziton, age eight, "You don't really know someone until you've had recess with him." Jesus said that taking a recess with Him was how to get to know Him, and that makes it a miracle that I've gotten to know Him at all because my adult habit is to stay in from recess to finish my work so my "teachers" will approve.

Christ lavishes beauty and help on me, but I remain self-absorbed like a spoiled child. "What's it going to take?" He must ask. Yet, He knows that what He's done for me is sufficient. He patiently waits for me to realize that as well.

Driving back at night from the hike around the lake, down and around the dark ribbon of the Winsooki River, it occurred to me that Christ's love for us is a spring from which rivers of grace arise. His water pours through the tight places of gorges, the spaciousness of peaceful valleys, and the churning rush of rapids in our soul. Logs and leaves alike float by as our seasons in their turn are dry with low water around the big rocks and are full to overflowing in flood stage. The river changes course only when given the means and the power to do so. So too does our life change in the power and purpose of Christ. "Praise God from whom all blessings flow!"

Questions for Reflection

1. Reflect on a time when you experienced God in nature.
2. How might your devotional reading and routines actually interfere with your intimacy with God?
3. In what surprising and unexpected way has God been revealed to you?

End Notes

Bible texts are taken from the New Revised Standard Version (NRSV) unless otherwise noted.

Introduction

1. Ephesians 6:18
2. 1 Thessalonians 5:17.
3. Philippians 2:10, 11.
4. Proverbs 14:10.
5. John 10:1–18.

Chapter 1

1. Madame Jeanne Guyon, *Experiencing God Through Prayer* (Springdale, Pa.: Whitaker House, 1984), 11.
2. John 14:6.
3. Matthew 6:5–8, NIV.
4. Andrew Murray, *The Believer's School of Prayer* (Minneapolis: Bethany House, 1992), 40.
5. Roberta Bondi, *A Place to Pray: Reflections on the Lord's Prayer* (Nashville: Abingdon Press, 1998), 23, 24.
6. Ole Hallesby, *Prayer* (Minneapolis: Augsburg, 1994), 148–150.

Chapter 2

1. Hallesby, *Prayer*, 13. (See chap. 1, n. 6.)
2. Hebrews 11:6.
3. James 1:7, 8.
4. Mark 9:24.
5. See Matthew 6:7, 8, NIV.
6. Matthew 7:7, 8, NIV.
7. Mark 1:35.
8. Matthew 18:15–20.
9. Mark 11:22–24.
10. 1 Samuel 12:23.
11. Richard Foster, *Prayer: Finding the Heart's True Home* (San Francisco: HarperSanFrancisco, 1992), 180, 181.
12. Genesis 18:17–33.
13. Exodus 33:11.
14. John 17.

15. Brennan Manning, *The Lion and the Lamb* (Tarrytown, N.Y.: Chosen Books, 1986), 126.
16. Psalm 35:27.
17. Frederick Buechner, *The Magnificent Defeat* (San Francisco: HarperSanFrancisco, 1985), 135.
18. Isaiah 54:10, NIV.

Chapter 3

1. Genesis 12; 13.
2. Exodus 33:11.
3. John 15:15, 16, RSV.
4. Hebrews 1:1, 2.
5. Revelation 3:20, NCV.
6. John White, *Daring to Draw Near* (Downer's Grove, Ill.: InterVarsity Press, 1997), 17.
7. Psalm 37:4.
8. Ecclesiastes 3:11, NIV.
9. Psalm 39:7.
10. Psalm 63:1.
11. Psalm 73:26.
12. John 17:3.
13. Psalm 84.
14. Matthew 6:31–33, NIV.
15. Psalm 42:8, *The Message*.
16. 1 Corinthians 1.30.
17. Acts 17:28.
18. 1 John 2:24, 25, 27.

Chapter 4

1. Psalm 66:18, RSV.
2. Luke 16:15, NIV.
3. Matthew 9:12, 13, NIV.
4. Hebrews 4:15, NIV.
5. Hebrews 4:16, NIV.
6. Psalm 19:12.
7. Luke 18:13.
8. Watchman Nee, *What Shall This Man Do?* (Wheaton, Ill.: Tyndale House, 1988), 64–67,

69, 70, emphasis in the original.
9. Psalm 51:15–17.
10. See Luke 18:19.
11. 1 Peter 5:5–7.
12. Romans 5:20.
13. See Revelation 3:16, 17.
14. 1 John 1:9, NIV.
15. Psalm 34:8.

Chapter 5
1. Told by Brennan Manning in *Abba's Child* (Colorado Springs, Colo.: NavPress, 1994), 19, 20, quoting Parker S. Palmer, "The Monastic Renewal of the Church," *Desert Call* (Crestone, Colo.).
2. 1 Corinthians 13:11.
3. Romans 15:1, 2.
4. Psalm 119:41, 42, NIV.
5. Galatians 5:14–16, 24–26, NIV.
6. John 14:18–20.
7. Psalm 59:14, 15, NIV.
8. Psalm 107:8, 9.
9. Psalm 65:9.

Chapter 6
1. See Luke 18:35–43 and Mark 10:46–52.
2. Luke 19:10, RSV.
3. Psalm 104:3.
4. Ephesians 1:20; 2:6; Hebrews 10:12; 12:2; 6:19.
5. Hebrews 4:16.
6. 1 Timothy 1:12–17.
7. 2 Peter 3:9.
8. 2 Peter 3:15, emphasis added.
9. Psalm 145:17–19.
10. Luke 19:7.
11. Luke 19:5.
12. 2 Thessalonians 3:5.

Chapter 7
1. Psalm 145:17–19.
2. Psalm 109:1, 2, 4–15, 20–22.
3. See Psalms 77:6–9; 102:6–11; 44:13–16; 88:1–18.
4. Matthew 6:7, 8.
5. Romans 8:26, 27, NIV.
6. Don Chapman, quoted by Brennan Manning in *The Ragamuffin Gospel* (Portland, Ore.: Multnomah Press, 1990), 155.
7. Ole Hallesby, *Prayer* (Minneapolis: Augsburg Press, 1994), 150.

Chapter 8
1. 2 Timothy 1:5–7.
2. Matthew 23:14–30.

3. Revelation 21:5–8.
4. Matthew 7:7–11, *The Message.*
5. Luke 15:11–32.
6. 1 John 4:8, 10.
7. 1 Corinthians 13:4–7, NIV.
8. Psalm 35:27, NIV.
9. Author unknown.
10. Psalm 46:10.

Chapter 9
1. Rabindranath Tagore, *Gitilani* (New York: Scribner Poetry, 1997), 62.
2. I adapted this story from one told by Anthony de Mello, *Taking Flight* (New York: Image Books, 1988), 103.
3. John 12:23–32, NIV.
4. See Matthew 12:20.
5. Brennan Manning, *Abba's Child* (Colorado Springs: NavPress, 1994), 126–128.
6. Luke 11:1–13; John 14:26; Revelation 3:20.
7. John 17:24, 25, NIV.

Chapter 10
1. M. Wayne Brown, *Water from Stone* (Colorado Springs: NavPress, 2004), 43.
2. Evelyn Underhill, *Concerning Inner Life* (Oxford, England: OneWorld Publications, 1999), 81, 82.
3. Exodus 32:31.
4. See Romans 6:4, 5.
5. Philippians 2:4–8.
6. Luke 6:35, 36.
7. 1 Corinthians 2:9, 16.

Chapter 11
1. Mark 11:12–14, 20–26, paraphrased.
2. Luke 13:6–9.
3. Genesis 1:1; John 1:1–17; Ephesians 1:3–10; Revelation 1:17, 18.
4. Ephesians 1:17–21.
5. Ephesians 2:6, 7; 1 Thessalonians 4:17; Revelation 21:25.
6. Matthew 6:14, 15.
7. Luke 15:24, emphasis added.
8. John 20:22.
9. Retold by Brennan Manning in the *Lion and the Lamb: The Relentless Tenderness of Jesus* (Old Tappan, N.J.: Chosen Books, 1986), 135, 136.
10. Matthew 18:23–35, paraphrased.

Chapter 12
1. Genesis 5:21–24.
2. Genesis 4:20–22.

3. Luke 14:16–20, paraphrased.
4. Luke 14:21–24, paraphrased.
5. Luke 14:25, 26, 33, paraphrased.
6. Matthew 6:31–33; 7:7–10.
7. Matthew 18:3, *The Message.*
8. Luke 15:17.

Chapter 13
1. Matthew 7:21–23, *The Message*; emphasis in original.
2. Matthew 5:20, NIV.
3. Zechariah 4:6.
4. Proverbs 19:21, *The Message.*
5. John 3:16, 17.
6. Exodus 34:29–35; Luke 15:11–13.
7. See John 10:10, 15.
8. John 17:20, 21, 23.
9. Matthew 22:36–39.
10. 1 John 4:21–5:2.
11. See 1 Corinthians 13:1.
12. Song of Solomon 2:10–13.

Chapter 14
1. Matthew 14:23.
2. John 15:5, NKJV.
3. Luke 10:2.
4. Matthew 26:11.
5. John McKinney, *Day Hiker's Guide to Southern California* (Santa Barbara, Calif.: Olympus Press, 1992), 150.
6. 1 Kings 19.
7. Luke 18:27.
8. Psalm 46:10.
9. Matthew 7:21–23, paraphrased.

Chapter 15
1. Genesis 28:10–17.
2. Genesis 28:20–22, emphasis added.
3. Genesis 32:22–32.
4. Tony Campolo, *Let Me Tell You a Story* (Nashville: Word Publishing, 2000), 59, 60.
5. Romans 12:1, 2.
6. Matthew 22:36–40.
7. Isaiah 64:8.
8. Philippians 3:21.
9. 2 Corinthians 3:18.
10. Acts 10.
11. 1 Peter 5:5–11.
12. Psalm 62:5–7.

Chapter 16
1. Anthony de Mello, *The Heart of the Enlightened* (New York: Image Books, 1991), 175, 176.
2. Isaiah 9:6.

3. Mark 1:35.
4. Psalm 46:10.
5. Isaiah 30:15.
6. Psalm 37:7.
7. 1 Corinthians 4:5.
8. Jeremiah 7:22, 23.
9. Deuteronomy 6:4–13, *God's Word.*
10. Hebrews 3:7–13.
11. Luke 9:35, 36.
12. 2 Timothy 3:16, 17.
13. Mark 4:9, 20.
14. Romans 10:14, 16, 17.
15. John 7:16–18.
16. John 5:46, 47.
17. Exodus 20:7.
18. 1 Samuel 15:23.
19. 1 Samuel 15:22.
20. Matthew 7:24, 25.
21. Isaiah 30:19–22.
22. Hebrews 8:10, 11.
23. Jeremiah 29:11–14.
24. Hebrews 4:16.
25. Psalm 125:1.
26. John 5:43, 44, NIV.
27. James 1:5–8.
28. Luke 23:23–25, NIV.
29. 1 Corinthians 13:8, 9, 12.

Chapter 17
1. Luke 24:49, NIV.
2. See John 20:19.
3. See Luke 24:47, 48, NIV.
4. Psalm 127, NIV.
5. Acts 1:3–5, NIV.
6. Acts 1:6, NIV.
7. Acts 1:7, 8, NIV.
8. See Acts 1:9.
9. Acts 1:12–26, NIV.
10. See Acts 9.

Chapter 18
1. Exodus 14.14.
2. John 5:44.
3. Jeremiah 7.
4. Proverbs 19:2.
5. Acts 12:1–19.
6. Matthew 7:7–11.
7. Matthew 6:5–18.
8. Luke 10:1–16.
9. Luke 10:2.
10. Robin Baird-Smith, ed., *Carlo Carretto* (Springfield, Ill.: Templegate Publishers, 1990), 68, emphasis in the original.
11. Galatians 6:2–5.
12. Eugene Peterson, *Traveling Light* (Colorado

Springs: Helmers & Howard, 1988), 162.

13. Parker Palmer, *Let Your Life Speak* (San Francisco: Jossey-Bass, 2000), 10, 11.

14. Brother Lawrence, *Practicing His Presence* (Beaumont, Tex.: The SeedSowers, 1973), 102.

15. Romans 12:1, *The Message.*

Chapter 19

1. Peterson, *Traveling Light*, 181 (see chap. 18, n. 12).

2. Acts 19.

3. Colossians 1:7.

4. Philemon 2.

5. Colossians 1:23.

6. Colossians 1:3, 4.

7. Ephesians 2:4–10.

8. Colossians 1:9.

9. Colossians 3:17, 23, 24.

10. 1 Corinthians 1:30, 31.

11. Colossians 1:9, 10.

12. John 17:1–3.

13. Colossians 1:11.

14. John 16:33, *The Message.*

15. Annie Hawks, 1872.

16. Colossians 1:11–14.

17. Psalm 39:7.

Chapter 20

1. Rabindranath Tagore (1864–1941), "My Voyage."

2. Kent Hansen, *Grace at 30,000 Feet* (Hagerstown, Md.: Review & Herald, 2002), 175.

3. Luke 18:11.

4. Carlos Caretto, *Letters from the Desert* (Maryknoll, N.Y.: Orbis Books, 2002), 7.

5. Luke 10:25–29.

6. See Luke 10:36, 37.

7. Philippians 2:1–8.

8. John 15:5, *The Message.*

9. Matthew 25:40.

Chapter 21

1. Exodus 3:1–6.

2. Bruce Feiler, *Walking the Bible* (New York: HarperCollins, 2001) 224–248.

3. Ibid., 229.

4. Psalm 114:4.

5. Elizabeth Browning.

6. John 9:39.

7. Exodus 2:11–15.

8. Exodus 4:3.

9. Psalm 36:9.

10. Philippians 3:10–12.

11. Exodus 3:13, 14.

12. Exodus 3:6, with my own notes.

13. Hosea 2:13, 14, NIV.

Chapter 22

1. Exodus 2:21, 22.

2. Exodus 2:23, 24.

3. Psalm 102:17.

4. Exodus 3:3, 4.

5. Exodus 3:11.

6. Blaise Pascal, *Pensées* (London: Penguin Books, 1966), 309, 310.

7. Mark 8:12.

8. Jeremiah 29:13, 14.

9. John 1:9.

10. John 1:10–13.

Chapter 23

1. Romans 8:26.

2. John Newton, "Amazing Grace."

Chapter 24

1. 1 Samuel 3:3, 4, 15–18, 21, NIV.

2. 1 Samuel 7:15–17, NIV.

3. See 1 Samuel 28.

4. Elisha A. Hoffman, "Is Your All on the Altar?"

5. 1 Samuel 12:17–25.

6. Matthew 6:31–33.

7. Henri J. M. Nouwen, *Making All Things New* (New York: Harper & Row, 1981), 41–43.

Chapter 25

1. Joshua 9.

2. Joshua 10:10–15.

3. Joshua 10:25.

4. See Psalm 15:4.

5. Joshua 10:40–42.

6. Philippians 2:5–8.

7. Luke 14:26, 27.

Chapter 26

1. 1 Kings 19:7.

2. Luke 15:25–32.

3. 1 Kings 19:9.

4. See 1 Kings 19:11, 12.

5. 1 Kings 12.

6. 1 Kings 19:15–18, paraphrased.

7. Harry D. Clarke, "Into My Heart."

Chapter 27

1. Ephesians 3:14–21.

2. Psalm 25:19–21.

3. Job 6:15–17, NIV.

4. Mark 15:34.

5. Luke 23:46, NIV.

6. Psalm 39:7.
7. Habakkuk 1:2–4, 13, NIV.
8. Habakkuk 2:1, NIV.
9. Habakkuk 2:4–20.
10. Habakkuk 3:17–19, NIV.
11. Oswald Chambers, *My Utmost for His Highest* (Grand Rapids, Mich.: Discovery House Publishers).
12. Job 17:6–9, *The Message.*
13. Exodus 14:14.

Chapter 28
1. 2 Kings 6:1, 2, *The Message.*
2. 2 Kings 6:2, *The Message.*
3. 2 Kings 6:3, *The Message.*
4. 2 Kings 6:3, *The Message.*
5. 2 Kings 6:4, 5, *The Message.*
6. 2 Kings 6:6, 7, *The Message.*
7. Isaiah 55:8, 9.
8. Proverbs 19:21.

Chapter 29
1. Genesis 33:19.
2. Based on John 4:1–42.

Chapter 30
1. See Mark 6:30–44.
2. See Mark 8:1–10.
3. Mark 8:12.
4. See Mark 8:14.
5. Mark 8:15.
6. See Mark 8:16.
7. Mark 8:17, 18, my paraphrase, emphasis added.
8. Mark 8:19–21, emphasis added.
9. Psalm 37:25, 26.

Chapter 31
1. Eugene Peterson, *Answering God: The Psalms as Tools for Prayer* (New York: HarperSanFrancisco, 1991), 27, 28.
2. Psalm 70:1, NIV.
3. Psalm 119:41, 42, NIV.
4. Psalm 138:8, NIV.
5. Psalm 61:1, 2, NIV.
6. Psalm 57:7, 8, NIV.
7. Robert Robinson.
8. Psalm 42:8, NIV.
9. Psalm 69:29, NIV.
10. Psalm 73:25, 26, NIV.
11. Psalm 141:3, NIV.
12. Psalm 23, RSV.
13. Psalm 85:6.
14. Psalm 69:5, 6.
15. John 15:5.

16. Psalm 63:3, 4, 7, 8, NIV.
17. Philippians 1:21, NIV.
18. Psalm 86:4, 5.
19. Luke 15:18, NKJV.
20. Psalm 35:24–26, NIV.
21. Psalm 39:7, NIV.
22. Psalm 51:10, NIV.
23. Psalm 139:23, 24, NIV.
24. Jeremiah 17:9, NIV.
25. Psalm 86:11.
26. See Matthew 6:24.
27. Psalm 25:21.
28. Psalm 143:10, NIV.
29. Isaiah 40:31.
30. Psalm 142:6, 7, NIV.
31. Luke 4:18, 19.
32. Psalm 131, NIV.
33. Psalm 4:8.

Chapter 32
1. *Black's Law Dictionary.*
2. Joshua 1:1, 2.
3. See Exodus 16:1–3; 17:1–7; 32; Numbers 11; 13:25–14:45; 16; 20:1–13, 22–29.
4. Numbers 13:25–33.
5. Joshua 1:3, 5, 9.
6. Fenelon, *The Seeking Heart* (Sargent: The SeedSowers, 1992), 85, 86.

Chapter 33
1. 1 Kings 17:1–7.
2. Deuteronomy 11:11, 13, 16, 17.
3. 1 Kings 19.
4. Jeremiah 15:18.
5. F. B. Meyer, *Great Men of the Bible,* vol. II (Grand Rapids, Mich.: Zondervan, 1982), 72, 73.
6. Psalm 31:14–16.
7. John 19:28, NKJV.
8. Revelation 22:1, 2, 17.
9. 1 Kings 18:1.
10. James 5:17, 18.

Chapter 34
1. Matthew 11:28–30.
2. Genesis 3:4, 5, emphasis added.
3. 2 Timothy 3:1, 2, 5.
4. Lewis Smedes, *Shame and Grace* (New York: HarperSanFrancisco, 1993), 78.
5. Fil Anderson, *Running on Empty* (Colorado Springs, Colo.: Waterbrook Press, 2004), 42, 43.
6. Genesis 2:9, 16, 17.
7. Matthew 13:14, 15, 17.
8. Psalm 50:7, 21, 22.

9. Psalm 53:2, 3.
10. Psalm 103:13, 14.
11. Philippians 2:5, 6.
12. Philippians 2:9–13.
13. See Ephesians 2:11–22.
14. John 14:19.
15. Galatians 2:19, 20.
16. John 5:19–21.
17. Psalm 32:8, 9.
18. Matthew 11:28–30, *The Message.*
19. Psalm 26:2, 3, *The Message.*

Chapter 35
1. Psalm 62:3–7.
2. Gordon MacDonald, *The Life God Blesses* (Nashville: Thomas Nelson, 1994), 225, 226.
3. Zechariah 4:10.

Chapter 36
1. See 1 Corinthians 12.
2. See John 15; 1 Corinthians 11:23–26; Ephesians 4:4–16.
3. Proverbs 4:18, 19.
4. 2 Corinthians 12:9.
5. Matthew 18:18–20.
6. 1 John 5:11, 12.
7. 1 John 5:18–21, *The Message.*

Chapter 37
1. Civilla Martin.
2. 2 Corinthians 4:6.

Chapter 38
1. Rabindranath Tagore, "Fruit Gathering."
2. Tagore, "Stray Birds."
3. See Psalm 104:19.
4. Song of Songs 6:10, NIV.
5. Psalm 89:37.
6. Daniel 12:4, see footnote.
7. H. W. Longfellow (1807–1882).
8. Genesis 1:16–18.
9. John 1:9.
10. John 1:3–5.
11. Mark 13:28, 29.
12. Hebrews 9:28.
13. Hebrews 1:1–3.
14. Mary A. Lathbury, "Day Is Dying in the West," #51 in *The Seventh-day Adventist Hymnal.*

Chapter 39
1. See Philippians 4:6.
2. John 2:16.
3. Habakkuk 2:20.
4. Psalm 3:1, 2.
5. Psalm 3:3, 4.

6. Acts 16:19–24.
7. Hebrews 13:12–15.
8. 2 Corinthians 2:14.
9. Watchman Nee, *Assembling Together* (New York: Christian Fellowship Publishers, 1973), 117–119.
10. Psalm 22:1–5.
11. Psalm 84:5–7.

Chapter 40
1. Psalm 3:5, 6.
2. Robert Durback, ed., *Seeds of Hope* (New York: Image Books, 1997), 73.
3. *Let Go* (Springdale: Whitaker House), 36.
4. Psalm 3:7.
5. Matthew 6:7, 8.
6. Matthew 6:14, 25, 33; 7:1, 5, 7.
7. Romans 15:3.
8. Philippians 4:6, 7.
9. Psalm 3:8.
10. Luke 18:26.
11. John 3:16.
12. Romans 7:24, 25; 8:1, 2.
13. R. Paul Stevens, *Seven Days of Faith* (Colorado Springs, Colo.: NavPress, 2001), 117, 118.

Chapter 41
1. Matthew 12:43–45.
2. John 11:17–25.
3. John 11:21.
4. John 11:39.
5. John 11:40.
6. Robert Capon, *Kingdom, Grace, Judgment: Paradox, Outrage, and Vindication in the Parables of Jesus* (Grand Rapids, Mich.: Eerdmans, 2002), 140.
7. Mark 3:1–6; Luke 13:10–17; John 9.
8. Matthew 11:16, 17.
9. Matthew 13:14, 15.
10. Matthew 13:31.
11. Matthew 13:33.
12. Matthew 13:47–50.
13. Proverbs 1:7.
14. 2 Corinthians 12:9.
15. Philippians 4:13, NKJV.
16. 1 Peter 5:10.
17. Hebrews 10:38.
18. Hebrews 11:13–16.
19. Hebrews 12:1–3.

Chapter 42
1. Genesis 44.
2. Mark 14:24.
3. Mark 14:36.

4. Mark 10:38–40.
5. Jeremiah 45:3.
6. Jeremiah 45:4, 5.
7. Romans 8:28.
8. 1 Corinthians 15:19.
9. John 18:11.
10. Psalm 116:9–14, 17.
11. Revelation 21:5–7.
12. Matthew 26:27–29.

Chapter 43
1. Philippians 4:5–7.

Chapter 44
1. Retold by Anthony De Mello, *Awareness* (New York: Image Books, 1992), 143.
2. Psalm 148:7, 8.
3. Romans 5:1–5.
4. John 16:5, 16–24, *The Message*.
5. *Prayer: Finding the Heart's True Home* (New York: Harper Collins, 1992), 24.
6. Isaiah 55:9–13.

Chapter 45
1. Thomas Merton, *Thoughts in Solitude* (New York: The Noonday Press, 1958), 87.
2. Isaiah 35:1–4.

Chapter 46
1. Robert Frost, "Stopping by the Woods on a Snowy Evening."
2. Titus 3:9.
3. Psalm 119:105.
4. Matthew 21:42, 44.
5. Zechariah 4:6.
6. Ellen G. White, *Education*, 288.
7. John 1:11–13.
8. Psalm 29:2.
9. Robert Frost, "The Road Not Taken."

Chapter 47
1. Luke 21:1–4; Mark 12:41–44.
2. John 8:29.
3. Johannes Metz, *Poverty of the Spirit* (New York: Paulist Press, 1998), 38.
4. John 4:32.
5. Mark 12:41–44.
6. John 10:17.
7. Philip Yancey, *Soul Survivor: How My Faith Survived the Church* (New York: Doubleday, 2001), 103.
8. Anthony DeMello, *The Song of the Bird* (Anand, India: Gujuarat Sahitya Prakash, distributed by Loyola University Press, Chicago, 1983), 130.

9. Luke 14:26.
10. Luke 14:27, 33.
11. Ephesians 1:7, 8.
12. See Philippians 2:5–8.
13. See Ephesians 2:4–10.

Chapter 48
1. Mark 14:12–16.
2. 2 Corinthians 10:10.
3. 2 Corinthians 11:16–21.
4. See Acts 10:9–16.
5. Acts 10:28.
6. Acts 11:15–17.
7. See Matthew 16:17–19, 23.

Chapter 49
1. John 2:1–11.
2. Ellen G. White, *The Desire of Ages*, 148.
3. See Philippians 4:6.
4. Ecclesiastes 7:8.
5. John 3:28–30.
6. Matthew 22; 25; Luke 12.
7. John 13:23.
8. John 1:16–18.
9. Quoted in *Christianity Today*, December 9, 2002, 53.
10. Luke 12:32; John 10:10.

Chapter 50
1. Psalm 42:8.
2. Romans 8:9–17; Galatians 5:16, 22–25.
3. G. A. Young.
4. Fanny J. Crosby.
5. 1 Thessalonians 5:16, 17.
6. 1 Peter 1:8, 9.
7. Annie Lamott, *Blue Shoe* (New York: Riverhead Books, 2002), 34.
8. Revelation 22:5.
9. Joseph Swain.

Chapter 51
1. Philip Yancey, *What's So Amazing About Grace?* (Grand Rapids, Mich.: Zondervan 1997), 51.

Chapter 52
1. Isaiah 40:26.
2. J. S. B. Monsell.
3. Zechariah 7:5.
4. Matthew 7:21–23.
5. R. Paul Stevens, *Seven Days of Faith* (Colorado Springs, Colo.: NavPress, 2001), 39.
6. Hosea 2:14.
7. Matthew 11:28–30, my paraphrase.
8. Matthew 12:1–6.

If you found food for thought in this book, you'll want to read these books, too.

Swimming Against the Current
Living for the God you love.
Chris Blake

The question is not, **What do I agree with?** The question is, **What do I need to hear?"** *Swimming Against the Current* contains stories, questions, and observations. Read these diverse messages and listen to the voice of the Holy Spirit urging you to spiritual growth and practical course corrections in your life.
Paperback, 256 pages.   0-8163-2141-8   US$15.99

Searching for the God of Grace
Stuart Tyner

Explore God's perfect gift as revealed in the plan of salvation, the pages of history, and the principles of God's character. Find out how and why some religious people—maybe even we, ourselves—have gotten off the gospel path and tried to find a different way to heaven.
Paperback, 304 pages.   0-8163-2152-3   US$17.99

Searching for a God to Love
Chris Blake

If you have questions or doubts, if you've been hurt, if you ache for something more than rhetoric, preaching, and simplistic reasoning, take the journey this book defines. *Searching for a God to Love* will surprise you.
Paperback, 256 pages.   0-8163-1719-4   US$11.99